T0364144

Clariant clareant

Anna Bálint studied Business Administration, History and European Ethnology and earned her doctorate in Art History in 1997. As an author, consultant and art expert, she values interdisciplinary relationships. When working on a book project, she performs all the conceptual, content and creative steps by herself. Anna Bálint has gained particular renown in the field of critical examination of contemporary corporate history.

Anna Bálint

Clariant clareant

The Beginnings of a Specialty
Chemicals Company

Translated from the German by Myrna Lesniak

Campus Verlag
Frankfurt/New York

ISBN 978-3-593-39374-2

Copyright © 2012 Campus Verlag GmbH, Frankfurt am Main.
All rights reserved. No part of this book may be used or
reproduced in any manner.
Cover design: Guido Klütsch, Cologne
Cover illustration: © Clariant AG, Muttenz, concept by Anna Bálint
Typesetting: Fotosatz L. Huhn, Linsengericht
Typeset in Minion Pro and The Sans
Printing: Beltz, Bad Langensalza GmbH
Printed in Germany

Also available as an eBook.
www.campus.de

Contents

Preface

Let businesses prosper, blaze, excel, succeed! That is what every businessman and every company wishes. To blaze, excel or become famous is called *clarere* in Latin. To express a wish that, it is thought, may possibly come true, one needs the present subjunctive: *clareant.*

Since its very beginning Clariant has been in a continual process of transformation forcing it to travel a rocky road to define itself and achieve its own culture and persona. Its roots go back a long way and could fill books.

Level-headed deliberation, diligence driven by the will to succeed, but chance, too, as well as long periods of lean and difficult times have brought the group considerable wealth, huge burdens and great responsibility. The chapters on its own past, no matter how problematic they might be, should not be swept under the carpet but addressed openly because a firmly established awareness of one's origins fosters professional confidence and a certainty of action and sustainability. History, to quote Lessing freely, "should not burden memory but illuminate the intellect."[1]

Thus, for the very first time and in accordance with this guiding principle, this book presents the beginnings of Clariant, which has its historical foundations in two corporations: Sandoz and Hoechst.

---

[1] Gotthold Ephraim Lessing in his preface to his translation of Voltaire, cf: Lessing, Gotthold Ephraim: *Werke und Briefe, Band 2 Werke 1751–1753*; edited by Jürgen Stenzel, Frankfurt a. M., 1998, p. 311.

The globalisation of dyeing:
How the dyeing trade developed[2]

The art of dyeing can be traced back to the Stone Age. The red-brown paintings of animals in the caves of Lascaux in the south of France dating from between 17,000 and 15,000 BC and the similar motifs of the rock paintings in Altamira in Spain are living witnesses to the prehistoric use of dyes and pigments. Archaeologists found bandages dyed blue, red and yellow on mummies in their 5,000-year-old graves in the Egyptian pyramids, too. The Etruscans, Greeks, Romans and other Mediterranean peoples were also familiar with a large number of dyes and techniques. There was a wide range of colours and from time immemorial our forefathers made use of a variety of raw materials from nature—plants, various types of wood, minerals or animal extracts.[3]

Cave paintings in Lascaux, from around 17,000–15,000 BC

---

2   This chapter was written in cooperation with Dr. Alexander Engel, Akademischer Rat (Academic Councilor, comparable to Assistant Professor) at the Institute for Economic and Social History, Göttingen University. See Alexander Engel: *Farben der Globalisierung. Die Entstehung moderner Märkte und Farbstoffe 1500–1900* (Doctoral Thesis, Göttingen University, 2007), Frankfurt a. M./New York, 2009.
3   Emil Ernst Ploss: *Ein Buch von alten Farben*, 3rd unaltered edition, Munich, 1973.

Purple dye *murex* from the Indian Ocean

The lotus tree and the madder root were used for red dye. Purple tones were achieved with the aid of litmus, walnut shells and pomegranate blossoms; the 'royal colour' purple derived from the snails of the genus *murex* had a special significance. Indigo and dyer's woad were suitable as a blue dye. The unassuming mignonette plant, also known as dyer's rocket, grows on rubble heaps and at the wayside. Its seed vessels and the saffron crocus produced a strong yellow.

In the beginning, dyeing materials were collected in the countryside and used for dyeing at home but over time it became customary to grow the dye plants oneself. In the biography of Charlemagne, written after his death in 814, it was reported that he strongly advised growing madder: a Mediterranean plant used in dying, which had been brought over the Alps to Northern Europe by Benedictine monks.

A wall hanging from around 1070, known as the Bayeux Tapestry, owes its great value both as a historical document and a work of art to its colour fastness.[4] The hanging is an embroidered picture story depicting the Norman conquest of England. The embroidery is in coloured wool, which has hardly faded even to the present day. The professional dyeing of textiles such as wool, linen, cotton and silk was provided by cloth makers. It was the Flemish in particular who plied this early craft and who were well-known for the high quality of their trade. Their work was first mentioned in documents in Vienna in 1208. The increase in finery meant that the guild of tailors became

Crocuses on the saffron fields in Mund/Valais

4   David M.Wilson: *Der Teppich von Bayeux*, preface by Jean le Carpentier, 2nd ed., Cologne 2005, p. 9–12.

Bayeux Tapestry (detail), around 1070

more and more important and from a historical point of view the proverb 'Clothes make the man' is less likely to be a cliché but rather a confirmation of the trade's importance.

From 1400 the dyers began to form independent guilds. As the individual processes in dyeing, i. e. washing, bating, rinsing and dying depend on water, the trade settled near flowing water. 'Blauhandgasse,' a street in Frankfurt, is thought to be one such site.

On account of their botanical and animal origins, textiles contained residual substances from the manufacturing of the fibres which made the materials look grey and yellowish. This meant that they needed to be bleached before being dyed. The bleachers—a specialist branch of the dyeing trade—mostly spread the textiles on the municipal bleaching green. Bleaching was effected by the sun and, depending on the type of weave, various aids such as sour milk, potash and water were added in turn; however, it could take weeks of treatment for the textiles to reach the degree of whiteness desired. Smoothing, i. e. pressing the bleached or dyed linen, was also part of the dyeing trade. It was to be some centuries before the dyers were in a position to avoid the time-consuming bleaching on the green and the arduous smoothing and replace these with efficient finishes.

Hides which had been tanned to make leather and then dyed were very popular at royal courts in the Middle Ages. Horse tack, shoes, and robust clothing were fashioned from coloured or gilded leather. Books, too, were given prestigious bindings, especially in sumptuous red. The leather from the Moroccan town of Fez was particularly valued for its suppleness and its uniform colouring. Even today tanneries there still use the old, traditional,

Dyers, 1482, illumination from a Flemish manuscript

energy-sapping methods: young men full the leather in large, brick vats filled with tanning agents, water and dyes.

In the Western World, mediaeval illuminations were based on brazilin, the dye from redwoods. Its origin was in East India and it was very much in demand. It reached Europe via the Silk Road before America was discovered. In the 16th century dye-producing woods were among the most coveted imports from the New World—the South American country of Brazil gets its name from the brazilwood.

A fall in the price of basic foods and an increase in real wages in Europe in the late Middle Ages encouraged the specialised growth of plants suitable for dyeing and trading. Consequently, supra-regional markets emerged for a limited number of popular, high-quality plants for the natural dyeing process. Needless to say, their transport, even over large distances, was worth the effort.

The comparatively high capital requirements could only be met with investments by merchants, who not only organised distribution but controlled the entire supply chain of the dye business. However, these agricultural pro-

Bleaching on the Green, 1890, painting by Max Liebermann

duction systems were unstable: When the price of a dye decreased, this could not be cushioned by innovations as there was no mechanism for developing new technologies. As a result, quality gradually deteriorated to reduce production costs, which, in turn, completely ruined any sales opportunities. By the end of the 17th century, the most important, marketable dyes of European origin—dyer's woad, dyer's rocket and safflower which is also known as false saffron, with the one exception of madder—had been ousted by non-European products: principally indigo, dye-woods and cochineal, the dried form of a scale insect which breeds on cacti.

In the medium term favourably priced Central American woods which could be easily felled became a key product on the European mass textile market. On the other hand, dyers not only made use of the European madder but also resorted to cochineal from Central America for high quality shades of red. Cochineal production was, unlike all the other major export articles from Latin America, in the hands of the indigenous population. The main reason for this was that hardly any economies of scales could be realized by producing cochineal on a large scale.

Due to the conquistadors, trade with the dried bodies of cochineal scale insects spread throughout Europe, too. At first, cochineal was used primarily in the dyeing of textiles, but soon it was used in cosmetics, too. In the Baroque period it was to be found on the colour palette of such artists as Jacopo Tintoretto, Jan Vermeer, Peter Paul Rubens or Diego Velázquez. In the region of origin, however, it was difficult to produce this natural dye stuff in large quantities and with consistent quality. Production on a larger scale caused problems in coordinating work, alternately high and low demand for labour, and brought about recurrent infestations of the cacti, all of which prevented cochineal gaining access to the mass market.

The situation was quite different when it came to the blue dye indigo, a highly concentrated plant extract and the only dye produced in the plantation economy of the Caribbean. Unlike European agriculture, this business was not interested in sustainable cultivation but only in the short-term maximizing of the capital invested. This led to a highly specialized, intensive monoculture. The accompanying inordinate strain on the land, the excessive exploitation of the slaves, the cost benefits resulting from the mass production and the synergy of a monoculture with integrated processing meant that an exceptionally high level of productivity was achieved. However, it was primarily the merchants engaged in overseas trade who made a profit. In their role as providers of capital and by dint of their involvement in various lines of business they acquired sufficient dominance on the market to be able to beat down producer prices almost to the level of production costs.

The planters were tied to the specific processing infrastructure required to produce the dye and to the frequently long growth cycles of the indigo plant. They were simply not able to switch over to growing a cash crop that would achieve a maximum profit either at short notice or just as the market required. Following the abolition of slavery and the political chaos in the Caribbean in the 19th century, indigo production for the European market shifted to British India.

Unlike the Caribbean, the areas in India over which the British gradually gained control in the mid-18th century were densely populated and, because of the caste system, property relations were sacrosanct. Accordingly, the Europeans restricted themselves to the processing of indigo leaves in factories built on rented land and run with the aid of paid labour. Plant materials were obtained by closing deals with peasant farmers who cultivated indigo at their own expense. However, the contractual relations, which were liberal in the beginning, were gradually replaced by procurement systems in which the peasants became dependent and were increasingly at the mercy of the European indigo producers. This caused social tensions and among other things boosted the protest movement around Mahatma Gandhi. In the end natural indigo lost its importance in the European dye industry: to begin with, it was gradually replaced by cheaper materials such as logwood and eventually other sources of tannin in the dyeing of black, which used to be achieved by combining deep blue with red. The botanical dye was finally supplanted by synthetic indigo around 1900. However, the crux of the change was not that industrial production was more cost-efficient, but that its marketing became way more effective.

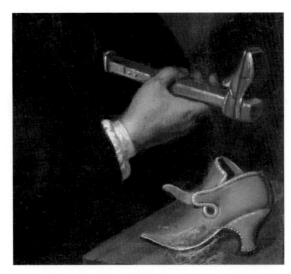

The Cobbler (detail), 1755, illustration from
the "Nürnberger Hausbücher"

Due to industrialisation, the market for dyes soared from the middle of the 18th century on. The dye manufacturers, who from the very start were suppliers to the weaving trade, the tanning and leather trade, paper makers and the building sector, and ritual and fashion makeup, developed their products and techniques with a view to meeting the requirements of their customers. At the same time, there were signs of a fundamental structural change in the market trend, which ultimately dated from a change in the perception of the nature of dyes. Dyes came to be regarded less and less as holistic natural products but rather as a combination of chemically defined substances. The scientific deconstruction of natural dyes had an immediate technological and economic impact as dye traders and dyers made use of analysis techniques on a commercial scale to obtain purer and more consistent dyes. Companies such as Geigy (1857) or what was later to be known as Ciba (1859) in Switzerland, Cassella (1798), Bayer (1863) and Hoechst (1863) in Germany were established either by traders specialising in natural dyes or by dyers themselves.

The early application of science to products and manufacturing methods was not restricted merely to dyes but also extended to bleaching and consequently to the manufacturing of substances such as soda and alum. The increase in methods for manufacturing pure chemical products was accompanied by a rise in the demand for chemicals, especially for basic commodities such as alkalis, acids, and, later, hydrocarbons distilled from tar such as phenol and aniline. Individual traders concentrated on such substances and

Washerwoman at the Well, about 1890, pastel by Giovanni
Segantini

amalgamated with producers and finishers under one roof. Companies like
the Badische Anilin- und Soda-Fabrik/BASF (1863) and the Aktiengesellschaft
für Anilinfabrikation/AGFA (1867) can trace their origins back to this period.

The outcome of the change in the trade with dyestuffs and in the traditional
chemical industry was the emergence of a new chemical industry which was
characterized by large-scale enterprises with a perceptible focus on business
with dyestuffs. The basis for this was provided by the increase in the range of
products, diversification, and the consolidation of production and distribution. Moreover, the fact that the companies were interested in uniting, if possible, as many of or even all the parts of the supply chain within one company
added another aspect: vertical integration.

In the pre-industrial era production and distribution systems were dominated by individuals who were connected to each other by means of market
and network relations. The degree of specialisation tended to remain low and
the complexity of economic activity as well as the demands regarding produc-

tion methods were not very exacting. As a result, the costly set-up of larger hierarchies or the organization of extremely well-funded companies was unnecessary. This changed with the shift to modern factory-produced dyestuffs. There was an increase in effort and expenditure in all sectors: in the development of new products, in their production and finally in their commercial exploitation.

The more complex the knowledge about dyes became, the more difficult the role of the aforementioned universal individuals proved to be. These were finally replaced by specialists whose work required co-ordinating. At the same time economies of scale and—in the supply of an entire range of dyestuffs— synergies could be obtained more effectively than in the traditional manufacture of natural dyes. All this led to the type of organization which consisted of a scalable, hierarchic corporation with multiple subdivisions, so that all the tasks of a manufacturing and distribution system could be carried out in one set-up. Modern companies evolved, just as they did in most other branches of the emerging industrial world.

The move towards modern companies with independent subsystems for marketing, research and development altered the market situation radically and created dynamic and competitive pressure to an extent that had previously been unknown. God-given, hardly processed natural dyestuffs gradually lost their importance on the markets and were replaced by the high-quality dyestuffs created and manufactured by chemists. At the same time, the transition from the traditional to the modern dye industry was a process lasting decades.

From the late 1840s and even more so from the late 1850s with the emergence of aniline dyes, entirely new artificial dyes were added to the early historical extracts and compounds obtained from natural dyestuffs. A pioneer in this field was August Wilhelm von Hofmann, who obtained his doctorate in Giessen under the aegis of Justus von Liebig in 1841. A few years later, at the behest of Queen Victoria and Prince Consort Albert, he accepted a chair at the Royal College of Chemistry in London. The German chemist developed an aniline synthesis based on benzene won from coal tar. In experiments in 1856 to produce quinine from the aniline bases of coal tar, Hofmann's assistant William Henry Perkin, who had just turned 18, accidentally discovered a process to manufacture 'mauveine'. After discovering how eminently suitable this first synthetic organic dye was for dyeing textiles on account of its intensity, Perkin took out a patent and soon afterwards he founded a small factory called Perkin and Sons in London. As violet was a very fashionable colour at that time, Perkin enjoyed huge success with his monopoly on the production of mauveine. Soon competitors began systematically to exploit aniline and to create further dyes such as fuchsine or magenta.

The so-called coal tar dyes—as they were originally derived from coal tar—proved, in the long term, to be a key innovation. At first they came under the category of particularly elaborate dyes and like all innovative and expensive dyes found their way onto the market via the niche provided by exclusive silk fabrics. In the 1870s, French and British companies lost their early market leadership to German and Swiss companies, due, among other things, to the superior knowledge management the latter possessed. That was even before tar dyes also gained importance on the mass market from the 1880s on. The foundation of Sandoz in 1886 dates back to this boom. At the beginning of the 20th century, coal tar dyes had drawn level with natural dyes and by World War I achieved a market share of more than 80 percent in Germany and Switzerland, which at the time produced around 95 percent of the tar dyes in the world.

The key to the success of tar dyes lay less in the alleged price advantage than in their innovative commercial exploitation. In the pre-modern period dyes were regarded as commodities, i. e. goods defined according to their range of uses. When dyers purchased dyestuffs, they tried to identify suitable materials on the basis of origin, external characteristics and testing procedures. In the case of extracts, compounds and tar dyes, which all required

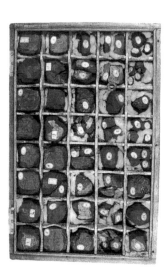 

Samples of indigo in an open case, ca. 1750

Tin with Indigo Brand from the Farbwerke vorm. Meister Lucius & Brüning, ca. 1900 greater processing, identification was even more difficult, especially as the range of products became more complex. At the same time, however, there was a fundamental change in production rights. Legislation protecting patents and brands strengthened the entitlement to individual rights to products; a liberal market approach predicated on clearly defined and protected rights (property rights) gained acceptance. Correspondingly, the visible and tangible characteristics of a substance which were important for the customer's decision faded into the background as information from the manufacturer was given priority in the marketing of dyes. Sealed tins with labels giving precise details of the contents replaced open showcases as a means of presenting the product—the vast number of long-established commodities defined by the demand side were supplanted by a flood of thousands upon thousands of new specialties with brand labels and defined by the supply side.

The transition from the comparatively static world of *commodities* to the dynamic world of *specialties* marked the beginning of an operating environment in which marketing became the permanent and principal task. Commodities were barely processed, produced in large quantities, and chosen by customers for their particular purpose on the basis of their visible and tangible qualities. Who produced them played a minor role at best. Specialties, on the other hand, were artificial dyestuffs: manufacturers set great store by their authorship being clearly recognizable. Usually it was impossible for the consumer to examine the contents beforehand, as the products were offered only in sealed packages. Instead, one relied on the labels attached by the manufacturer, by which the latter informed about and guaranteed the characteristics and the quality.

Woman Ironing, 1904, painting
by Pablo Picasso

The Bookworm, around 1850, painting by Carl Spitzweg

Dyers had to be actively informed of the potential uses of new products and persuaded of their inherent advantages. Because of the speed at which the market was developing, manufacturers could not wait for consumers to explore the possibilities for themselves, as had been the case before industrialization. It was also important to gear innovation and research to customers' requirements. A prerequisite for success on the market was the successful linkage of the R&D department and the marketing department—a company fell behind if it did not grow and made no effort to develop the market further.

The transition from the traditional dye industry to a modern one was virtually complete just prior to the outbreak of the First World War. After that, the patterns of activity in the industry remained almost constant for decades. However, there were changes in market structures. The First World War meant that all connections between German dye factories and the global markets were severed. Switzerland's major manufacturers Ciba, Geigy, and Sandoz benefited from the situation while the USA, Great Britain, France, Italy and Japan built up or expanded their own production facilities substantially—partly by confiscating German-owned plants abroad. After the war, Japan and Italy covered most of and the other three states covered all of their own demand with their own factories. At the end of the 1920s Germany's share of the global market had shrunk by almost half to a good 40 percent compared with its share in 1913; Switzerland's share almost doubled rising to almost one seventh. At the same time, competitive pressure on the dye markets decreased both nationally and internationally due to mergers and the creation of cartels. The latter were particularly typical of the period. The three main Swiss companies entered into a syndicate; in France the dye syndicate CMC (Centrale Matières

Spray, 1962, painting by Roy Lichtenstein

Colorantes) was set up. In 1925 the members of the German cartel amalgamated as *I. G. Farbenindustrie AG* (demerged again in the early 1950s), while in Great Britain ICI (Imperial Chemical Industries), the gigantic chemical company, was formed. Together these four large-scale organisations entered into cartel agreements, thereby gaining control of approximately two-thirds of the world's dye market; the remaining third was dominated chiefly by U.S. companies.

Securing the traditional core business afforded the participating groups and companies the opportunity to develop, more intensively, other lines of business such as basic chemicals, fertilizers, pharmaceuticals, photo-chemicals etc. This diversification caused the share of the turnover generated by the dye business in Germany's chemicals companies to slump by almost half from nearly two-thirds in 1913 to just under one third around 1930. From the 1940s to about 1990 the share in turnover remained constant at just under one sixth of total business. That the share in turnover remained stable was partly due to a diversification of the actual business with dyes; not only textile dyes gained in significance but also veneer and gloss paint, textile auxiliary agents, paints and printing inks, and masterbatches, too, when synthetics triumphantly entered the market as from 1950s.

Meanwhile, U.S. chemical companies enjoyed considerable but temporary success in the 1950s and 60s; however, by about 1980 their market position had dwindled again and they were superseded by Ciba-Geigy, Bayer, Hoechst, BASF, Sandoz and Japanese manufacturers. In the wake of the increasing relocation of the world's textile manufacturing to Asia, new producers from Korea, Taiwan, Indonesia, Pakistan and above all India and China gained increasing significance, first of all on their home markets and soon on export markets. Making use of low wages and some state subsidies,

Kamisuki (woman combing her hair), 1920,
woodcut by Goyô Hashiguchi

Asian manufacturers—principally small and medium-sized businesses—
conquered the mass market while Western producers, on account of their
greater expertise, concentrated on more expensive specialties. In 1994 Asian
dye manufacturers boasted a global market share of 41 percent—among
these manufacturers China had 19 percent, Japan 7 percent and India 5 percent. In comparison, only 35 percent was shared more or less equally by
Western Europe and North America. Producers in Latin America, Eastern
Europe, Australasia and Africa accounted for the remaining 24 percent.

This transformation of the dye market coincided with a restructuring of
the traditional Central European chemicals companies, which had been subject to considerable pressure in various business segments in the 1990s and
consequently repositioned themselves as life-science companies after shedding traditional lines of business.

The prevailing doctrine of 'the more and the bigger, the better', got out of
hand with the result that over time many a chemical company started to re-
semble a convenience store. The British entrepreneur Denys Henderson was
the first to save a group listed on the stock exchange when he demerged the

"You might be larger than me, honey, but I am bigger for sure." Basel Marriage, 1972, cartoon by Hans Geisen in the Basler Zeitung

company and yet contributed to increasing its shareholder value.[5] He divided ICI[6], which had been established in 1930, into two completely independently run and listed companies: Traditional chemicals remained with ICI whilst Zeneca, which had been spun off, stood for life science, with pharmaceuticals and pest control products as its main pillar.

With this in mind, Bayer and Hoechst spun off their textile dye divisions and combined them to form DyStar GmbH, at that time the second largest supplier in the world next to Ciba-Geigy; BASF's dye production, which ranked fourth in the world in 1995, was added in 2000. DyStar went bankrupt in 2009 and was bought by an Indian company, Kiri Dyes and Chemicals, at the beginning of 2010.

---

5   Wilfried Kratz: "Wundersame Spaltung," in *Die Zeit*, 5 Mar. 1993, no. 10.
6   See Geoffrey Owen/Trevor Harrison: "Why ICI Chose to Demerge," in *Harvard Business Review*, vol. 73, no. 2, Mar.-Apr. 1995, pp. 132–142.
    See Geoffrey Owen: "Parting of the Corporate Ways," in *Financial Times*, 13 Mar. 1995.

ICI parts with Zeneca, cartoon by Ingram Pinn in the *Financial Times,* 13 Mar. 1995

The traditional Swiss companies Ciba-Geigy and Sandoz merged to become Novartis in 1996 and in the course of their orientation towards life sciences transferred Ciba-Geigy's specialty chemicals and their dye production to a separate company; Ciba AG has since become part of BASF. Before the merger Sandoz had already spun off its specialty chemicals business to form Clariant AG, which acquired Hoechst AG's specialty chemicals business in 1997 and Ciba AG's Masterbatches Division in 2006.

The focus on specialist dyes which has resulted from competition from Asia and the manifold restructuring of the industry in the last 15 years has changed the traditional face of the industry. Cultural and institutional friction losses from these various restructurings have left their mark on the companies that are heirs to the major dye companies. Nevertheless, it is still possible to draw on their accumulated knowledge and experience: The thread is still intact, the colour has not faded.

The history of Sandoz

Grandmother

When the achievements in the economic history[7] of Switzerland are scrutinized closely, it is very obvious that many striking courses have been charted since the foundation of the Federal State of Switzerland in 1848. Among these outstanding events are the introduction of the Swiss franc in 1850; the opening of the 'Eidgenössische Technische Hochschule' (the Swiss College of Technology) in 1855; the foundation of the 'Schweizerische Kreditanstalt' (the Swiss Credit Institute) on the initiative of Alfred Escher in 1856; the breakthrough in alternating current technology which led to the founding of Brown, Boveri & Cie. in Baden in 1891; the merger between Nestlé and the Anglo-Swiss Condensed Milk Company in 1905; the concept with which Gottlieb Duttweiler revolutionized the food industry, his consumer-friendly Migros retail store chain in 1925; Arnold Isler's vision of consolidating all those engaged in aviation in Switzerland into one company, Swissair, which became reality in 1931; the 'Peace Treaty' in Swiss industry in 1937; the rescue of Switzerland's watch and clock industry by Nicolas Hayek, who put it back on its feet in 1983, and finally the merger between Ciba and Sandoz to form Novartis in 1996. This merger, the so-called 'Basel Marriage' on 6 March 1996, was at the time the largest merger the world had ever seen and marked the beginning of a new era at the 'Rhine's Knee' and the irreversible farewell to the traditional chemical industry.

However, before the strict, legendary patriarch Marc Moret could pull off the biggest coup of his career, a solution had to be found to the 'grandmother' problem. The problem was the former core business—the extraction of dyes from tar, which had been the reason for starting the company in 1886. The

---

7 "Historie: Zehn Meilensteine. Vom Start des Frankens bis zur Pharma-Fusion: die wichtigsten Weichenstellungen aus 150 Jahren Schweizer Wirtschaft," in *Bilanz* 04/2006, 28 Feb. 2006.

dyes were renamed chemicals a century later, in 1985, and in the course of diversification as of 1990, it became evident that they were less viable as a division in the set-up at that time and were therefore no longer sustainable.

'Grandmother' refers to Kollektivgesellschaft Chemische Fabrik Kern & Sandoz, the company established in the 19th century, whereas 'mother' is used to refer to the modern company of Sandoz with its many divisions- pharmaceuticals, food, seeds, chemicals, agriculture, construction and environment. Finally, the term 'daughter' refers to the young company of Clariant.

The location in Basel

Basel's early economic development was determined by politics and goes back to the time of the Salians when Henry IV elevated the Burgundian nobleman and cleric Burkhard von Fenis to the office of Bishop of Basel in 1072.[8] They were not only friends but were also declared enemies of Pope Gregory VII. When Henry became Emperor, Burkhard, who supported him in the Investiture Controversy, accompanied him on his journey to meet the Pope at Canossa in the winter of 1077. In addition to his secular commitment, Burkhard always had a sympathetic ear for the interests of the church in Basel. In reply to the wishes of the population, he consequently called Benedictine monks from the reform monastery Cluny to his diocesan town in the north of Switzerland. It was thus that the first monastery in Basel, which was built in Sankt-Alban-Tal (St. Alban's Valley), came into existence. Thanks to the monks, the power of the River Birs could be harnessed, and they built a canal which from the 12th century served to operate several mills and attracted all kinds of craftsmen. That laid the foundation for the settlement there of a local paper manufacturing industry somewhat later.[9]

The Council of Basel which convened in 1431 employed around one hundred secretaries, who had to record every meeting. The considerable demand for paper that was involved drew the attention of Heinrich Halbysen, a Basel merchant, to a niche in the market with the result that he bought the 'Allenwinden' mill at the Riehenteich, a mill which he then proceeded to convert into a paper mill. Later he moved the flourishing business to the St. Alban's Valley and used the 'waterworks' built by the former Cluniacs. Halbysen faced

---

8   René Teuteberg: *The History of Basel*, 2nd ed., Basel 1988, p. 100 ff., 135 ff.
9   See Peter Tschudin: *Basler Papiermühle*, Schweizerisches Museum für Papier, Schrift und Druck (the Swiss Museum for Paper, Writing and Print), Basel 2002.

local competition from the Galliziani brothers, two paper manufacturers who had immigrated from Italy and who likewise rose to great wealth through their trade. Another contributing factor was very likely the paper consumption at the university, which was founded in 1460. Because of its high quality, paper from Basel was held in great esteem throughout Europe from the 15th/16th centuries on.

Significant impulses for the economic development of Basel also came from the Huguenots who, after the repeal of the Edict of Nantes in 1685, found a new home in what was considered to be a religiously tolerant town. They also brought weaving and the dyeing of silk ribbons to the region. For a long time the manufacture of the ribbons was a cottage industry: i. e. the ribbons were woven on hand-operated weaving looms in the homes of so-called 'ribbon-weaving' families, but gradually in the 1830s the fabrics were manufactured in factories on weaving looms driven by water and steam. This economic sector was highly influential in helping to establish the manufacture of dyes in Basel.

Salt

However, before it was possible to even think of such an important industry as chemicals in the north of Switzerland, one basic prerequisite was essential: salt. In Switzerland this raw material was known merely as an expensive import. Actually the mineral had been hidden in the ground for more than 250 million years but it had never been brought to the surface. In 1837 the discovery of salt deposits at a depth of 107 metres on the Rothaus estate in Muttenz by Carl Christian Friedrich Glenck,[10] a German saline expert, freed Switzerland of the necessity of importing salt and heralded in the industrialization of the region. Glenck, who was inspired by the example of Schwäbisch Hall, his home town, quite simply called the place of his first Swiss discovery Schweizer Hall. The name is verifiably not the historical name of any district.

Further decisive conditions for a site[11] where a dye industry could develop were sales and consumer orientation, the various patent regulations, the border location, the number of inhabitants, skilled staff and expertise, the River

---

10 *Hessische Biografie*, Data Set No. 5499; see Bernhard Ruetz/Armin Roos: *Carl Christian Friedrich Glenck 1779–1845: Salzpionier und Gründer der Saline Schweizerhalle*, Zurich 2009.
11 Christian Zeller: *Globalisierungsstrategien. Der Weg von Novartis* (Thesis, Hamburg University, 2001), Berlin/Heidelberg 2001, pp. 102–108.

Rhine as a convenient waste dump, communication and transport facilities, the capital market and the attitude of the authorities.

One of the pioneers of dye manufacturing in Basel is considered to be the silk dyer Alexander Clavel, who, in 1859—three years after William Henry Perkin in London accidentally discovered how to manufacture mauveine—began to produce fuchsine and opened his own factory for the production of aniline dyes in 1864. However, in 1873 he sold this manufacturing facility to Bindschedler & Busch, later known as Ciba, so that he could again devote himself to dyeing silk.

Another tar factory on the Rhine ...

In 1885 the paths of Alfred Kern, a chemist, and Edouard Sandoz,[12] a businessman, crossed. This fortunate meeting laid the foundations for starting up a company, which was later to be referred to as 'mother' and was called Sandoz AG. It was from this company that Clariant was spun off.

Kern,[13] who was born in Bülach in 1850, had studied chemistry at the Swiss Polytechnic, now the ETH (Swiss College of Technology) in Zurich.

After completing his studies he went abroad to work in a chemical plant which distilled dye from the raw material, tar. The plant, 'Chemische Fabrik Karl Oehler,' was established in Offenbach in 1842 and was the first independent plant in Germany to manufacture asphalt. In 1905 it was acquired by 'Griesheim-Elektron,' which belonged to the founder members of I. G. Farben in 1925 but was assigned to Farbwerke Hoechst after its demerger. When 'Hoechst Specialty Chemicals' was spun off in 1997, it became the property of Clariant until it was sold by Rolf W. Schweizer to Karl-Gerhard Seifert in 2001. Since then it has been a division of AllessaChemie.

Thus it was that Alfred Kern began his career in the chemical industry in Offenbach in 1872, became a member of the Frankfurt Chemische Gesellschaft (Frankfurt Chemical Society), gained his doctorate at the university in Giessen—because the Polytechnic in Zurich was not entitled to award doctor-

---

12 "Festschrift Sandoz (Sandoz's Commemorative Publication): 100 Jahre für ein Leben mit Zukunft," in *Sandoz Bulletin*, vol. 22, 1986; Renate Riedl-Ehrenberg: "Alfred Kern (1850–1893). Edouard Sandoz (1853–1928). Gründer der Sandoz AG, Basel," in *Schweizer Pioniere der Wirtschaft und Technik*, no. 44, ed. by the Verein für wirtschaftshistorische Studien Zürich (Society for Economic Historical Studies), Zurich 1986; "110 Jahre Sandoz: Ein historischer Rückblick," in *Sandoz Bulletin*, no. 112 (last number)/1996, pp. 6–31.

13 *Neue Deutsche Biographie*, vol. 11, Berlin 1977, pp. 517–518.

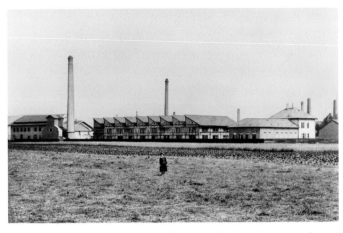

Sandoz's factory site around 1900

ates at the time—and after six years returned to Switzerland with a wealth of experience at his disposal. Scarcely had he taken up his post at the dye factory of Bindschedler & Busch in 1879 than he succeeded in coming up with a number of major inventions. Among other things, Kern had developed the field of ketone dyes and in the process discovered crystal violet, which caused quite a sensation. It is, therefore, all the more inexplicable why his employer, well known as the predecessor of the future Ciba, terminated his contract in 1884. It is quite likely that there were differences of opinion with regards to the use of Kern's patents. Kern seems to have recognized the hard game being played, because when he was dismissed, he took various company documents including valuable laboratory journals with him and began negotiations with Durand & Huguenin, a dye factory in Basel, with a view to setting up a new dye factory together.

Edouard Sandoz, who acted as an intermediary at the talks, was born in Basel in 1853. He was the son of a cloth merchant and had served a commercial apprenticeship in a raw silk business in Basel. After that he had found employment with Poirier & Dalsace, an aniline dye factory near Paris. After extensive business trips which had taken him as far as North America, he had returned to Basel in 1880 and had taken up a post with Durand & Huguenin. When the negotiations between Kern and the dye factory broke down, Sandoz and Kern decided to go it alone: they established the Kollektivgesellschaft Chemische Fabrik Kern & Sandoz, which commenced work with three chemists, a bookkeeper, a foreman and 10 tradesmen in a plant in the St.-Johann-Viertel (St. John's Quarter) in Basel on 1st July 1886. This date marks the birth of the later Sandoz and the beginning of the manufacture of textile dyes.

Thanks to the manufacture of the well-known basic dyes alizarine blue and auramine using Kern's new technique, the company quickly enjoyed their first major successes. At the same time, Edouard Sandoz set off on numerous business trips to establish contacts throughout the world. In order to win through in the face of foreign competition, especially from Germany, the company very soon began to engage in extensive research and to manufacture new products. Their first development was the violet dye 'prune pure' which was patented in 1888. In the meantime the young company was already producing 6 different dyes, two of which- the Victoria Blue brands- proved to be very successful in the years that followed. In 1889 Edouard Sandoz was able to report record earnings to his co-partner who was on holiday at the time: "ledger showed CHF 112'000 today!!! Colossal, unprecedented, fabulous, monumental …" he wrote. In 1892 the range of products comprised 28 different products for dyeing wool, silk, cotton and linen at a total weight of 380 tonnes.

In 1893 the up-and-coming company was shaken by a great calamity when Alfred succumbed to a heart condition. As a result, Edouard Sandoz decided to continue running the company as a limited partnership called Sandoz & Cie. Basel. However, it was only two years later that Sandoz, too, was forced by ill health to withdraw from active participation in the management. Consequently the company was converted into a public company and traded as Chemische Fabrik vormals Sandoz. Sandoz was elected President of the Board of Directors at the constitutive Annual General Meeting on 9th July 1895, handed over this post to Robert Gnehm after three months but continued to exert influence on the fortunes of the company as a majority shareholder.

In the same year, the company created a second pillar in addition to the dye department and began to manufacture antipyrine, the first antipyretic pharmaceutical substance of its kind. Meister Lucius & Brüning, Hoechst's predecessor, had already included a medication called Antipyrin in its product range[14] since 1884

In 1897 Chemische Fabrik vormals Sandoz applied for a patent for a violet and blue dye which enabled the company to gain a foothold in the emerging group of direct dyes for cotton and paper. In 1911 the first foreign subsidiary, Sandoz Chemical Company Ltd., was established in Bradford, Great Britain. The sales company situated in Yorkshire, the centre of the wool industry at the time, principally sold dyes, but sales also included some pharmaceuticals. The outbreak of the First World War meant that further plans to expand had to be

---

14 Anna Elisabeth Schreiner/Manuela Wex: "Chronik der Hoechst Aktiengesellschaft 1863–1988," Special edition from *Dokumente aus Hoechst-Archiven*, Ed. Klaus Trouet, Frankfurt a. M. 1990, p. 33.

Share certificate of the *Chemische Fabrik vormals Sandoz AG*, 1895

shelved. However, in 1919 not long after the war ended, a second branch, Sandoz Chemical Works, Inc., was opened in New York. Initially this branch was only to be an import and sales company for dyes, but from the very beginning the production of dyes, chemical and pharmaceutical products was provided for in the trade register. The British subsidiary also started to manufacture dyes and chemicals in 1921. Over the next few years further subsidiaries were established in Italy, France, Spain and Germany.

During the First World War the company was able to maintain production despite the difficult circumstances and even managed to step it up somewhat as competition from Germany ceased. Furthermore, by setting up its own research and development facilities, Sandoz began, in 1917, to expand its pharmaceutical activities which until then had been rather negligble and in 1921 launched Gynergen, the first drug resulting from its own research.

International competition, which intensified after the war ended, caused the three local dye manufacturers Ciba, Geigy and Sandoz, to team up in September 1918 as the so-called Basler Interessengemeinschaft (Basel Syndicate) to streamline their activities in research and development, production and sales. With this in mind, a common pooling of profits and a set quota allocation were arranged. As a result joint plants were established in Switzerland, England, Italy, Canada, Spain and the USA. During this time, Sandoz recognized the economic significance of anthraquinone dyes and as a result Samuel von Allmen, a young chemist, was given the task of organizing research into them. The work was divided among the three companies involved, within the framework of Basler IG, whereby Sandoz[15] was given the task of processing the acid anthraquinone dyes

In the beginning they primarily copied the successful products of competitors, but soon the researchers managed to develop their own high-quality dyes. In 1922 Sandoz launched two alizarine light blue brands, the first in this category of dye. In the course of the years it became apparent that the members of the syndicate were expanding in different fields. Tough negotiations on a reorganization of the syndicate lasted for years but an agreement could not be reached so that the contract was finally annulled by a court of arbitration at the end of 1950.

During the 1920s Sandoz, with great foresightedness, bought a huge area of the Rothaus estate in Muttenz—it was there that the Schweizerhalle plant was to be built; in addition 14 dyes were patented and included in the range of products. Sandoz's dyes department remained, for a long time, the market leader in the field of anthraquinone dyes, in which 'Sandolan Walkblau NGL', 'Brillantalizarin Reinblau BS' and 'Sandolan Walkviolett NBL' proved to be particularly successful and were still being sold by Clariant decades later.

With the onset of the Great Depression at the end of the 1920s Sandoz was faced with difficult times which resulted in short-time working and redundancies. The dye department underwent essential reorganisation whereby research and production were separated from each other; thus the chemist's field of activity experienced a considerable change as he was now no longer in charge of the entire process from the development to the manufacture of a product. Specialisation had gained a foothold in these fields, too.

Obviously, the boom in dyes ebbed perceptibly when the First World War ended so that Sandoz was forced to look around for new production opportunities. So-called textile auxiliary agents, in which some experience had already been acquired, were a useful and, at the same time, a forward-looking addition to the portfolio. These involved chemicals for the textile, leather and paper industry as well as the manufacture of cosmetic products and synthetic detergents. For that reason, a department for this production field was established in 1925. In 1929 it was run as an independent chemicals department and over the years became the third pillar of the company. Even during the Second World War this business division generated about 20 percent of turnover. Through time the emphasis of the department shifted from wetting agents—

---

15 Paul Erni: *Die Basler Heirat. Geschichte der Fusion Ciba-Geigy*, Zurich 1979, pp. 23ff; Tobias Straumann: "Die Novartis-Fusion aus historischer Sicht" in *Basler Stadtbuch* 1996, Christoph Merian Stiftung (Ed.), pp. 37–42.

Dye production at Sandoz, around 1940

these agents reduced the surface tension of water—to detergents and to optical brightening agents, which are so closely related to dyes that the chemicals department was disbanded at the end of 1968 and amalgamated with dyes again.

In 1939 'Chemische Fabrik vormals Sandoz's was renamed Sandoz AG. At the outbreak of World War II the dyes department had an excellent organization at its disposal both at home and abroad and this enabled the company to continue business almost as usual during the war despite the (prevailing) difficulties in obtaining energy and raw materials. At the end of the 1930s Sandoz gradually began to engage in pest control but only on a small scale.

In the post-war era, the company confronted with fierce international competition. To enable the company to keep pace with its competitors, major investments were made in modernising production facilities and in the gradual development of the area in Muttenz, where production started in 1948. In 1952 Hans Lehmann, the first and only dye chemist among the ten Sandoz presidents so far, took up his post. But just as he took over as head of the company, sales in the dye department were outstripped by those of the younger pharmaceutical division and, from that time on, it had to surrender its supremacy forever.

1956 saw the setting up of production facilities for pigments and additives in the French town of Hüningen, close to the Swiss–French border. That was the time when Walter Schweizer was deputy director of the dye department and his son Rolf, who was born in 1930, was acting as an assistant at the Handels-Hochschule (Commercial Academy) in St. Gallen where he took his oral examination as a postgraduate. After obtaining his PhD, the ambitious and talented young recruit joined the dye department at Sandoz in 1958.

Simultaneous events

Taking over Biochemie GmbH in Kandl, Tyrol in 1963 provided Sandoz with the foundation stone for its dominant position in the biotechnological manufacture of pharmaceutical ingredients. From that year on, it is worthwhile following the careers of the crucial players in this story because their paths crossed to some extent in the 1960s, and the environment in which they were to develop was naturally similar.

That was also the year when Jürgen Dormann submitted an application to Hoechst. A newspaper advertisement[16] from 10th August 1963, carefully cut out and since yellowed with age, was the reason for his application to Farbwerke Hoechst AG vormals Meister Lucius & Brüning. The company was looking for "young men with scientific qualifications", an aptitude for sales and humane qualities for the management duties of the seventies. The advertisement promised "full employment as a member of staff after completion of training and a probationary period and the chance to grow into management positions in sales and distribution both at home and abroad." It goes without saying that Dormann grew into it.

In 1967 Sandoz acquired Wander AG in Bern, which provided access to dietary products and the hospital supplies business. In 1967, Rolf W. Schweizer, just like his father before him, was appointed deputy director of the same division. In the period from 17th to 23rd September Rolf W. Schweizer assembled all the Sandoz dye sales representatives at the 'Bürgenstock' at the Vierwaldstätter Lake for the first international workshop in the history of the company. It was attended by Dr. Ernst Merian, Dr. Ernst Bretscher, Oskar Nicolet, Dr. E. Kern, Theo Knecht (Brasil), Dr. E. Fileti (Italy), R. Bernasconi (Argentina), Dr. Hans Jörg Frank (India), Pablo Gysin (Chile), Juan Morin (Spain), Ruedi Mathys (Argentina), Ernst Strobel (Brasil), Max Hediger, Rolf W. Schweizer, E. Probst (Italy), Jean Pierre Sorg (France), Dr. Adolphe Kaufmann, Arthur D. Ferns (England), Frau G. Schultheiss, Dr. Hans Eggenberger, R. Lindenmeier (USA), Max Gossweiler (USA), Jean Pierre Hayoz, Dr. William Lüthy (USA), J. A. Clarke (England), B. Weatherston (Canada), Kurt

---

16 Interview with Jürgen Dormann in Winterthur on 17 Feb. 2010.

Meeting of the Sandoz dye sales representatives at the 'Bürgenstock,' 1967

Leimgruber, R. Erzinger (Japan), Dr. Arthur Locher, Fritz Hohl (Japan), W. J. Waldie (Australia), Walter Staufacher, I. Vassey (Canada), J. Prat (Spain).[17]

At the same time that Rolf W. Schweizer was posing with his colleagues in front of a camera at the 'Bürgenstock,' Herbert Link joined Sandoz as a project engineer in the pharmaceutical department after completing his studies as a process engineer at the ETH, the Swiss College of Technology. Martin Syz,[18] too, found employment that year as plant manager of the Dye and Chemicals Division in St. Johann. When he started his job, it was quite normal in Basel and elsewhere to still feel proud when lots of smoke was belching from the factory chimneys and there was a decided smell of chemicals in the air. After all, they were obvious signs that the chemical industry was doing well.

After many years of experience in the food industry, Marc Moret, at that time 44 years old, was looking for new job perspectives. In 1967, when a friend suggested that there might be good opportunities in industry in the north of Switzerland, Moret began to examine the annual reports of the 'Big Four' in Basel and discovered that Sandoz was the weakest of all. As far as he was concerned, there was absolutely no doubt what his decision would be: "It seemed to me that that was where I should make my next move—not to one of the prima

17 *Sandoz Bulletin,* no.11, 1968, p. 63
18 Interview with Martin Syz in Muttenz, 10 Dec. 2009.

Marc Moret, pre-1970

donnas of this group of companies, but to the one that needed the most help."[19]

By contrast, Jürgen Dormann,[20] who was then 27 and a salesman selling fibres, saw fewer and fewer prospects in his job with Hoechst. The unexpected offer from a customer, who wanted to lure him away, arrived at an opportune moment and prompted Dormann to consider just what his market value might be. The representative of NINO, the Niehues family-owned business in Nordhorn—at that time NINO was a major textile company with customers like Karl Lagerfeld and the German national football team—got in touch with Dormann and asked whether he might be interested in changing jobs. Dormann was most certainly interested and had an interview with Alfred Herrhausen, the then chairman of NINO's board of directors, in the executive suite of Deutsche Bank in Frankfurt.

Regardless of the offer from Nordhorn, Dormann applied to Sandoz in Basel. During the interview[21] for this book, Dormann laid a photocopy on the desk: "That's a contract between Sandoz and me, dated 2nd November 1967. It states that I was to start work there on 2nd January 1968. My salary was CHF 22,800, plus child allowance; that made CHF 30,000 a year." Asked why he had applied to Sandoz more than 40 years ago, Dormann replied rather drily: "Because it was very boring in Hoechst and I didn't have enough money."

With the contract from Sandoz in his pocket he asked for an appointment with the appropriate director at Hoechst and in the interview explained that in view of his large family his income was not high enough and that in his eyes there were no very clear perspectives for his career. After this rather daring statement he was given an immediate percentage rise in income and an outline of what his next assignment might be.

It is an appealing idea to imagine what might have happened if Jürgen Dormann had actually started in the marketing department of the pharma-

19 David Finn: "A Conversation with Marc Moret" in *A Tribute to Marc Moret. A Collection of Essays,* preface by Daniel Vasella, New York, 1996, pp. 71–80; for further information on Moret see Raymond Petignat: *Marc Moret – bewundert, verehrt, gehasst,* in Basler Stadtbuch 2006, pp. 74–77.
20 Jürgen Dormann, 17 Feb. 2010.
21 Ibid.

ceuticals division at Sandoz on 2nd January 1968. One thing is certain: Marc Moret from the French-speaking part of Switzerland joined Sandoz on 1. April 1968 and by a whisker would have become the colleague of Heidelberg-born Dormann. It is and remains idle speculation to run through the history of Hoechst *without* Dormann and the History of Sandoz with both Moret *and* Dormann. However, it is extremely interesting and instructive to trace how these two entirely different characters with their varying qualifications and prerequisites, even with regard to their age, influenced the industry in the next few decades.

In the autumn of 1970, the so-called 'Basel Marriage'[22] was announced. The two companies which merged were almost equally strong. Ciba's turnover amounted to CHF 3,693 million and Geigy's was CHF 3,257 million. Sandoz's turnover at the time amounted to CHF 2,751 million.

As far as Sandoz's development was concerned, the company relied mainly on insecticides in its agricultural chemistry sector right into the 70s. Additionally, it also accomplished pioneering feats in the field of biological pest control. In the middle of this decade, Sandoz began to venture into the seed business. The first oil crisis erupted in 1973—some consumers may remember that driving on Sunday was prohibited—and rising prices and the throttling of mineral oil production plunged the world economy into a long period of stagnation. Nonetheless, this was also a time when there was in fact a considerable increase in investments in chemicals as is evident from the following: Sandoz's Spanish plant which went into operation in Prat near Barcelona in 1974, the establishment of production facilities in Martin, South Carolina, USA in 1978 and the acquisition of K. J. Quinn GmbH in Germany which dealt in leather chemicals, and Sarma S.p.A. in Italy which was active in the field of masterbatches.

Overhead value analysis 1981

After Marc Moret had been put in charge of corporate finance in 1976 and had been elected to the Sandoz Board a year later—thus succeeding Yves Dunant—he came to realise that he would have to do something about the divisions that were sustaining losses and tackle the disproportionate size of the parent company. In 1981 Marc Moret commissioned McKinsey to carry

22 Erni 1979, pp. 23 ff., 229.

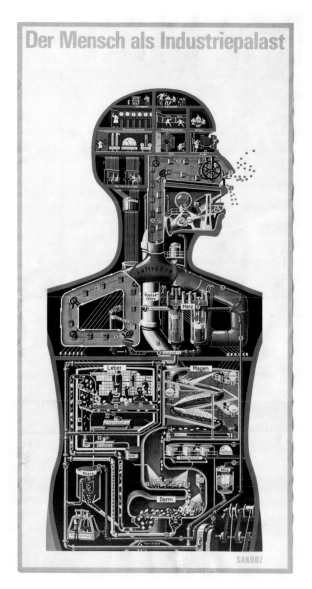

Man as an Industrial Palace, a Sandoz poster from around
1975

out the so-called overhead value analysis[23] which was a novelty in the history
of industry in Switzerland. These reorganization measures were to counteract
the increasing bureaucratisation and to improve productivity and effective-

---

23 Werner Meyer/Felix Erbacher: "Bei Sandoz pfeift ein anderer Wind, Interview mit Marc
    Moret," in *Basler Zeitung*, 9 Apr. 1983.

ness. Moreover it was important to prepare for the future in good time and to forestall the emerging inflationary trends.

During the actual analysis in 1981, 5,850 jobs were examined at Sandoz and in the Pharmaceuticals Division at Wander AG, the Sandoz subsidiary in Bern, all in the course of a few months. The cost-saving options which were identified were implemented by the end of 1982. But when the reorganization was announced, it caused concern not only among the workforce but also among the general public as redundancies were expected. There was an outcry in the whole country on account of the lack of information and even the *Neue Zürcher Zeitung* spoke of treatment à la 'Eisenbart' (famous for his radical treatments with negative effects). For the very first time, a company in Switzerland had resorted to 'using the axe' to cut costs where outwardly there appeared to be no need. The initiative originated with McKinsey partner Hans Widmer and his then assistant Lukas Mühlemann; the project management on the part of Sandoz was in the hands of Rolf Soiron.[24] Dominik von Bertrab, Heiner Meier and Herbert Link were also actively involved.

In actual fact, 900 jobs were to be axed at the head office in Basel as a result of the overhead value analysis. However, as promised by the management, the job-cuts were absorbed by natural fluctuation, internal transfers, early retirement, individual cuts in working hours or placement with external companies. Letters of dismissal were merely issued in four instances where the employees concerned had rejected the jobs which had been offered to them as an alternative. All in all, the overhead value analysis cut expenses at Sandoz by CHF 70 million annually. Moret's management style was committed to cost transparency and constituted a radical and courageous break with the previous era.[25]

German-Swiss chemical talks

From the 1980s until the mid-1990s, the so-called German–Swiss Chemical talks[26] took place once as year and were attended by six companies: Sandoz, Ciba-Geigy and Hoffmann-La Roche from Switzerland and Hoechst, BASF and Bayer from Germany. As a rule the CEOs and their deputies met not within their companies but on neutral ground—sometimes in Switzerland,

---

24 Ibid.
25 Daniel Vasella: "Nachruf. Dr. Marc Moret zum Gedenken," in *Novartis live*, 4/2006.
26 Interview with Günter Metz in Sulzbach on 26 May 2010.

sometimes in Germany. They dined together on the evening before the conference which lasted all morning and ended with lunch.

The meetings of these competitors enabled the participants to become acquainted and to exchange views on themes of mutual interest to the chemicals sector. All the companies were members of CEFIC, the European Chemicals Association. The talks were essentially concerned with basic legal conditions, aspects of economic policy, general investment policy, environmental protection issues, market trends and regional conditions.

For years, Günter Metz, in his capacity as deputy CEO of Hoechst AG, accompanied his CEO Rolf Sammet and later his successor Wolfgang Hilger to the sessions. Marc Moret was likewise a participant of the German-Swiss Chemical Talks as of 1985 when he was appointed president of the Sandoz Board. Metz found him not only to be a man with a mind of his own but also decidedly strong-willed.

Metz recalls that Moret, in contrast to his Swiss colleagues, Alexander Krauer from Ciba-Geigy and Fritz Gerber from Hoffmann-La Roche, seldom appeared at the meetings in the company of one and the same person. After the fire at Schweizerhalle, Rolf W. Schweizer, too, was present at one of the meetings. It was, of course, only natural that the representatives of the other two Swiss companies, Ciba-Geigy and Hoffmann-La Roche, had more contact with each other than to Sandoz due to the fact that Sandoz's structure and range of products were somewhat different; the focus was more on numerous minor products.

Rendezvous: Airport

The considerations following the overhead value analysis and the exchange of information at the German-Swiss Chemical Talks promoted an early willingness to discuss a variety of issues and specific alliances: the idea of merging Sandoz dyes with Hoechst dyes is 25 years old. The idea, which was decidedly audacious in the mid-1980s, originated in the heads of business economists; they were fully conversant with the businesses and figures of the other participants but until then they only knew each other perforce from conferences, from reports in the press and from customers. Through time, closer contacts were to develop through the German-Swiss Chemical Talks. It was, however, in the summer of 1986 that the future partners met for the first time specifically to hold talks. The following little story about this meeting is worth reading.

One day Rolf W. Schweizer,[27] who was a dedicated yachtsman, decided to sell his old boat, a Mediterranean one, and buy a Scandinavian model instead. His eldest son, who shared his father's intense love of yachting and the sea, had managed to arrange an appointment to view a boat which appeared to be suitable and which was lying at anchor on Lake Constance. Schweizer was abroad on business and after his flight home was to meet his wife and son at Zurich Airport so that they could drive straight to Lake Constance. There must have been a hitch of some sort because even though the plane landed on time, he was decidedly late in putting in an appearance. When he did finally arrive at the appointed venue, he was literally beaming all over his face and was in the best of moods. His wife and son learned that he had just had an important meeting with someone in the airport building and was highly delighted that the discussion at the meeting seemed to have gone very well indeed. Pressed for time, his son simply accepted the explanation and no further questions were asked.

Thus it was that two businessmen met at Zurich airport in the summer of 1986—their aims were compatible and the chemistry between them was right. They parted feeling quite positive and even inspired, and looked forward confidently to a continuation of the talks. However, things didn't turn out the way they expected. Scarcely had the Hoechst CEO begun to implement the concept at home by the River Main than in the course of his endeavours he met with huge resistance especially in one of his oldest plants. At the same time, the Sandoz CEO by the River Rhine set to work on the project, too, but was stopped abruptly by an unforeseen event.

The company centenary

Prior to 1986 Sandoz was a typical *business-to-business* company, which mainly manufactured intermediates for processing plants. Emphasis was placed on cultivating close contacts to customers in the chemicals sector and doctors in the pharmaceuticals industry and there was cooperation with customers from agriculture. The only company run by Sandoz which had dealings with the general public was rooted in nutrition by way of such brands as Ovaltine, Isostar and Wasa. The company was convinced that its work based on science and dedication was of a high standard. It paid its taxes, defined itself as a good

27 Conversation with Juerg Schweizer in Oberwil on 24 Mar. 2010.

citizen and as a *corporate citizen*—but the importance of the general public, i. e. public relations, still had to be discovered. The centenary celebrations in 1986 afforded a golden opportunity.

For various reasons the jubilee was to be something special. Events had been arranged to take place throughout the entire year. However, basically, there were three highlights. The official opening ceremony took place in the large festival hall of the Mustermesse in Basel on 27th May 1986. In his official speech, Marc Moret predicted a change in information policy, i. e. from an employee-orientated company to a public-orientated one.[28]

On 7th June there was a private function, the 'Centenary Saturday,' at the entire factory site in Muttenz. Only those in possession of the 'Fest-Tüechli,' festive polyester scarves imprinted with Sandoz's Foron dye, gained admission and were entitled to free public transport to the centenary area. Even though it was pouring out of the heavens, more than 18,500 employees with their relatives and special guests paid a courtesy visit to Sandoz, where they were received and entertained in style. It may be justifiably claimed that never before had there been such a concentration of show business in Basel as there was on that centenary Saturday in Muttenz. There were performances by around 1,300 artists; a real highlight was provided by the Hubstapler-Ballet in choreography by Heinz Spoerli, the director of the Basel Ballet.

On 13th September, a week after the private function in Muttenz, Sandoz held an open day at its premises in Basel so that the general public in St. Johann could take a look behind the scenes at the laboratories and production facilities.

The fire at Schweizerhalle 1986[29]

During the early hours of 1st November 1986, only six weeks after the open day in Basel, the company was shaken to its very foundations by a catastrophe in Muttenz, seven kilometres from Basel cathedral as the crow flies; shortly after midnight on that Saturday, a fire, the cause of which has remained a mystery to this day, broke out in Building 956, a store at Sandoz's Schweizer-

---

28 "Festschrift Sandoz" 1986; see the *Basler Zeitung,* 28 May 1986.
29 *Sandoz-Gazette,* vol. 18, No. 243a, Special Issue, 26 Nov. 1986; See the Basler Zeitung (Ed.): *Die Katastrophe von Schweizerhalle; Zwei Wochen im November 1986: Eine Dokumentation aus Originalartikeln der Basler Zeitung,* zusammengestellt von Roger Berger, Basel 2006 (A collection of original articles from the *Basler Zeitung* on the catastrophe at Schweizerhalle compiled by Roger Berger).

The fire at Schweizerhalle on 1 Nov. 1986

halle premises, where agricultural chemicals were kept. The police reported the fire at 19 minutes past midnight and two minutes later sent out a general fire alarm. For more than four hours, several hundred firemen were in action; more than 1,300 tonnes of burning chemicals had to be extinguished; about 25 m³ of water per minute were used in the attempt to put out the fire.

There were no casualties, but widespread pollution extending 250 kilometres down the Rhine caused the massive death of fish. The Schweizerhalle plant had no collecting tank so that water used to extinguish the fire, now a deep red in colour, was able to get into the Rhine without being treated. Further consequences were widespread odour nuisance and pollution of the air and soil. Damage amounted to CHF 17.8 million; third party liability, the disposal of debris from the fire and the subsequent soil decontamination were put at CHF 122 million. According to the 'Wissenschaftlicher Dienst' (scientific services), the most likely cause of the fire was the shrinkage of a pallet of 'Berlin Blue'. A counter-opinion set out other possibilities but the examination ordered by the public prosecutor found insufficient proof of the actual cause.

In the previous decade there had been three major incidents that had shocked the chemicals industry and brought it into disrepute. On 10th July 1976, there had been a leak in a factory run by Icmesa, a subsidiary of Givaudan, near Seveso in Italy. An unknown quantity of highly toxic dioxin had escaped and contaminated a large, densely populated area. Years later, the incident was still uppermost in the minds of the public when barrels containing toxic substances disappeared in 1982 and could not be located for a considerable time. Union Carbide was responsible for a further incident which occurred in Bhopal, India, on 3rd December 1984. Due to a technical mishap methyl isocyanate had escaped taking a huge toll on human life. Then, on 26th April 1986, just a few months before the fire in Schweizerhalle, there was the explosion in Chernobyl, the nuclear power station in Ukraine, which had such fatal consequences.

Apart from all these incidents, the fire in Schweizerhalle, too, was considered to be one of the worst ever environmental disasters. It not only shattered belief in the safety of the chemical industry but also damaged the reputation of both Sandoz and the chemical industry in Switzerland in general. The company was increasingly subjected to criticism from the media and the public; the population was up in arms.

However not only the management but the employees, too, came under fire. Suddenly people were ashamed of working in the chemicals industry. It even reached a stage where some chemists felt compelled to have details of their profession deleted from the telephone directory. Feelings ran high and there was a real smear campaign, something which was completely new for Sandoz and which worried Marc Moret considerably as he found it hard to deal with.

Sandoz was greatly shocked by the accident at Schweizerhalle and its aftermath, which was also due to the inadequate communication on the part of the company. Hoechst AG had a similar experience after the so-called 'Shrove Monday Incident' in Griesheim seven years later.

The disaster on the Rhine attracted an avalanche of annihilating press reports in which Switzerland was depicted, throughout Europe, in a negative light. At the same time, it was an inducement to rethink protection measures in the case of hazardous incidents, water pollution and crisis management. According to Martin Syz,[30] the incident, against all the odds, had no lasting detrimental effects on day-to-day business; instead, it heightened the profile of the company and its products globally so that its impact on turnover figures was, contrary to expectations, favourable rather than unfavourable.

Sandoz drew lessons from the devastating fire disaster and systematically put them into operation; professional environmental measures e. g. the 'Rhine Funds' were introduced: the new awareness of the attendant risks led to a gradual relocation of production facilities to out-of-town sites.

Within the company, the accident at Schweizerhalle also functioned as an accelerator, because all the alterations which followed at Sandoz were not only

---

30 Martin Syz, 10 Dec. 2009.

industry-specific and dictated by the spirit of the times but were also actuated by the 1986 fire, which forced the pace significantly.

Ringaskiddy

It cannot be denied that Marc Moret was a strategic genius, who recognised trends early on and and acted accordingly: science developed from organic chemicals towards synthetic chemicals, and then to *biosciences*. Aware that the profitable business of pharmaceuticals would change he tackled the topic without further ado. After Ireland joined the EU—still the European Community at the time—in 1973, numerous international chemical groups settled their subsidiaries in County Cork, in the south of the island. A *new enterprise zone* emerged, a textbook example of clustering. Johnson & Johnson, Eli Lilly, Misui Schering-Plough, Henkel, Pfizer and SmithKline Beecham were already located there when Marc Moret applied, in 1989, for permission to build on 40 hectares of wasteland in Ringaskiddy[31] near the port of Cork. Almost simultaneously he began to streamline the structure of Sandoz and make it more flexible. He divided the company into various separate legal entities in a holding company. The former business units were divided into six divisions: Chemicals, Pharmaceuticals, Agriculture, Seeds, Food, and Construction and Environment. This restructuring was called 'Sandoz-90-Reorganisation' and was to last until 1995.[32]

Sandoz-90-Reorganisation

Moret prefaced his ultimate goal, at that time not clearly perceptible, with a quote from Blaise Pascal, the French philosopher: "We anticipate the future as too slow in coming, as if in order to hasten its course" as it appears in the Sandoz *Annual Report* of 1989.[33] It would appear that Moret could not wait for the future to happen. Comparable to the overhead value analysis of 1981 when things were by no means going badly for Sandoz and yet strict restruc-

---

31 See Christian Zeller: "Beyond Globalization: Scales and Speed of Production in Pharmaceutical Industry," in: ESPACE. Economies in Space, Working Papers in Economic Geography no. 2007–2, Bern 2002, p. 11.
32 *Annual report of Sandoz 1990*, pp. 6–7, 12–13.
33 *Annual Report of Sandoz 1989*, p. 7.

turing measures and downsizing in personnel were put into effect, Moret was in a strong position and therefore acted deliberately when he explained in the subsequent *Annual Report* why he was undertaking the reorganisation and restructuring of Sandoz: "We anticipate a more difficult business environment. When reaching such decisions it is essential to be farsighted and to choose the right moment, otherwise they can easily become lost opportunities."[34]

The 'Sandoz-90-Reorganisation' i. e. the transformation of the six existing divisions into stock corporations and their amalgamation in the Sandoz Holding, was the first step towards a later focusing of activities on the Life Science Division and the demerging of non-priority lines of business. The restructuring also meant a geographical reorganisation of the group: e. g. the Chemicals Division was moved from Basel to Muttenz, Huningue and Prat in Spain.

The Chemicals Division and its future had occupied Sandoz for years before it was actually spun-off. Herbert Wohlmann[35] remembers that when Director of Finance Raymand Breu was a guest at a meeting in Alsace of lawyers from Sandoz Legal Department in autumn 1989, he was asked over an aperitif: "What has the Chemicals Division still got that Sandoz has to keep it?" Wohlmann, who at that time had just moved from pharmaceuticals to chemicals, quickly forgot this incident but he did remember it when Clariant was established in 1995. In retrospect Wohlmann also figured out that the demerger process had been put in motion as early as 1990 because in the course of diversification he was given the task of establishing subsidiaries for the Chemicals Division in the Far East and of breaking loose from the earlier distributors, which is what happened in Thailand, Singapore, Malaysia and Taiwan.

By the way, there were some sharp-tongued wisecracks during the 'Sandoz-90-Reorganisation'. One of them was that Schweizer wanted to become a '*Divisionär*,' which was why '*divisionalisation*' was taking place at Sandoz. A '*Divisionär*' is an officer's rank and is the name of a major general in the Swiss army.

"We are going to sell you"

On the morning of 6th January 1995 the phone rang in Albert Hug's[36] office at Sandoz and he was asked to come with Martin Syz to the main building. Rolf W. Schweizer and Raymund Breu were already waiting and announced to the

34 Ibid.
35 Interview with Herbert Wohlmann in Muttenz on 9 Feb. 2010.
36 Interview with Albert Hug in Muttenz on 13 Jan. 2010.

two of them: "We are going to sell the Chemicals Division." To all intents and purposes the news was totally unexpected, but Hug was the controller and had had an inkling of what was going on behind the scenes. For some time there had been a large number of hints, questions and signs, which would have explained many a thing to him earlier but which only made real sense now.

It was under these circumstances that Hug learned of the spin-off. But as early as 1990, when the reorganisation into divisions began officially at Sandoz, Victor Bischoff, the then Director of Finance and Raymund Breu's predecessor, had sent for Hug and hinted in the subsequent conversation that in fact the Chemicals Division no longer fitted into the group.

Hug reports that on that January morning in 1995 Syz was instructed to work out a business plan and he himself was to present a comprehensive bank-compliant financial background. As the five-year plan had just been drawn up three months earlier, Hug used this as a basis to create, on paper, a pro-forma company consisting only of the Chemicals Division. Breu lent Hug his support by specifying the prerequisites he could take as a starting point. For example, the new company was to continue, for a limited period, to make use of such services at Sandoz as bookkeeping, payroll accounting and the pension fund against payment in cash.

Martin Syz reports that with the demerging of chemicals, whose profitability was 15 to 20 percent below the company average, there was hope of increasing the total profitability of the parent company, which would have a favourable impact on the share price of Sandoz. It was the intention of the Board to achieve high proceeds from the sale of the Chemicals Division on the one hand but to retain the social environment for the workforce on the other hand. With this in mind, there were two possibilities: to sell the division to a strategic investor or to float it on the market.

Initial public offering 1995

What exactly was SSC?

Marc Moret intended to focus the strategic alignment of his group on pharmaceuticals and food. As a result it was decided either to remodel the Chemicals Division as a completely independent, listed company or to sell it in its entirety to a strategic purchaser.

Just before Clariant was founded in 1995 Moret, along with Schweizer, approached Pierre Borgeaud,[37] the former President of the Board of Directors of Sulzer, the long-standing engineering group. In the period from 1987 to 1993 Borgeaud had held office as chairman of Vorort, the local economic umbrella organisation,[38] which preceded today's Economiesuisse. After outlining to the man from Winterthur the plans to demerge Sandoz Specialty Chemicals (SSC) in the very near future and the exciting task of putting a new company on the right track, the two Sandoz men asked him whether he would be prepared to take a seat on the Board of Directors of the future company.

Borgeaud was decidedly interested in becoming acquainted with another industrial sector in addition to engineering. However, he did not see his function on the Board as only attending the four meetings a year but rather as a committee member because that would demand much more from him. Clariant was not to have a committee but a presidium consisting of Rolf W. Schweizer, Markus Kündig and Pierre Borgeaud. This triumvirate determined and guided the fortunes of Clariant until 2001. Usually Roland Lösser, in his capacity as CFO, also participated in the meetings of the presidium.

---

37 Interview with Pierre Borgeaud in Winterthur on 28 Jul. 2010.
38 See Bernehard Wehrli: *Aus der Geschichte des Schweizerischen Handels- und Industrievereins 1870–1970: Zum hundertjährigen Bestehen des Vororts*, Zurich 1970.

Borgeaud[39] describes Moret and Schweizer as entrepreneurial personalities, two powerful minds who got on well with each other but who also met head on. The relationship between Moret and Schweizer becomes somewhat clearer when we read Borgeaud's description of Schweizer's attitude to the new challenge of spinning off Sandoz Chemicals in 1995: "I only know from Mr Schweizer that he told me at that time that he had not actually been looking for a new challenge." Anyone who is aware of Moret's way of delegating responsibility will know that it is likely to have been a case of the Sandoz Chairman quite simply telling his CEO: "You'll take charge of it."

The announcement was made officially on 23rd March 1995: "Sandoz is planning to spin off the Chemicals Division; this will enable the company to set its own priorities."[40] Thus it was that the Basel chemical companies—Sandoz and Ciba-Geigy—gained a fourth member: SSC.[41]

What was behind SSC? The former Sandoz Chemicals Division, Sandoz Specialty Chemicals, later Clariant, described itself as a leading international manufacturer of specialty chemicals that was among the top global companies in the field of dyestuff chemicals. The company developed, produced and distributed a wide range of products from dyes and chemicals for the textile, paper and leather industries; pigments for the plastics, man-made fibres, printing ink and paint industries; to additives and masterbatches for the plastics and man-made fibres industries.

On a pro-forma basis, SSC generated a turnover of CHF 2.3 billion in 1994. Operating profit amounted to CHF 214 million; net profit totalled CHF 103 million. While business in Europe had contributed 41 percent to the total turnover, sales in North America constituted 22 percent. The Asia-Pacific Region accounted for 21 percent and Latin America/Africa 16 percent. As of 31st December 1994 Sandoz Specialty Chemicals had assets worth CHF 2.4 billion. The head office was to be in Muttenz and the new company had around 8,700 employees worldwide.

According to Herbert Wohlmann,[42] who as future Head of Clariant Legal was permitted to participate in the talks but had no negotiating power whatsoever, the future Clariant men were objects rather than subjects in the spin-off proceedings. The drivers sat in the legal department of what remained of Sandoz, under the aegis of Urs Bärlocher, Peter Rickli, Gerhard Schmid and lawyer Rolf Watter; these were the driving force. The entire concept was

39 Pierre Borgeaud, 28 Jul. 2010.
40 *Sandoz Information intern* , 23 Mar. 1995, p. 1.
41 Urs Aeberli: "Da waren's plötzlich vier," in *Handelszeitung*, 1 Jun. 1995, p. 3.
42 Herbert Wohlmann, 9 Feb. 2010.

drawn up by Sandoz, where it was decided which equipment Clariant was to take with it and the amount of debt and burdens it had to carry. It soon became clear that life would not be a bed of roses for the young company.

Moreover, Herbert Wohlmann reports that what Moret was prepared to grant to Clariant was far from abundant. He only provided them with sparse funding and with the bare necessities as far as buildings were concerned. Even before things started in earnest it was clear: reorganisation was the first priority and costs would have to be reduced even more. To crown it all, Moret gave the future Clariant employees the feeling of being cast out. A meagre starting point! Only in one respect did Moret facilitate the new start: at least they did not have to share responsibility for the old deposits of toxic waste from the dumping ground of the plant in Basel.

The first men appointed

The first men who were appointed to lead SSC to success were six experts with work experience abroad, in their mid-fifties, from the second and third management levels, who knew precisely that their future field of activity, as Sandoz's plans went, was not particularly attractive and that they could not exactly be regarded as the 'crown jewels', the best of what the parent company had to offer. The jewels, the top managers, Moret kept for himself. The others were put in a tiny boat that appeared no bigger than a nutshell and abandoned on the high seas of the chemical industry. The paddle was seized by Rolf W. Schweizer as President of the Board of Directors, who was still a member of the Sandoz Board of Directors at the time.

Martin Syz, who had been in charge of the Chemicals Division at Sandoz since 1993, became CEO; Roland Lösser, at that time still Head of Finance in the USA, became CFO. Other members of the Board of Management were Hanspeter Knöpfel, Peter Brandenberg, Albert Hug and Herbert Link.

With the articles of corporation dated 24th May 1995, Clariant AG, based in Zug, with a share capital of CHF 150.1 million, was published in edition 109/1995 of the 8th June 1995, page 3,184 in the Swiss Commercial Gazette (Schweizerisches Handelsamtsblatt). The persons registered were Rolf W. Schweizer, Raymund Breu and Alexandre Jetzer. The purpose of the registration: 'Acquisition of an interest in companies which are active in the field of chemicals and related fields; entitled to acquire, pledge, exploit and sell real estate and intangible rights.'

The first men appointed: Hanspeter Knöpfel, Albert Hug, Peter Brandenberg, Martin Syz, Herbert Link, Roland Lösser (l-r), 1995

Junctim

Sandoz conducted the spin-off of its Chemicals Division under the code name: *Junctim*. The Latin word *iunctum* means more or less 'connected to' and is a legal term describing the coupling of rules and conditions which are inherently independent. In legal practice, the term is used to describe the linkage of contracts and laws which are only dealt with together. In simple terms, the view is taken that the one isn't possible without the other.

Applied to the example of the Chemicals Division, the code name *Junctim* can be understood programmatically as follows: without getting rid of the Chemicals Division, Sandoz was hampered, had too much ballast and not enough room to manoeuvre in coming strategies. Without doubt the spin-off in 1995 was an important prerequisite for future developments in 1996. One wasn't possible without the other.

It was planned that in the event of a share placement Sandoz Chemicals Division would assume financial liabilities amounting to CHF 750 million. The parent company would not only have benefited from the assumption of these debts by the business unit that was being spun off but at the same time was also to receive the proceeds from the sale of the shares.

The intention to spin off SSC from Sandoz was commonly known when

Jürgen Dormann announced in the *Frankfurter Allgemeine Zeitung* on 13th June 1995 that Hoechst was examining options such as joint ventures, going public or even a possible sale in marginal activities and in such areas where a leading position could not be achieved in the foreseeable future. This statement particularly applied to Hoechst Specialty Chemicals, which found itself in a similar position to Sandoz Specialty Chemicals in Basel.

In view of the great excitement which prevailed in the Sandoz head office at the time, this news probably did not arouse any special feelings because everything centred round SSC in St. Johann. Clariant's IPO was the largest there had ever been in Switzerland and never before had anyone at Sandoz had anything to do with a transaction of this kind. Sandoz had imposed a very tight schedule for the enormous and extensive preparation demanded by the project.

Christoph Mäder,[43] employed in 'Corporate Legal,' remembers that Sandoz had a very lean organisation, which quickly and efficiently pressed ahead with decisions once they had been reached: "Sandoz was a company that made bold decisions and followed them through immediately. Schedules were always decidedly ambitious." If nothing else, this consistent approach bore Marc Moret's hallmarks. Mäder, who with Herbert Wohlmann and Martin Henrich under senior lawyer Peter Rickli was involved in the preparations, reports that work was carried out night and day to support the spin-off and Clariant's IPO and to have the necessary resources involved in place.

Going public

Sandoz showed originality in the course of the spin-off and transition of the Chemicals Division from the group to independence: in accordance with the bookbuilding method, the shares were offered to institutional investors who determined the share price in an auction beforehand. What was new was the fact that this method, which had been tried out abroad a few times, provided for a slice of the shares being set aside for private investors. Likewise, during the entire process, the Chemicals Division could have been acquired *en bloc* by one of the existing potential buyers. Had an offer been made that was higher than the share price determined in the bookbuilding process, Sandoz might have had to accept it in the interest of the shareholders. Head of Finance Raymund Breu actually put the chances of this option at 50 percent.

---

43 Interview with Christoph Mäder in Basel on 1 Mar. 2010.

After it became known that Sandoz intended to sell their Chemicals Division or float it, some private equity companies also expressed an interest. These private equity investment companies frequently bought up a promising start-up, waited for a few years until it obtained good results and then resold it at a profit.

These potential buyers naturally wished to become acquainted with the company and so for a small exclusive number of guests there were several presentations at Sandoz which always followed the same pattern. The future management team was introduced and business figures and prognoses were discussed. Usually the private-equity investors required the management team to participate financially to ensure that the management would do its utmost to make a success of the company. Herbert Link[44] reports that the promises made were always the same: "It's safe to say that we will keep the company for five or six years and then it will be sold. Either we go public or we find another investor, who will take you over and integrate you like ICI, like DuPont." At the same time the investors referred in particular to the leverage effect resulting from the financial participation: if the Clariant management invested two years' salary, it would mean a return of 50 years salary in the case of an IPO. The Sandoz men had to listen to this at every presentation.

Once, at one of these events, Raymund Breu,[45] as a representative of the organisation that was selling, took up position at the wall behind the private-equity investors. When they began the same old song, Breu could not help waving his arms behind them pretending to play the shawm and the fiddle to indicate: "Don't believe these charlatans!" Even today Herbert Link can still picture Breu pretending to play the shawm and the fiddle. Although the promises made by the potential investors could not be believed entirely, it was essential to listen to their proposals as there might, after all, have been an attractive offer for Clariant among them.

The IPO was preceded by three weeks in which two teams each, made up of three members of the future Clariant management, set off on a road show as of 7th June to introduce the young company to potential investors at major international financial centres. The aim was to encourage investors to buy shares. Roland Lösser, Hanspeter Knöpfel and Martin Syz[46] comprised the group which visited Europe and America; Peter Brandenberg, Albert Hug and Herbert Link travelled throughout the Asia-Pacific region. Both groups were accompanied by bank representatives.

44 Interview with Herbert Link in Muttenz on 13 Apr. 2010.
45 Interview with Raymund Breu in Basel on 27 Jan. 2010.
46 Martin Syz, 10 Dec. 2009.

The order of events followed the same pattern: the presentation which had been well prepared was given in a hotel, after which the protagonists had to be ready to answer questions from the potential buyers so that the latter could see for themselves whether an investment in the new company would be worthwhile or not. After that the so-called book-building began: i. e. the investors had to lay down how many shares and to what price they would be prepared to buy. Some of them were not prepared to pay more than CHF 200 while others might be prepared to pay CHF 400. On the basis of this data, the banks gained considerable insight into the purchasing interest worldwide and were able to calculate the best price for placing the share on the market. Obviously the budding Clariant men had little influence on the fixing of the issue price. Unlike Sandoz they would have preferred a lower entry level price.

The biggest ever IPO in Switzerland, which had been prepared in minute detail, was carried out by the Schweizerische Bankgesellschaft, the Schweizerische Bankverein and S. G. Warburg from Great Britain, who presided over a consortium of eleven banks. The spin-off and the process of going public were preceded by a press conference in the 'Haus zum Rüden' in Zurich on 6th June 1995. Rolf W. Schweizer, Sandoz CFO Raymund Breu, Martin Syz and Roland Lösser gave a lecture on 'Newco', the future *new company*, before invited economic journalists and the international press. The four men were accompanied by Alexandre Jetzer, who was the CEO at Sandoz, and representatives from UBS and Warburg.

At that point, SSC published a preliminary placement brochure containing comprehensive details on the business, the strategy and the financial benchmark data of the new firm. Based on a very tight schedule, the initial public offering took place as follows: after price discovery until 15th June, the price framework was fixed and announced during the week that followed. As of the 16th, institutional investors handed in details of their offers with prices and the number of shares. This part of the proceedings is termed bookbuilding. The precise issuing price—CHF 385—was determined on 26th June after night-long negotiations with the banks. The public offer for small shareholders, the retail placing, took place in Switzerland from 27th to 28th June. Allotment was to be on 29th June and the three Swiss Stock Exchanges recorded a strong new admission on 30th June 1995: the Clariant share was listed and trade could begin. The shares were also traded on the SEAQ in London.

The first official quotation appears to have come from the exchange in Geneva and amounted to CHF 387. In Basel the price started at CHF 388 but in the end dropped to CHF 387 and it was at this level that the exchange in Zurich opened. Then the share rose to CHF 389 and closed at CHF 388. On the

Stückelung		ISIN (Int. Val.-Nr.)	Serie Nr.
1 00 0000002	CH0003760888	00 000001	

Clariant AG
Clariant SA
Clariant Ltd.

Zertifikat Nr.	1	über	*2*	**Namenaktie(n)**
				von je hundert Franken
Certificat No		pour		**action(s) nominative(s)**
				de cent francs chacune
Certificate Nr.		for		**registered share(s)**
				of hundred Francs each

Herr
Martin Henrich

Basel

ist im Aktienregister der Clariant AG als Eigentümer(in) dieser Aktie(n) eingetragen.
est inscrit(e) au registre des actions de Clariant SA comme propriétaire de la (des) présente(s) action(s).
is registered in the share register of Clariant Ltd. as owner of this (these) share(s).

Clariant AG
Clariant SA
Clariant Ltd.

Für den Verwaltungsrat:
Muttenz, 25.07.95   Pour le Conseil d'administration:
For the Board of Directors:

Der Präsident: Ein Mitglied:
Le président: Un membre:
The chairman: A member:

Der Indossant: Übertragungsvollmacht
L'endosseur: vorhanden
The endorser: vorbehältlich Widerruf

Dr. R.W. Schweizer   P. Borgeaud

100 000	10 000	1000	100	10	1
*******	*******	*******	*******	*******	zwei

000004

<425.0001/8515>

The first Clariant share certificate dated 25th July 1995

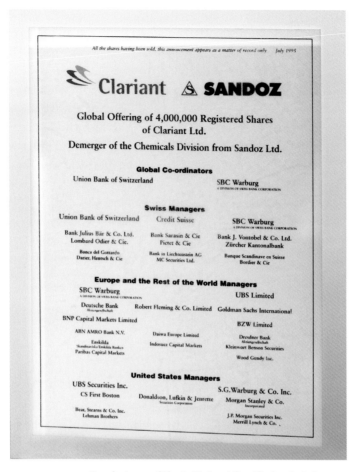

Tombstone of the initial public offering in July 1995

grey market the securities had been valued at CHF 392. Traders reported price management by the Schweizerische Bankgesellschaft. The issue price reached CHF 385 with a nominal value of CHF 100. Around 60 percent of the 3.56 million shares on offer were placed in Switzerland.

According to agency reports almost 40 percent were acquired by international investors. However, the demand in the USA turned out to be surprisingly low. The shares were listed on the exchange in Frankfurt[47] from mid-1997, too.

---

47 Although trade with the Clariant share took place predominantly on the Swiss Exchange, it was temporarily listed on the small and mid-caps segment of Frankfurt security exchange from 1 Jul. 1997. This measure meant little additional expenditure and in the course of the merger with Hoechst's Specialty Chemicals served to bring the share of the Swiss company to the attention of German retail investors. As the cost of listing in Germany did not decrease and the volume of shares traded on the German exchange remained very low, it was decided to restrict trading

Today, shares are no longer available in certificate form, which renders the Clariant share number 1 all the more beautiful. It was placed at our disposal by a long-serving Sandoz employee from Litigation at Novartis International AG to act as an illustration.[48]

In July 1995 Clairant was awarded its first *tombstone* and further *tombstones* were to follow. As a rule, the so-called *financial tombstones* are highly transparent geometric shapes which are awarded by banks to business partners or employees in honour of and as a bonus for successful deals or consultations. The blocks which are the size of a hand are inscribed with the date of the deal, the logo and frequently characteristic motifs of the object which had been negotiated.

Clariant's first award of this kind was related to the IPO. The white foil laminated with acrylic displays the logos of both Clariant and Sandoz, the number of shares subscribed—4,000,000 in total—and the names of the 32 banks in the order of their participation in the transaction.

Naming

Finding a name was unknown territory for all concerned because no one had ever been involved in such a process before. Consequently the search for a suitable idea proved, at first, to be very rough and ready: the Sandoz men who were being spun off were called upon to suggest a name for the new company which they were to fax or hand in at the gates. A prize was offered to encourage employees to participate: the one to create the future company name would win a weekend trip. As a result, many people in Basel and abroad got together and began trying to create a word.

However, it was by no means the competition which provided an incentive to participate and do some thinking, but rather the feeling of having been cast out and the fear of losing one's identity. It is important to realize that in the process of cutting all ties and becoming independent the loss of their name was one of the greatest shocks for the staff—a circumstance which was extremely painful and triggered a sense of collective embarrassment. Up to that time employees could be proud of their job at Sandoz—even the circle of family and friends acknowledged this status. Sandoz was a name everyone

---

to Switzerland. The share was delisted on 25 Sept. 2003. See e-mail from Philipp Hammel on 26 Nov. 2010.

48 At this point my sincerest thanks to Mr Martin Henrich of Basel.

knew, but suddenly they did not belong anymore. The hand which had offered protection for so long now pointed its forefinger in no uncertain terms to an uncertain future. It was not just a matter of no longer being entitled to use the name, but the fact that no one even knew what the company would be called at all in future.

Personal anxiety about the future was one aspect and worry about loss of business was the other. They saw themselves faced with huge problems and were convinced that the change of name would be a gigantic obstacle and the familiarity engendered by the name would be lost in the market. "The whole spin-off team and even the employees fought fiercely for the right to retain the name of Sandoz Chemicals," Herbert Link reports. "We feared there would be huge economic disadvantages if we had to use a different name." Link had travelled the world and he knew from experience that the brand name of the Basel company meant something to the dyer or leather worker even in the backwoods of China or India: "Ah, Sandoz. Yes, yes, we know."[49]

That is the reason why in most suggestions either part of the word *Sandoz*, at least the letter *S* , a dyes concept or the location were included in some way: i. e. every effort was made to pass on something of its origins to the new company. Early in April 1995 the spin-off team had already received several hundred suggestions, which were put into lists and discussed by a committee. The mile-long catalogue of imaginary names and compound words contained creations such as *Aceco* (= *Autonome Chemical & Color AG*), *Forsan* (= *formerly Sandoz*) or *Safa* (= *Sandoz Fabrik*), noteworthy because of their triviality.

All in all, the attempt to find a name within the company proved to be rather unsuccessful and after one of the leading banks involved suggested, in a memo, putting the matter into professional hands, the proposal was taken to heart and the two companies that were recommended were approached. One of these was prepared to give a presentation in Basel within a few days. Thus it was that Siegel+Gale was chosen, an advertising agency which had been established in New York in 1969 and had rapidly become the leader in strategic branding in the world. Siegel+Gale was the agency that created the brand name for Microsoft's computer software, coming up with the name Windows with its four distinctive undulating coloured windows. The brand identities of Yahoo!, Danone, IBM, the US Air Force, American Express, Dell, and 3M were also created by Siegel+Gale. Novartis which was established in 1996 can still be found as a reference on their homepage.

---

49 Herbert Link, 13 Apr. 2010.

It was at the end of April 1995 that the London branch office of Siegel+Gale received the request from Basel to create a new name for Sandoz Specialty Chemicals, which was being demerged. As a basis for the promising creation of a new name the branding experts outlined strategic and conceptual prerequisites to the spin-off team. The most important of these was making the future employees aware of the fact that the future did not lie in the past and that it was not a question of them liking the new name but rather that it was an undeniable fact the name would have to assert itself on foreign markets far, far from home. It was important that there should be no negative connotations worldwide; it should be easy to pronounce and read; it should be ageless and distinctive, but above all it should suit the purpose and objectives of the company.

Siegel+Gale began the creative process with dozens of names which had been researched beforehand. These were then reduced to a total of six—CLARIZON, CLARIUS, IRIZON, CHEMOSOL, SYMOX and of course CLARIANT—which were to be subject to a very thorough analysis. The spin-off team had a decided preference but suddenly the choice was made by Marc Moret: the new company was to be called CLARIANT.[50] Now it was up to the advertising agency to create the visual identity, the logo and the company trademark. On 15th May Siegel+Gale finally presented the name in three different forms, lettering and colours. At first the lettering was to be blue but Martin Syz refused to accept this as this colour had originally been used by Sandoz. Syz suggested green instead and thus it remained.

There were two concepts for the logo: a traditionally figurative one and a modern, implemented geometric signet. For the figurative portrayal the branding experts took their creation from the traditions to be found in the history of dyes and depicted the hexaplex trunculus, the banded dye murex, in front of the Clariant lettering. The presentation was given on a transparency on the aforementioned 15th May 1995. The association of the experimental Clariant logo with the traditional chemicals giants Bayer, Ciba, Hoechst, BASF, the Duisburg Kupferhütte, ICI and Zeneca, which had been spun off just before Clariant was founded, is particularly vivid.

Björn Edlund[51] reports that the logo, i.e. the symbol, was presented to Moret in the presence of Schweizer at a meeting of the designers. The design in colour on a sheet of A3 paper by British designer Nick Shaeff, who refers

---

50 "At Sandoz, the name Novartis had been one of the names short-listed for the chemicals business which was being spun off and which was, in the end, christened Clariant." See Albert Steck: "Novartis Teil 1, Die Fusion," in *Bilanz* no. 4/2006, 28 Feb. 2006.
51 Interview with Björn Edlund in Pratteln on 7 Sept. 2010.

Naming process, presentation transparency of
15 May 1995

to his authorship[52] in a website directory from Edinburgh, depicted four coloured feathers. At the meeting, those present tried to explain the significance of the plume of feathers, its form, the number of the recurring motifs and the colours. Planning must have been far advanced because a set of business cards with the name of Martin Syz, the new CEO, had already been printed. When deliberations became more and more lengthy and tedious, Moret intervened and rejected the number of motifs. He covered over the fourth, lilac-coloured feather with a sheet of paper, and the swoosh, as it was also known, was in turn pasted over and eliminated. Moret's argument was compelling: firstly, there were three and not four basic colours in dye chemicals and secondly—here he pointed to his nose with his index finger—his *intuition présidentielle* told him that his decision was the right one. That was how the fourth swoosh came to be missing. Later Walter Vaterlaus[53] had a glimpse of the large-sized sheet of cardboard with the aforementioned draft in Clariant's archives.

A clear(ant) answer

The new name *Clariant* came into force as of 7th June and replaced the temporary label *Sandoz Specialty Chemicals*. The logo was also completed but was not allowed to be used until 1st July 1995. It was defined as follows: "The elegant, dark green of the name reflects the quality and tradition of the young

52 http://uk.linkedin.com/pub/nick-shaeff/18/b84/579 (6 Apr.2010), "Clariant – name creation and branding identity for de-merger of Sandoz Chemical Dyestuff," Basel 1995."
53 Interview with Walter Vaterlaus in Zurich on 25 May 2010.

company and the plume of 3 feathers in yellow, red and blue stands for its momentum and entrepreneurship."[54]

Herbert Wohlmann[55] remembers that the employees who had responded to the appeal to find a name for the Chemicals Division which was to be spun off felt they had been passed over and in retrospect perceived the action as a fake because in the end the name chosen did not come from the staff but from an advertising agency. According to a modern legend, however, Clariant owes its name to the following occurence: an anxious, bewildered production worker from the Chemicals Division at Sandoz asked a manager what would happen to him after the spin-off and when he would finally get a precise answer to his open questions. The worker stammered and said, in his Swiss accent: "When do w-we g-get a c-clea-rant …, a c-clariant … a *Clariant-Wort* (a clear answer)?"

54 Clariant *Interne Mitteilung* (Internal Memo), 7 Jun. 1995.
55 Herbert Wohlmann, 9 Feb. 2010.

Fending for itself

Big Linkers

On 1st July 1995 the former Sandoz AG Chemicals Division began operations as a newly created and independent stock corporation trading under the name of Clariant. In the first phase of its existence, the management underwent a full-scale learning process as it was a gargantuan step from the running of a division to the management of an entirely independent company. Even if the management entered the scene of action with considerable trepidation, at least the Board of Directors was not lacking in experience.

The Clariant Board was composed of well-known personalities from the Swiss economy. The close corporate interrelations and interconnected activities of the so-called *Big Linkers*, about whom Swiss economists, historians and sociologists at the universities of St. Gallen, Zurich and Freiburg have produced complementary academic papers over the past few years, played a decisive role[56] in Rolf W. Schweizer's dealings and his company policy.

Measured against the population figures, there are a relatively large number of major international companies listed in Switzerland. Consequently, as there is only a small elite in economics and politics, it is often necessary for these people to hold multiple offices not only in companies but also on political, military and cultural committees.[57] Members of the Clariant Board were: Rolf W. Schweizer (Board of Directors and CEO Sandoz, Board of Directors Schweizerische Bankgesellschaft), ship-owner Eric André (Execu-

---

56 Michael Nollert: *Unternehmensverflechtungen in Westeuropa. Nationale und transnationale Netzwerke von Unternehmen, Aufsichtsräten und Managern.* Soziopulse – Studien zur Wirtschaftssoziologie und Sozialpolitik, vol. 3 (Post-doctoral Thesis, Zurich Univ., 2002), Berlin/Münster 2005, pp. 259–316.

57 Manuel Ammann/Daniel Matti/Rico de Wyss: "Performance Schweizerischer Verwaltungsräte anhand der Aktienkursentwicklung" in *Financial Markets and Portfolio Management*, no. 17/1, Mar. 2003, pp. 43–75.

tive Partner of André & Cie. SA, Chairman of the Suisse-Atlantique Société de Navigation maritime SA), entrepreneur Truls Berg (Board of Directors Attisholz-Gruppe, Biber Holding AG, Hakle AG, Schweizerische Mobiliar, Schweizerische Volksbank, Tela Papierfabrik), entrepreneur Pierre Borgeaud (Chairman of the Board of Directors of Sulzer Ltd., Board of Directors Bühler Ltd., Schweizer Bankgesellschaft, Société Internationale Pirelli SA, Winterthur Versicherungsgruppe), entrepreneur Urs Bühler (CEO Bühler-Gruppe, Board of Directors Schweizerische Bankgesellschaft, Sulzer Ltd., Winterthur Versicherungsgruppe), banker Hans-Ulrich Doerig (Vice-Chairman Crédit Suisse, Board of Directors Alusuisse-Lonza Holding AG, Elektrowatt AG, EXOR GROUP), Member of the St. Gallen Council of States Paul Gemperli (Council of States CVP St. Gallen), management consultant Jean-Claude Gisling (consultant), Member of the Zug Council of States Markus Kündig (Board of Directors Landis & Gyr AG, Merck AG, Metro International AG, Pelikan Holding AG, UBS Union Bank of Switzerland, Zurich Versicherungen) and two bankers Marcel Ospel (Member of the Group Executive Committee of Schweizerischer Bankverein) and Pierre de Weck (Vice-Chairman UBS Union Bank of Switzerland, Board of Directors Alcatel STR AG).

Thus, Rolf W. Schweizer had a Board of Directors *ad personam*: four bankers, five other companions from the old days, and suppliers. Most of them, however, were closely connected as *big linkers*. The only one who was entirely new and only known to Schweizer by sight rather than personally was Paul Gemperli, a tax expert, politician and army colonel from St. Gallen. Gemperli was surprised at his appointment to the Clariant Board of Directors, but regarded it as an honour and dealt with tax issues at meetings.

Cutting the cord

In addition to the duties which were an inherent part of the everyday business of a medium-sized company in the specialty chemicals trade, Clariant was to create innumerable organisational and legal rules and regulations during the transition period of several months.

For the time being contracts remained valid for employees, who also continued to be insured in the Sandoz AG pension fund. However, it was planned to introduce a new system in due course. At the same time, the benefits acquired at Sandoz to date were retained. Sandoz Pharma AG continued to take charge of Clariant's payroll but Clariant took over the administration of employees' accounts. The employee's identity card also remained valid. The Clariant logo only had to be pasted over the Sandoz logo. The same applied to business documents, invoices and other printed matter.

In view of the fact that Clariant had its own Board of Directors and shareholders, it seems decidedly odd and rather lacking in independence that the group had no staff of its own for press releases and, as far as communication was concerned, still relied on the parent company. When Schweizer still held the post of CEO at Sandoz, Björn Edlund,[58] the Chief Communication Officer there, did a lot for him in media relations. At Moret's instigation, the Swede acted as Communications Consultant for Clariant's management team before and for a long time after the IPO. Edlund was also to recruit a Communications Manager on behalf of Schweizer—but whom to choose? At that time, Dagobert Cahannes, now Media Officer of the Solothurn Governing Council, was a member of Edlund's communications team at Sandoz. He recalled a colleague with whom he had worked at IBM in Zurich. This colleague was tracked down and approached by Schweizer on the phone.

Learning by doing

By his own account, Walter Vaterlaus'[59] job at Clariant just fell into his hands. He was Chief Communications Officer in the textile engineering industry at Saurer in Zurich where in the early summer of 1995 the then
CEO, Melk Lehner, had left the company from one day to the next. Out of a sense of loyalty he asked to be released from his contract and looked forward to six months' leisure. Scarcely had he resigned from Saurer and was cycling in the Zurich lowlands on a wonderful afternoon in August 1995 when his mobile rang. It was Rolf W. Schweizer at the other end. He said he was CEO at Sandoz and told the unsuspecting Vaterlaus that a company called Clariant was to be floated on the exchange in a few weeks' time and was on the lookout for a communications manager.

Vaterlaus thought he had not heard right for up to that point he had had nothing to do with the pharmaceuticals industry or with chemicals. At all events, chemicals only came to mind in connection with the fire at Schweizerhalle in 1986. His father was a fire-brigade commander in Winterthur and

---

58 Björn Edlund, 7 Sept. 2010.
59 Walter Vaterlaus, 25 May 2010.

he himself had served in the voluntary fire brigade as a fire equipment operator. The accusations levelled at the fire brigade that the toxic substances from the fire in the storehouse in 1986 should not have been allowed to get into the Rhine with the water used to put out the fire had deeply hurt the feelings of the entire profession and given rise to a great deal of discussion.

Walter Vaterlaus was thinking of that when Schweizer asked him whether he was interested in the job and whether he could come to Sandoz in Lichtstrasse in Basel at 9 o'clock. As he had not even started to look for a job, Vaterlaus said yes, but he did wonder what had made Schweizer think of him. It was only later that he learned that the offer had been due to a former colleague. Vaterlaus arranged his résumé and references in an application file and during the night tried to obtain some information on Clariant. The data was sparse because the company had no website at that stage.

Next morning Vaterlaus drove to Basel and passed through Doris Hufschmid's outer office and was admitted to the old wood-panelled office where Rolf W. Schweizer and Martin Syz were sitting. After an interview of about 30 minutes Schweizer asked Vaterlaus when he could start work as Head of Communications at Clariant. Actually Vaterlaus would have liked to enjoy his six months' holiday, but he accepted the post on one condition—he wanted to see his future workplace at head office in Muttenz. A few days later Martin Syz showed him the plant in Muttenz.

When Vaterlaus took up employment at Clariant on 1st November 1995, Edlund[60] recommended Schweizer to involve the new Head of Communications in the work of the Board of Managers. After all, Vaterlaus could only give a good briefing if he could get an idea of what was going on at Clariant. Thus it was that Vaterlaus[61] became both Communications Manager and Secretary to the Board of Managers. Despite the fact the he was a complete stranger to the industry, he was to take the minutes at the meetings of the Management Board. He was unfamiliar with many expressions with the result that after the meetings he talked to each of the speakers personally to ensure that what he had written was in fact a true report of what had been said. Later, he was also asked to take the minutes in the Executive Committee of the Board of Management when it was established by Rolf W. Schweizer. Schweizer had initiated the committee, which also included the CEO and the CFO, so that he did not have to take part in the meetings of the Board of Management, which were much too time-consuming. It sufficed if he was informed of events in a

---

60 Björn Edlund, 7 Sept. 2010.
61 Walter Vaterlaus, 25 May 2010.

concise and compact form and he could focus on discussing major issues in a small group.

After the IPO, it was important to lend substance to and to make the name Clariant known and to showcase its products and services. Until then the preceding road shows had, at most, made the name familiar on the financial markets but not among the general public. Even the staff still felt they were deeply rooted in Sandoz and the new name still had to become a part of their hearts and minds. On the second or third day in his post, something caught new Communications Manager Walter Vaterlaus' eye. Looking out at the plant grounds from Martin Syz's office he noticed that the outline of the old Sandoz logo, which had hung there for years and which had only recently been taken down, could still be seen clearly and distinctly. "As long as that is up there, none of the employees are going to believe in the new company," Vaterlaus thought and in one of his first official acts tried to persuade the CEO to have a huge neon sign costing CHF 50,000 and with the Clariant logo on it put up in the same place instead. Although Syz pointed out that actually there was not such a sum of money available for this purpose, the Clariant logo was in fact put up.[62]

Start up, please!

Round about the same time as Vaterlaus was being interviewed by Schweizer at Sandoz's head office, American trade journal *Chemical Week* reported on Clariant's IPO in the issue dated 30th August to 6th September 1995 and published an interview with fledgling CEO Martin Syz.[63] The cover was very cleverly illustrated: on the blue ocean is a ship called *Sandoz* depicted as an aircraft carrier. The bird's-eye view of the runway emphasises the power and thrust of a pale jet with the inscription *Clariant* which is flying off in the opposite direction. The headline of the front-page story poses a question and voices, with reservation, the general thinking on Clariant, which has only been in existence for a few weeks: "The Shape of Things to Come?"[64]

The move from being a division within a group to an independent company was exceedingly challenging and from an IPO point of view well thought out

62 Ibid
63 David Hunter: Clariant: "Out on its own. Moving where the market is," in *Chemical Week*, 30 Aug. to 5 Sept. 1995, pp. 30–34.
64 The headline is purely and simply a play on words; the article has nothing to do with the futuristic novel of the same name by the English science-fiction author H. G. Wells.

EXXON Expands U.S. Polypropylene ♦ DUPONT Faces Benlate Fine ♦ MOBIL's *Para*-Xylene Process

chemicalweek

THE WORLDWIDE NEWS SOURCE FOR CHEMICALS MAKERS AND PROCESSORS   Aug. 30/Sept. 6, 1995 $8 U.S., $10 elsewhere

U.S. Trio Tries
Ethylene Harmony

Dendrimer Discovery

Clariant
The Shape of Things to Come?

Martin Syz, CEO

The headline of the front-page story in the trade journal
Chemical Week, 30 Aug./6 Sept. 1995

and unique in Switzerland. The company stood in the limelight, and the expectations placed in the young company and the employees were high. From an objective point of view, all the necessary conditions for a quick start were in place, but there was one thing which still had to be clarified.

To be sure, the little jet took off from the mothership, but what was to happen next? Simply put: the prerequisites were there, but where was Rolf W. Schweizer when it was time to get cracking? He spent the first six months in the history of Clariant at Sandoz. What was the reason? Had it to do with a successor for Moret or had the positions not been clearly defined?

It was as if no one was prepared to believe in the start-up of the company. When Clariant was founded, Schweizer had taken over the post of President of the Board of Directors in the new company but unlike his management he did not move to Muttenz but retained his office at Sandoz's head office in

Lichtstrasse. At that time many looked upon Schweizer as Marc Moret's potential successor.

According to Björn Edlund,[65] who held the post of Head of Communications at Sandoz in the period between 1993 and 1996, the relationship between Moret and Schweizer was characterized by mutual respect but defined by clear boundaries. Schweizer knew precisely where the boundaries lay. Moret could be demanding and difficult and it was not always easy to work in close proximity to him. On account of his strategic skill, however, his occasional, erratic moods were regarded by his associates with indulgence. For Edlund, for example, it was a pleasure to work in a company where decisions were taken and implemented that were really sound. The strategic focus could be palpably felt. There was never just talk; the appropriate action was taken also.

But, according to Martin Syz, Moret always 'played on two stages': he let two horses run to see which was the better. To a certain extent it came as a surprise at the end of 1995 when Schweizer was not the one to be appointed Head of Sandoz. Instead, it was proposed that he play a more active part in Clariant in future, which is what happened in the end.

"Schweizer Dismissed as Head of the Sandoz Group" could be read in the *Basler Zeitung* on 15th December 1995. Sandoz did not extend Schweizer's mandate. This was how he explained his 'resignation' as a member of the Board of Directors and CEO. Alexandre Jetzer was appointed to succeed him as CEO. Seen in retrospect, it looks as though Moret wanted to make use of other brain power in coping with the further measures which were still to follow at Sandoz. Moret's timing was, as ever, intentional.

After that Schweizer assumed the post of Chairman of the Clariant Board in addition to his post as President. He finally moved his workplace from Basel to Muttenz, where, for a start, there was no office available for him. For that reason Hanspeter Knöpfel made way for his boss, who was given the famous corner office on the top floor of Building 907.

Not media-shy

An important person, who accompanied Rolf W. Schweizer and Clariant's fortunes from the very beginning, is veteran economic journalist Felix Er-

---

65 Björn Edlund, 7 Sept. 2010.

bacher.[66] He describes Schweizer as a very ambitious man. Under Marc Moret, it cannot have been easy for him to curb his ambitions. Obviously he would have preferred to become Moret's successor. Perhaps he did something wrong there but evidently his tactics were very skilful and shrewd so that at least he became Head of Clariant, which was the second-best position in that constellation.

Felix Erbacher also knew Marc Moret from conducting several interviews with him and also from press conferences and press briefings on financial statements even though Moret was sometimes loath to attend meetings with the media. Erbacher believes that the Head of Sandoz did not have a very high opinion of journalists. It seems that Moret had a certain charm, but it was difficult to relate to him. He was a singular character.

Rolf W. Schweizer was entirely unlike Moret; at least that is what Erbacher experienced. Moreover, Schweizer regularly sought personal contact to journalists. The two of them had been in touch ever since Schweizer's time in pharmaceuticals from the 1990s and they had had lunch together on a number of occasions. Schweizer had a lot to talk about: amusing stories about parties with Russian colleagues in the industry or about overindulgence of vodka were one topic, business strategies which Schweizer put forward were another. The problem was that Erbacher did not always get the point immediately because the manager presupposed a lot of expert knowledge. For example, when Schweizer tackled the masterbatches project, Erbacher was permitted to attend a meeting of the division where everything was discussed so very openly as if the economic journalist were not present. Erbacher considered this to be an act of faith. Perhaps Schweizer had a fine instinct as far as Erbacher was concerned or he simply wanted Erbacher to be in a better position to understand the business on which he had to write a report afterwards. An almost symbiotic relationship developed between the two men, which was of mutual benefit.

To be sure, Clariant wished for favourable press reports and perhaps "he liked to see his photo in the newspapers and his name in print—that is a possibility," Erbacher comments, "but as far as I was concerned, I was given access to material that the others didn't have. It was our job to report on the chemicals industry in Basel in as much detail and as often as possible. We could not afford to miss anything and that was a way for our newspaper to make a name for itself. Without a doubt, we were, to a certain extent, on the same wavelength even though we were totally different types… He was actually the first

---

66 Interview with Felix Erbacher in Basel on 26 Feb. 2010.

manager I experienced in action at close quarters; he thought along strategic lines and in terms of the company, and I have to admit in all honesty that he was the greatest manager at that time, and that was not just in my eyes: other journalists were of the same opinion. The deal with Hoechst surpassed everything that had gone before!"[67]

Few people in Basel were aware of the fact that Rolf W. Schweizer and Jürgen Dormann from Hoechst had known each other since 1986. It was at that time that they had considered merging the dye divisions of Sandoz and Hoechst. However, it was not just business that connected them. They got along right from the start, words were not necessary. "There was esteem on both sides," Björn Edlund[68] says when describing the relationship between Dormann and Schweizer. Karl-Gerhard Seifert, too, became acquainted with Schweizer only a few years after the fire in Schweizerhalle.

But who were these people, where did they come from and above all, what did they have to offer that enabled Schweizer to become the greatest manager of his time?

67 Ibid.
68 Björn Edlund, 7 Sept. 2010.

The history of Hoechst[69]

The foundations for Hoechst AG,[70] as it subsequently came to be known, were laid as early as 1863: after several attempts, chemist Eugen Lucius and merchant Carl Friedrich Wilhelm Meister started up business together. In their employment were five workers, an office clerk and a technical director. Lucius was born in Erfurt in 1834. His father ran a spinning mill, a weaving mill, a printing works and a business importing English yarns in Thuringia and Saxony. After studying chemistry he graduated from Heidelberg with a PhD under the guidance of Robert Wilhelm Bunsen, his thesis advisor. Born in 1827, Meister came from a long-established Hamburg merchant family and had gained international experience in his father's trading houses in the Caribbean, Cuba, Venezuela and England.

Lucius and Meister met during their years of apprenticeship in Manchester and became brothers-in-law when they married[71] daughters of the Frankfurt painter Jakob Becker, who taught at the Städel Art School. When they were not even 30 years of age, Lucius acquired citizenship of the free town of Frankfurt on Main, took up residence there and together with his friend Meister and Ludwig August Müller, an uncle of their wives, commenced business with dyes in neighbouring Höchst on Main in 1863—at that period in history belonging to the Duchy of Nassau. Thus, only seven years after William Henry Perkins accidentally discovered mauveine, the tar dyes factory Meister Lucius & Co was founded beyond the gates of Frankfurt.

---

69 This chapter was written in cooperation with Dr. Wolfgang Metternich, keeper of Hoechst AG's archives between 1984 and 1999 and the manager of HistoCom GmbH, Frankfurt, between 1999 and 2009. Metternich was also involved in the draft of Stephan H. Lindner's book: *Hoechst: Ein I. G. Farben Werk im Dritten Reich*, Munich 2005, and in the editing of archives and sources. See Holger Vonhof: "Ein Beitrag zum Verstehen. Das Werk Höchst im Dritten Reich," in *Höchster Kreisblatt*, 18 Mar. 2005, p. 14; Ernst Bäumler: *Die Rotfabriker. Familiengeschichte eines Weltunternehmens*, Munich 1988; Schreier/Wex, 1990.

70 Interviews with Jürgen Dormann in Winterthur, 17 Feb. 2010 and 3 May 2010.

71 Wolfgang Metternich: *Der Maler Jakob Becker – Der Lehrer der Kronberger Maler*, Frankfurt a. M./Kronberg 1991, pp. 44–50.

The Empress Eugénie around 1860, painting by
Franz Xaver Winterhalter

The first product to be manufactured in the factory was fuchsine, a red-violet tar-based dye which earned the company the nickname 'Rotfabrik' (the red factory). Gradually a wide range of dyes was developed and these were soon being sold and distributed all over the world. In the year of foundation chemist Eugen Lucius already managed to invent aldehyde green, which was supplied in huge quantities to the textile industry in Lyon. This was the breakthrough for the young company; a decisive factor was a visit to the opera by Empress Eugénie of France in an evening gown, dyed in Lucius' aldehyde green, which retained its hue even in the gas light which was in use at the time.[72] The beautiful Empress's decided preference for green can be easily recognized in the famous portrait by Franz Xaver Winterhalter.

In 1869, only a few years after the company was founded, the premises were

72 Wolfgang Metternich: "Höchster Farben – Lyoner Seide. Was den Damen der Pariser Gesellschaft die Tränen in die Augen trieb," in *Festschrift Höchster Schlossfest* (Commemorative Publication on the occasion of the Höchst Castle Festival) Frankfurt a. M.-Höchst 2011, pp. 38–42.

Bird's-eye view of the dye works *Meister Lucius & Brüning* in 1897

bursting at the seams, so that the building of a new modern factory was begun just one kilometre from the previous location. Relocation was completed in 1874. The space which was now available sufficed to permit the further extension of the company in the following one hundred years.

From the very beginning the company placed great emphasis on social benefits for its employees. Immediately after the move to the new premises, a housing development programme was started, in the course of which around 1,400 dwellings consisting almost entirely of detached and semi-detached houses with kitchen gardens were built. In 1879, the Kaiser-Wilhelm-Augusta-Foundation was set up to provide a pension fund for staff.[73]

In 1880 the company was converted into a stock corporation called Farbwerke vormals Meister Lucius & Brüning. The company shares were traded on the stock exchange from 1888 on but the equity majority remained in the hands of the founding families until the establishment of I. G. Farbenindustrie AG in 1925.

Step by step, the company began to change from being nothing but a dye works to a chemicals company. In 1880, the construction of a new factory for inorganic acids facilitated the production of its own primary and intermediate products. In 1884 Antipyrine, an antypretic agent, was launched on the market and proved to be a huge success, thus making a not inconsiderable contribution to the company's excellent reputation in the pharmaceuticals

---

73 Eva Maria Blum: *Kultur, Konzerne, Konsens. Die Hoechst AG und der Frankfurter Stadtteil Höchst*, Frankfurt a. M. 1991 (Thesis, Tübingen Univ., 1991), p. 94–95.

A working-class house by *Farbwerke Meister Lucius &
Brüning* at the World Exhibition in Paris in 1900

sector and enabling it to acquire the sobriquet of 'The World's Pharmacy' in
the years that followed.

The first plant to be established abroad was opened in Moscow as early as
1878 but protectionism and patents legislation in Europe necessitated the setting up of further subsidiaries abroad. In 1883 a factory was opened in Creil
near Paris. This was followed by a subsidiary in Ellesmere Port near Manchester in 1908. In Germany, too, the construction of a branch factory began in
Gersthofen[74] in 1900. The plant was to make use of hydro-electric power from
the River Lech for the energy-intensive production of indigo.

---

74 Wolfgang Metternich: *Vom Chemiewerk zum Industriepark. 100 Jahre Chemieproduktion in
Gersthofen 1902–2002*; with a contribution by D. Wagner, Gersthofen 2002

During a trip to America in 1903, Bayer's Chairman Carl Duisberg explored the trusts there and committed his impressions to paper. His objective was the formation of a cartel of German dyeing companies, a cartel which was to avoid unwanted competition and friction loss. Although the German dye manufacturers were very interested, they did not want to give up their independence. In addition, they feared the anti-trust actions by legislators according to the American example—as a result no solutions were reached. In 1904, however, AGFA, Bayer and BASF formed the so-called *Dreibund*, a loosely defined cartel of three, while the dye works in Höchst and Cassella in Frankfurt formed a *Zweibund*, an association of two, which also became a *Dreiverband* when Kalle in Wiesbaden joined in 1907.

In 1913 Farbwerke vormals Meister Lucius & Brüning in Höchst on Main celebrated its 50th anniversary. By that time the company had already achieved a remarkable growth. In Höchst, there were almost 9,000 employees in the parent plant alone and turnover amounted to more than 100 million reichsmark.

But soon a shadow was to fall on the prosperous company for the anniversary year saw the death of Gustav von Brüning, the senior manager. This ushered in the gradual withdrawal of the founding families from the management. The outbreak of the First World War in 1914 was the prelude to a phase in which the entire chemicals industry in German suffered severe setbacks. A large number of the employees exchanged their jobs for the trenches. British naval blockades brought the export-orientated dye market almost to a standstill. Only few specialty products found their way overseas and sometimes by very adventurous routes: e. g. by merchant submarine. In addition, the industry had to defer to orders from the War Ministry and was forced to manufacture chemical warfare gas and to produce explosives on a saltpetre basis according to the new Haber-Bosch method. In the Höchst plant, huge facilities for manufacturing saltpetre, nitric acid and ammonium nitrate were established.

In those countries which were enemies of Germany, patents, trademarks and factories were confiscated and due to the loss of supplies from Germany, entrepreneurs in those countries set up their own dye and pharmaceuticals industry. As a result, the industry in Germany perceived early on that the competitive situation would be much tougher in future. For that reason, the two major groups in the chemicals industry in Germany, Farbwerke Hoechst/Cassella/Kalle and BASF/Bayer/AGFA joined with Griesheim-Elektron and Weiler-ter-Meer in forming a syndicate in 1916. The member companies remained independent legal persons but together they made important decisions on the supply of raw materials, the control of the range of products, and on sales and distribution strategies.

Symbol of Hoechst AG: Tower and Bridges by Peter
Behrens, 1924, framed by Administration Building C 660,
built in the 1970s

The situation was aggravated even more by the Treaty of Versailles in 1919
and the resulting reparation claims of the victorious allies of World War
I. Nevertheless, the dye works did achieve some success even in this difficult phase due to a perceptible edge they had in research and development
over their competitors. The company managed to build up its production
of fertilizers based on nitric acid and launched the first pesticides. In the
pharmaceuticals sector, the analgesic Novalgin was invented. In 1923, on account of its longstanding research achievement, the company was granted
its first licence entitling it to manufacture insulin in Germany. Between 1920
and 1924 architect Peter Behrens constructed the technical administration's
building, with its longstanding logo of tower and bridges. The Expressionist

red-brick building is considered to be one of the major industrial buildings in the world.

Despite the favourable trends, the chemicals manufacturers in Germany had to work even more closely together. In 1925 the syndicate which had been established in 1916 merged to form I.G. Farbenindustrie AG with head office in Frankfurt on Main. It thus became Germany's second-largest and the world's fourth-largest non-state-owned enterprise. Its range of products was extensive, from dyes to pharmaceuticals, and to synthetic fuels and rubber. Thanks to considerable research funding,[75] it was possible to enlarge the range constantly.

A perceptible drop in turnover and the Great Depression led to a multitude of rationalisation measures and an amalgamation of production facilities as of 1929. During this period, the Höchst plant lost a significant part of its range of dyes but was able to expand promising fields of activity in the Pharmaceuticals, Fertilizers, Solvents and Artificial Resin Divisions.

After Adolf Hitler seized power in 1933, the company, which was geared towards international business and was decried by the new rulers as being under 'Jewish capitalist' domination, attempted to adopt a neutral attitude towards the Nazi regime at first, but the NSDAP's influence in the plants and at managerial level grew constantly. Moreover, there was also the Wehrmacht's demand for products by I.G. Farben such as Buna synthetic rubber and synthetic fuel from the Leuna factory, both of which constituted a lucrative business. In addition to these products, which were essential to the war effort, man-made fibres, raw materials for ammunition, camouflage paints, artificial fog, and other military supplies were also produced. In 1943 the group with its numerous subsidiaries and investments both at home and abroad generated turnover[76] worth 4 billion reichsmark. During the war, half of the 330,000 employees at I.G. Farbenindustrie AG consisted of German conscripts, foreign workers, forced labourers and concentration camp prisoners, many of whom later died in concentration camps. I.G. Farben was not directly responsible for the manufacture of the toxic gas used in the gas chambers, but it did have an equity investment of 42.5 percent in Degesch, a company run by Degussa, which manufactured the gas.[77]

The living conditions of the forced labourers in the Höchst plant of I.G. Farbenindustrie AG were very hard, as were those of the foreign workers—al-

75 Stephan H. Lindner: *Hoechst, Ein I. G. Farben Werk im Dritten Reich*, Munich 2005.
76 Lindner 2005, pp. 65–211.
77 Lindner: Preface, p. X, in Lindner 2005, pp. IX–XV; see Peter Hayes: *From Cooperation to Complicity. Degussa in the Third Reich*, New York, 2004, pp. 272–300.

most 9,000 in number and from many nations—towards the end of the Second World War.[78]

After the war ended, charges were brought against 23 senior staff of I. G. Farben before an American military court, which led to several of them being sentenced to prison terms. The group of companies was placed under the control of the Allies and demerged with a view to allowing new, viable and competitive companies to develop in the tradition of the original companies prior to the foundation of I. G. Farben.[79]

On 7th December 1951, six years after the end of the Second World War and more than two years after the foundation of the Federal Republic of Germany, the new business of Farbwerke Hoechst AG vormals Meister Lucius & Brüning started up. The five founders were notable in the world of German business and were appointed by the Allies in agreement with the Federal German government; Karl Winnacker took up the post of chairman in 1952.

The following years were characterised by growth in every respect, from research and development to sales and distribution. This was the beginning of the era of petrochemicals; the basic raw material changed from acetylene to ethylene. New fields of activity and markets were tapped: synthetic fibres, plastics and foils opened up undreamed-of possibilities that nature could not provide. Brands such as Trevira and the many Hosta products were synonymous with high-quality fibres and consumer goods. A further expansion of the traditional business sectors of dyes, pharmaceuticals and agriculture was generated by innovative products.

In addition, Farbwerke Hoechst AG also expanded its commitments abroad—a process which had already begun at the end of the 40s. The first step towards restoring Hoechst's foreign organizations globally after 1945 was taken in the direction of Switzerland with renewed contact to Plüss- Staufer AG in Oftringen in the canton of Aargau in 1949. The Swiss were actually more interested in chemicals and dyes while Hoechst was primarily interested in an agency for their pharmaceuticals. In 1948, Plüss-Staufer had already begun distributing medicines for Hoechst. A year later, a general agency agreement was signed, which gradually extended to all of Hoechst's divisions and subsidiaries.

After the new start-up in 1951, the former I. G. Farben plants which were primarily located in the American zone of occupation in southern Germany, the chemicals factory in Griesheim and Napthol Chemicals in Offenbach,

78 Lindner 2005, pp. 218–258.
79 Schreier/Wex 1990, p. 193.

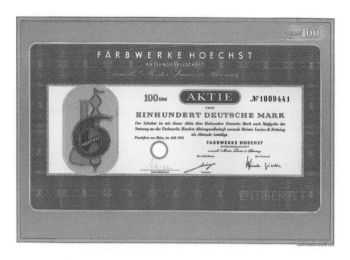

One of the first Deutsche-Mark-share certificates of
Farbwerke Hoechst of 1955

Kalle in Wiesbaden, the factory in Bobingen, Anorgana in Gendorf and the Behring plants in Marburg were allocated, along with Knapsack near Cologne, to the new company. The demerger of I. G. Farben was wound up when more than 75 percent of Cassella was acquired in 1970. Further investments such as Wacker-Chemie in Munich and the plant and construction firm of Uhde in Dortmund not only contributed to the range of products but also to the turnover generated by Farbwerke Hoechst AG, which was in the process of being transformed from a chemicals company into a group of companies. Adolf Messer GmbH was incorporated into Messer Griesheim in 1964. The foreign organisations, too, were characterised by steady growth. From 1950 the subsequent Société Française Hoechst was set up and from 1954 the first manufacturing facilities and sales and distribution outlets were established in the USA.[80]

Employee benefits kept pace with the success of the company thus promoting employee loyalty. Like the forefathers in the 19th century, social policy was a major component of Hoechst AG's corporate culture. In 1956 the 'Silobad' swimming pool opened its doors in Unterliederbach—a gift from the group to the employees and inhabitants on the occasion of the 600th anniversary of the district of Höchst. In 1948 the construction of dwellings for employees was resumed again, a measure which was of the utmost importance in war-damaged

---

80 Kurt Lanz: *Weltreisender in Chemie. Erfahrungen in fünf Kontinenten*, 2nd rev. ed., Düsseldorf/Vienna 1980, pp. 34 ff.

Frankfurt. In 1953 the Board of Management and the works council agreed on new regulations for the annual bonus in the form of a new profit-sharing scheme linked to the dividend payout. In 1955 the 5-day week was introduced with Saturday off. Shares for employees and loans to help them buy their own homes were also offered. In 1963, Farbwerke Hoechst AG celebrated its centenary. An outward mark of the company's financial position was the building of the 'Jahrhunderthalle'—the Jubilee Hall—not far from the parent plant.

The international presence of the Hoechst group was expanded considerably from the 60s on. In 1968, for the first time ever, turnover generated abroad and amounting to 51 percent exceeded the business volume transacted at home. In the same year, starting with a 40 percent stake, the group began, step by step, to acquire the majority in French pharmaceuticals company Roussel-Uclaf in Paris. This acquisition, completed in 1974, helped Hoechst attain the leading position on the world market in this sector. In addition, its organisational structure was changed to meet the requirements of the global market. Likewise, in 1974, the name was changed to Hoechst A. G.

As a result of the oil crises in 1973 and 1980 there was a slump in the fibres business and there were problems with the sales of oil-based products. Considerable efforts were required to put this corporate division back on a successful course. In 1982 it was announced that the oil exporting state of Kuwait had acquired a minority stake of 24.5 percent of Hoechst's capital stock. In spite of these upheavals, the first half of the 80s was characterised by weaknesses in economic activity and sales problems. Failure to tap new fields of activity, too much government regulation, and obstructions to the introduction of genetic modification methods made themselves felt.

In 1987 the acquisition of Celanese, the American chemicals company, which constituted the largest-ever single investment by the group, afforded a perceptible improvement in Hoechst's position on the American market. In 1988, Hoechst celebrated its 125th anniversary with brilliant turnover figures.

Nevertheless, the group was still in need of restructuring. The general upswing in the second half of the 80s and the special boom subsequent to the fall of the Berlin Wall and German Reunification in 1989/90 could not compensate for its weaknesses. It was not only the inadequate valuation on the capital market which caused the company a lot of bother; it lacked blockbusters from its own research and development as well as promising innovative products based on genetic engineering. Cumbersome bureaucracy, with highly graduated inner hierarchies and long, tortuous paths in the decision-making process did not help either. In this period a man gradually took centre stage; it was Jürgen Dormann, who, from 1994 on, was to transform the

Hoechst Group radically. He had joined Hoechst in 1963, took over the ZDA department (business and regional co-ordination and corporate planning) in 1980 and was appointed to the Board of Management in 1984. There he was responsible for the Fine Chemicals and Dye Division and also the region of North America. In 1987 he took over management control of the Departments of Finance and Accounting and Informatics but continued to be responsible for North America, where at his instigation Celanese was acquired.

It was also during this period that Dormann developed his own ideas on the future of the company: in a lecture at the *Schmalenbach-Tagung*, a conference held in 1992, he put forward the concept of business segmentation for discussion. "Build tents, not palaces" was his dynamic concept of restructuring measures—the lecture was published in the following year.[81]

In 1993, on the Monday before Lent, there was an accident at the plant in Griesheim[82] when ten tonnes of hazardous chemicals escaped via a safety valve into the atmosphere and contaminated a large residential area and numerous allotment gardens in the southwest of Frankfurt. Even though the very serious environmental damage could be remedied in the end, the impact on Hoechst AG's image was disastrous. A change in management and urgently needed reforms were required to put the group back on the winning track.

The most comprehensive reorganisation in Hoechst's[83] history began with the appointment of Jürgen Dormann as Chairman of the Managing Board in 1994 and the implementation of his restructuring programme *Aufbruch'94*. A corresponding measure had been introduced by Marc Moret in Basel when he announced the *Sandoz-90-Reorganisation* at the Annual General Meeting in 1989. Both Moret and Dormann were aiming at decentralisation and concentration on their respective core business activities. In contrast to Sandoz, however, the structures and the size of Hoechst meant that a different path had to be taken to achieve this goal.

Within a relatively short time, Dormann planned the concentration on pharmaceuticals, agrochemicals and industrial chemicals, the withdrawal from all business divisions where Hoechst was not one of the three leading suppliers, and decentralisation and a reduction of bureaucracy within the company. At the same time, it was necessary to strengthen the position on the major markets and growth regions of Europe, North America and Asia. To this end, hard-

---

81 Jürgen Dormann: "Geschäftssegmentierung bei Hoechst," in *Zeitschrift für betriebswirtschaftliche Forschung*, no. 45, 12/1993 (rev. ed. of the lecture at the Schmalenbach Conference in Neuss on 6 May 1992), pp. 1068–1077.

82 Hans Mathias Kepplinger: *Störfall-Fieber. Wie ein Unfall zum Schlüsselereignis einer Unfallserie wird*, Freiburg i. Br./Munich 1994.

83 Natasha Alperowitz: "Dormann leads a revolution at Hoechst," in *Chemical Week*, 15 June 1994.

Front page of *Hoechst persönlich*, the company magazine,
June 1994

hitting business units were to be created which were capable of taking action. These flexible business units, with their greater market expertise and know-how, assumed essential functions from the previous business divisions.

The takeover of Marion Merrell Dow, the American pharmaceuticals group, in 1995 served at first to effect an improvement in the sales organisation in the USA, but it was also an important step in the future positioning of the group in the field of life sciences. At the same time Hoechst parted with numerous fields of activity and investments. In 1996 the Board decided to turn the company into a strategic management holding and convert the sites used by several business divisions until then into industrial estates. All the remaining operative businesses were demerged into independent companies; that also included the specialty chemicals business, which was sold to Clariant in 1997.[84]

---

84 Annual report *Hoechst* 1996; Wolfgang Metternich: *Ideenfabrik. Von den Farbwerken zum Industriepark Höchst*, Frankfurt a. M. 2007.

High time for Hoechst!

Critical size

After 37 years with Sandoz, Rolf W. Schweizer moved his workplace to Clariant in Muttenz at the beginning of 1996. The critical size of his company, i. e. the circumstance that Clariant was rather small, caused him quite a headache. His business needed to grow and he did his utmost to achieve this. His credo was: Expand via acquisitions!

For that reason, Schweizer, despite the austerity measures, appointed a further new employee to give added strength to Clariant. He recruited Alfred Münch,[85] a lawyer who had been employed as a divisional lawyer in Sandoz's Building + Environment Division for seven years. As Rolf W. Schweizer had been in charge of this division for a long time, he knew the young man, who was almost thirty years younger and was Divisional Secretary to all the Boards of Directors of the Swiss subsidiaries. In September or October 1995, Schweizer enquired whether he would like to move to Clariant to become his assistant and secretary to the Board and to help him build up the new company. Münch knew that working with Schweizer would not be easy but the job and the challenge appealed to him. According to Münch, Schweizer had a really brilliant mind as well as keen and never-ending business acumen, but he was very difficult to please and even feared by his subordinates at times.

Münch found his first day at Clariant in January 1996 somewhat strange as no one knew that he was to start work on the first day after the holidays—Schweizer was still on holiday—and so there was no office for him when he arrived. Remembering the time, Münch says that obviously communications within the company had not quite worked. However, despite the rather rough start, the scope of his responsibilities, which was composed of three areas, was

---

85 Interview with Alfred Münch in Pratteln on 12 Aug. 2010.

Partners prefer Clariant

[Ihre erste Adresse]

Exactly your chemistry.

Poster motifs over a decade: 1996: *Faces;* 1998: *[Ihre...];*

really interesting: firstly he acted as Schweizer's assistant, secondly as secretary to the Board and thirdly he was put into the Business Development Division with a view to finding suitable candidates for mergers because Schweizer intended to expand the company via acquisitions.

When Münch joined Clariant, Head of Communications Walter Vaterlaus was already working feverishly on the first Annual General Meeting, which was to take place in the St. Jakobshalle. The most important question was how the company was going to position itself at all. As dyes were the basis of the core business at the time, the choice fell on a colourful appearance. For that purpose the colours to be found in the logo were used and were employed again and again as visual stylistic devices e. g. in the form of coloured surfaces. In this way the most important presentation fundamentals, as for example the first annual report, were compiled. According to Vaterlaus, the first presentations were altogether rather simple and restrained as there were no funds to splash out in style.

Posters with faces

The new identity required an outer appearance, an outer skin. Firstly, because it was entirely unknown, the company needed to acquire a face. Secondly,

2004: *Transition concept;* 2006: *What do you need?* (l–r)

Clariant wished to look entirely different from its competitors and thirdly it turned its back on the conventional photos of beautiful plants, reactors, pistons, and laboratories. How to familiarize people with specialty chemicals was a complex communications task and was contracted out. However, Vaterlaus could not approach Interbrand or any other agency which operated worldwide because, as he put it, the management was not prepared to "stir it with a big spoon" in order to promote the company.

Due to this tight-fistedness in which Vaterlaus could hear echoes of the Sandoz spirit, a local advertising agency was approached. This led to the first Clariant posters from 1996. The idea was to show objects from everyday life in which specialty chemicals were used and to create, from the final products of the respective industries, faces which would in turn personify the personality of each Clariant business division. For example, a shirt became a face, the casing of a mobile phone was the nose, a rolled-up leather belt the hair, a bundle of cables the mouth and plastic clothes pegs were the eyebrows. Taking the products or parts of products and using them to form faces was, in the final analysis, the idea of communications agency Gruner & Brenneisen in Basel. They had also designed the first annual report.

Like a bolt from the blue: Novartis

After a quiet start to the year, events came thick and fast. In March 1996 Marc Moret presented the newly established Novartis[86] to the world. The news caused a sensation and completely changed all the perceptions in the industry. When it suddenly became known that Ciba-Geigy and Sandoz had merged and that the Specialty Chemicals Divisions had been demerged, the fear of a takeover grew out of all proportion at Rothausstrasse 61. "Our friends next door, who now work for BASF, thought very carefully about doing that immediately," several employees at the company[87] reported. Moreover it was clear to everyone: if Ciba-Geigy and Sandoz had merged to form Novartis before Clariant was demerged, then the chemicals divisions of Ciba and Clariant would have been united immediately.

The fact that the concept of Ciba as the enemy intensified even more had a great deal to do with the company shares. In the case of Clariant, the shares were acquired by the banks after demergence and sold on the stock market. Thus Sandoz chose a different course of action than Novartis did later when Ciba Specialty Chemicals was spun off. In 1996 every Novartis shareholder automatically received Ciba shares. This had advantages and disadvantages. Ciba had the advantage that from the very beginning it could rely on the same regular Swiss shareholders as Novartis and as a result it was more firmly anchored in the region. Clariant, on the other hand, was thrown all the faster into the rough waters of the stock market, had a completely different range of shareholders from the very start and possessed international investment funds. While a lot of things at Ciba continued at the same old pace, things at Clariant were, according to Herbert Wohlmann,[88] very different.

A further event in the first half of 1996 which Schweizer could not fail to see or hear was an edition of the *Chemical Week* in May with the front page story about "Transforming Hoechst". In the article Jürgen Dormann[89] was quoted as saying: "The world around us is changing dramatically, there is no room for patience."

---

86 See Straumann 1996, pp. 37–42; Daniel Vasella: Novartis – Spitzenleistung in "Life Science", in *Basler Stadtbuch* 1996, Christoph Merian Stiftung (Ed.), pp. 11–17
87 Albert Hug, 13 Jan. 2010.
88 Herbert Wohlmann, 9 Feb. 2010.
89 Natasha Alperowicz: "Transforming Hoechst," in *Chemical Week*, 22 May 1996.

Press conference on the occasion of the foundation of Novartis on 7 March 1996,
Rolf A. Meyer, Daniel Vasella, Alex Krauer, Marc Moret, Raymund Breu (l–r)

The Sandoz band

The world was changing with noticeable rapidity; de facto, Sandoz no longer
existed but the old Sandoz spirit could still be sensed at Clariant. For years the
sentence could be heard frequently: "But that's not the way we did it at Sandoz." This was also evident in the preparations for the first Annual General
Meeting, which was to be held in the St. Jakobshalle on 20th June 1996. Walter
Vaterlaus[90] was flabbergasted when Werner Flükiger, the colleague helping
him with the organisation, informed him during a meeting on the order of
events: "And then the Sandoz band will play"; after all, that was the tradition.
Vaterlaus, however, was not of the same mind and crossed out a performance
by the musicians immediately, for the Sandoz brass band really had no business being at Clariant's Annual General Meeting. Nevertheless, Sandoz was

90 Walter Vaterlaus, 25 May 2010.

represented at the meeting. Because of a shortage of ballot boxes, Flükiger had borrowed some from there—and on them the inscription 'Sandoz's' was displayed in no uncertain terms.

Some 400 shareholders attended the Annual General Meeting, accepted the motions by the Board of Directors with an overwhelming majority and approved among other things a gross dividend of CHF 4.50 per registered share à CHF 100 for the short fiscal year from 1st July to 31st December 1995. This particular business year was a cyclical one. Around 8,400 employees generated turnover of CHF 2.1 billion and a profit of CHF 106 million. EBIT amounted to CHF 152 million. In the first six months after the IPO, the share price fluctuated between CHF 346 and 396, with an initial offering price of CHF 385 and a year-end price of CHF 378.

As stated in the annual report, Clariant was still searching at that early stage as it intended "to hone its corporate image and invest it with additional contours." It followed that there would not only be strategical and structural consequences but also new objectives for all those in authority. Therefore, the management structure was divided into three divisions: Textile/Leather/Paper, Pigments/Additives and Masterbatches. Furthermore, a new office on a full-time basis was created on the Board of Management to determine and realize growth projects. Victor Sanahuja was appointed to the post.

New plans

Rolf W. Schweizer worried about acquisitions. As a result, Alfred Münch[91] was to look into the matter as part of Business Development and present the chairman with a list of potential 'candidates'. The recommendations, within the limit of Clariant's budget, were in the region of CHF 100 to 800 million. There was not a single multi-billion company on the list, only solid respectable companies, whose acquisition would have made sense to Münch and so it was absolutely beyond the secretary's comprehension when Schweizer swept the propositions harshly from the table.

Actually, Schweizer was interested in pigments and under certain circumstances could have become enthusiastic about leather. His plan was, thanks to the profit-yielding starting position of pigments, to soar to the top of the global market by means of an ingenious acquisition and thus outstrip his competi-

91 Alfred Münch, 12 Aug. 2010.

tor Ciba. That was why he approached his 'good old friend' Jürgen Dormann. However, the reply from Hoechst was: "We are not prepared to discuss pigments only. If we talk, then it will be about everything." According to Walter Vaterlaus,[92] Schweizer returned to Muttenz feeling absolutely depressed after learning of this in Frankfurt. In actual fact, Dormann was extremely interested in the deal and when very lucrative financing models were brought into it, Schweizer willingly became involved after all.

1996 was to be something of a touchstone: all Clariant's business divisions took up their positions on the markets thus creating the conditions for systematic further development. The target was firstly to split the company and its management into divisions, secondly to increase turnover in all fields of activity and thirdly to expand business with masterbatches. The affinity to masterbatch went back to the Sandoz period when Sarma was acquired in 1979 and combibatch was developed on the occasion of the World Football Championships in 1990.

In fact, Clariant strengthened its position in the Masterbatch Division by putting into operation a new plant in Phoenix, Arizona, in March 1996. This was followed in May by the takeover of the Bay Resins Corporation in Millington, Maryland, USA. This was a small, innovative company specializing in compounding custom colours and afforded a first access to the promising compounding business. July saw the successful conclusion of the *Nordlicht* project: i. e. the masterbatch plant of the German company of Zipperling Kessler & Co in Ahrensburg, Schleswig-Holstein was taken over. Zipperling Kessler & Co., under the management of Bernhard Wessling, was a leading medium-sized manufacturer of concentrates with which synthetic materials could be coloured or furnished with special properties. It had around 260 employees. It also had a second plant in Trebbichau, Sachsen-Anhalt, which also became one of Clariant's properties.

In order to strengthen its position in China, Clariant opened a plant in Caohejing Hi-Tech Park, Shanghai, in May 1996, a plant that reflected the steadily growing importance of the service sector. This centre served customers in the textile, leather and masterbatches sectors. The plant in Tianjin, south of Peking, the capital, was still under construction in 1996 but was nearing completion.

One day, the special relationship between Rolf W. Schweizer and Basel business journalist Felix Erbacher[93] culminated in the question whether Er-

92 Walter Vaterlaus, 25 May 2010.
93 Felix Erbacher, 26 Feb. 2010.

bacher wanted to accompany Werner Wittlin, the head of Asian operations, on a business trip. That was indeed unusual preferential treatment of a journalist. Thus it was that for a week in November 1996 Erbacher travelled widely in Hong Kong, saw various localities in Peking, paid visits to customers in Inner Mongolia and talked with trade union representatives in Shanghai. The itinerary also included a visit to the Caohejing Technology Centre, Shanghai. The highlight was a visit to the first fully synthetic plant of a joint venture in Tianjin; textile dyes were to be manufactured in the factory which constituted the largest investment by Clariant at that time.

Upon his return, there was of course a detailed report about Clariant in the *Basler Zeitung*.[94] What Rolf W. Schweizer hoped to achieve with this trip to Asia did not exactly cause the journalist any sleepless nights. Naturally he hoped for a favourable report on Clariant and possibly it was a matter of "perhaps he liked to see his face and his name in the paper ..."

In autumn 1996, the plant in Muttenz marked its 50th anniversary with an exhibition of historical photos and objects and a celebration for the employees. Sandoz had shown considerable foresight when it had bought the area in 1917. The first sod for the construction of a complex of three factories was cut in 1946. Large-scale extensions to the plant were carried out in several stages over the years. More than 1,200 employees in an area of 400,000 m^2 generated turnover of around CHF 550 million.

On 1st July 1996, a year after its successful IPO, Clariant's shares were admitted to the Swiss Market Index (SMI) by the stock market commission. Thus Clariant became one of the 20 major Large-Caps listed. The then share price of CHF 451 rose by 27 percent to CHF 573 by the end of 1996.

In 1996, Clariant also took a step towards Europe. In keeping with EU law, a European works council was set up. The members, staff representatives from the various Clariant companies within the European Union, 1make use of the council to exchange information about and opinions on current trends within and without the company.

The merger

Rolf W. Schweizer's endeavours to provide Clariant with the necessary size were finally rewarded. Whereas Martin Syz had planned minor acquisitions

---

94 Felix Erbacher: "Clariant hat in Asien Großes vor," in *Basler Zeitung*, 27 Nov. 1996, p. 17

to enable the company to grow slowly, Schweizer said, "That's no use."[95] Instead, he made use of his relationship to Jürgen Dormann and ensured that, even if he did incur considerable debt, the little company of Clariant acquired the big company of Hoechst Specialty Chemicals, which amounted to nothing other than a *reverse takeover*. Syz admits ungrudgingly that Schweizer pulled off a tremendous coup.

On 10th December 1996, it was announced that Clariant and Hoechst had reached an agreement in principle on the contribution of the major part of Hoechst AG's specialty chemicals business to Clariant. The project was called *Barolo* in its preparation phase: *Barolo* would acquire *Rioja* and this would result in *Chianti*. The discussions in the Schlossrestaurant in Höchst had progressed considerably when the matter of the code name was raised. And so it came to be that the wines which were served lent their names to the project.

Shortly before the acquisition, which had been a closely kept secret, was due to be made public, there was a glitch: on Friday, 6th December 1996, an email which was intended for Hans-Bernd Heier in the Communications Department at Hoechst and contained a draft of the official press release was accidentally sent to an employee of the same name in the Applications Technology Department of what was later known as the Functional Chemicals Division.[96] Upon his return from a business trip on Monday, 9th December, this employee was astounded by the very revealing contents of the email in his inbox. Needless to say, it was not difficult for him to realize that the 'historic' message was intended for his namesake but first he wanted to show it to his boss, who was, however, not in his office.

Reading through the message once more, he came across the footnote: "Cleared for the genuine morning editions of 10th December." "Well, after that, I thought that if the contents of the e-mail are going to be in the newspapers tomorrow morning anyway, then I can tell my mates about it," Heier says recalling this 'aha' experience. So he forwarded the interesting text to two colleagues in the plant in Höchst and to one colleague in Gendorf. It goes without saying that he probably did not expect the email to spread like wildfire through the plant in Gendorf in particular and in the plants in the entire Rhine-Main area, and to escalate to such an extent. It was not long before he received a telephone call from Karl-Gerhard Seifert, the manager in charge of the deal, who asked him what on earth he had been thinking of.

The premature leakage of this explosive, highly price-sensitive information

95 Martin Syz, 10 Dec. 2009.
96 Interview with Michael Grosskopf in Muttenz on 8 Feb. 2010; augmented by Karl Heinz Heier on 19 Nov. 2010 and by Hans-Bernd Heier on 21 Nov. 2010.

confronted the publicly listed company with a huge problem, because suddenly there were lots of insiders who were not sworn to secrecy and who could put their knowledge to good use on the stock markets, which was in violation of the obligation to publish and disclose information according to paragraph 15 of the German Securities Trading Act (WpHG). Moreover, if there were no timely countermeasures, this would have led to a considerable loss of corporate image as far as the investors were concerned. Besides it could have resulted in a penalty imposed by the Federal Supervisory Office for Securities Trading and have led to possible claims to recourse from investors. Fortunately, prompt reaction was able to avert such serious consequences.

On the following morning, 10th December 1996, swift action had to be taken. Then there was a further mishap, but this time it was the fault of the stock market. At ten o'clock, Hoechst informed the Frankfurt Stock Exchange that at eleven o'clock—during trading hours- it intended to issue a short press statement relating to price-sensitive information which could not be postponed until after the market closed. Herbert Wohlmann[97] remembers that at the same time Clariant approached the Swiss Stock Exchange: "We are going to make an important announcement. Stop trading the moment the Frankfurt Stock Exchange stops trading."

At the time appointed, company spokesman Hans-Bernd Heier issued the stock markets with an ad-hoc release that Hoechst intended to dispose of its specialty chemicals business to Clariant but the Supervisory Board of Hoechst AG still had to agree. As soon as the sale was approved, there was a second ad-hoc release to inform the stock markets, which meant that within two hours on one and the same day two ad-hoc statements on the same situation were issued—a novelty and a unique event in the history of Hoechst. In point of fact, trading in Frankfurt was stopped punctually at eleven o'clock, but the Swiss Stock Exchange followed suit only three minutes later. Smiling in amusement, Herbert Wohlmann reports that this short period sufficed for the share price to rise from 390 to 440, as many traders had immediately taken the opportunity to purchase.

After this exciting start, the staff of 'old' Clariant was informed of the forthcoming acquisition and the special features of the future partner. The Specialty Chemicals Division contributed about 16 percent to the entire turnover of Hoechst AG in 1996 and around 15 percent to the operating result of the group. In those days, production was carried out in approximately 100 plants, most of which were located in Europe and in Germany in particular,

97 Herbert Wohlmann, 9 Feb. 2010.

in North and Latin America and increasingly in the Far East, too. From a geographical point of view, the presence of Hoechst Specialty Chemicals in South America was an ideal addition to the existing Clariant strengths in the Asia-Pacific area.

Hoechst contributed six fields of activity to Clariant: surface-active agents and auxiliaries, pigments, polymers/alkylose fine chemicals, masterbatches, and additives. The majority of these products were sold throughout the world. Hoechst had associated companies and agencies in 48 countries. The share of turnover generated in Europe was 58 percent of the total turnover in 1996, North and South America contributed 26 percent, Asia 14 percent and other regions 2 percent. At that time Hoechst Specialty Chemicals had a staff of ca. 23,000. In the course of the transaction, manager Karl-Gerhard Seifert, until then in charge of pharmaceuticals, was to transfer to Clariant as CEO.

The Frankfurt stock market daily *Börsenzeitung* praised Jürgen Dormann's dynamism and emphasized with approval that the company which had been taken over was one of the top companies in the pigments and additives as well as in the masterbatches sectors. The remaining divisions such as textiles and leather chemicals would no longer be 'rolled through the region' in Hoechst's barrels but in Clariant's barrels. As one analyst put it when describing the merger with Clariant,[98] Hoechst had succeeded in marrying off a "less attractive daughter" to a "strong fellow."

The transaction took place in several stages after it had been approved by the cartel authorities in charge. Firstly Hoechst spun off their specialty chemicals activities in Germany and transferred them to a legally distinct subsidiary called Virteon Spezialchemikalien GmbH in which Hoechst held 100 percent interest. The transfer was effected retroactively on 1st January 1997. This step was necessary on account of the German Temporary Employment Act and took place at book value on the basis of the German Reorganisation Tax Act.

The next stage was the transfer by Hoechst of their 100 percent interest in Virteon to Clariant by way of an *in specie* contribution against shares. After the capital increase, Hoechst held 45 percent of the all the shares in the enlarged Clariant. At the same time, Hoechst had agreed to certain restrictions, which included the obligation to consult the Board of Directors in Switzerland prior to any sale of Clariant shares before 2005. Clariant borrowed capital amounting to around CHF 3.1 billion, whereby the net debt of the extended group rose to a total of approximately CHF 3.8 billion.

Clariant still retained its entrepreneurial independence and complete free-

98 *Börsenzeitung*, 11 Dec. 1996

dom of action. With this in mind, Hoechst agreed to 10 percent of the voting rights, and 33.4 percent in certain decisions, which was achieved by altering the statutes. Hoechst was represented by three members on the Board of Directors. The company remained a listed Swiss stock corporation with head office in Switzerland. On the whole, the 'new' Clariant was organised according to the same principles prior to its expansion. The major organisation units remained Corporate Management, Divisions, Business Units, Regions and Plants.

In actual fact the deal between the two companies was an acquisition by Clariant in which it bought the specialty chemicals business from Hoechst. For tactical reasons, the word 'acquisition' was seldom used. Instead, it was always referred to as a 'merger'.

Preparations for the acquisition of Hoechst Specialty Chemicals required numerous negotiations. The EU Commission for Anti-Trust Law had been informed of the transaction and given their approval as early as January. The contract which was finally signed on 16th June 1997 was to take effect retroactively on 1st January 1997. But just prior to this, the Federal Cartel Office intervened because the acquisition by Hoechst of the 45 percent share in Clariant would lead, in the dyes sector, to a competitive situation with DyStar in which Hoechst also had a share. Thus the entire transaction began to totter; but fortunately Clariant was given the opportunity to explain the competitive situation in greater detail. Herbert Wohlmann[99] says that the competitive situation in the Far East, the structure of DyStar and the competition in the services sector were outlined, whereupon the civil servant in charge said: "Well, service competition is also competition." This answer meant that the doubts harboured by the Cartel Office were disposed of once and for all in October 1997.

The tombstone created to celebrate the completion of the deal was a crystal-clear acrylic cube designed in July 1997. The data on the framed foil provide information on the deal: Hoechst Specialty Chemicals was acquired by Clariant in a transaction worth DM 5.4 billion which was supervised only by SBC Warburg Dillon Read. Embedded behind the inscription is a tasteful little glass flask, filled with a turquoise-coloured liquid. The fact that it has not lost its intensity and transparency in 14 years testifies to the excellent quality of the dyes.

---

99 Herbert Wohlmann, 9 Feb. 2010.

Tombstone, Clariant acquires Hoechst
Specialty Chemicals, July 1997

Drawback

However, there was one huge snag to the Hoechst deal: the Hessian revenue department imposed a mandatory holding period of seven years which severely obstructed Clariant's business activities in Germany and to a certain extent restricted integration of the newly acquired company. When Karl-Gerhard Seifert retired in April 1999, it was rashly announced that "integration work in connection with the takeover of Hoechst's specialty chemicals business has been successfully completed."[100] In retrospect, however, it was actually admitted in the company magazine *Palette* that even years later Hoechst's activities still had not been sufficiently integrated into the group.[101]

At that time, as far as the exchange of shares was concerned, there were no rules in German tax laws to make it possible to avoid disclosing the undisclosed reserves in the shares which went to Virteon. Here it was a question of assets which, according to tax law, are shown in the business assets as an amount—the so-called book value—which is below the actual value. Accord-

---

100   Clariant *Annual Report 1998*, p. 7.
101   "10 Jahre Clariant – eine dynamische Dekade," in *Palette* 2/2005, pp. 16–18.

ing to the general rules, the transfer of Virteon stock from Hoechst to Clariant had to be subject to the same tax laws as a sale at market value, in which case Hoechst would have been liable for tax amounting to between three and four-digit millions and Hoechst AG wanted to avoid this at all events.

It was for this reason that Johannes Müller-Dott, the Head of the Tax Department at Hoechst, got in touch with Jochen Täske, the Assistant Head of the Hessian Ministry of Finance in Wiesbaden, to negotiate for the tax neutrality of the exchange of shares. They reached agreement that in this case the so-called "Tauschgutachten" (report on the exchange of shares) by the Federal Fiscal Court of 16th December 1958 was to apply. According to this piece of legislation, the exchange of shares at 'book value' should be possible if the shares which are given and received in exchange are identical in kind, values and function.[102] Täske agreed to apply the findings of the report, with the proviso, however, that Clariant was not allowed to sell the Virteon shares for a period of seven years after the exchange and was obliged to maintain and not undermine Virteon as far as its economic substance was concerned.

To compel Clariant to observe this mandatory holding period Hoechst included a corresponding clause in the contract, in which the relatively narrow 'thresholds of materiality' were laid down in precise terms. For example, Clariant was not allowed to reduce turnover generated by Virteon, later renamed Clariant GmbH, by more than DM 400 million annually and by more than DM 1.6 billion within seven years. In the event of measures which would lead to a violation of the limits stipulated, Hoechst AG's assent had to be sought.

In the subsequent time this mandatory holding period proved to be something of a 'straitjacket.' There are numerous examples of this. As early as 1997 Virteon, which was renamed Clariant GmbH after the exchange of shares, planned to transfer its sales and distribution activities to Clariant (Germany) GmbH as a commission agent. Moreover, the former Hoechst masterbatches business and the Masterbatches Division of 'old' Clariant were to be amalgamated in a general partnership which was to be set up. Between 2000 and 2002 there was talk of the sale of several product fields and interests, including emulsion paints and emulsion powder, monochloroacetic acid and terpenes. When it came to all these projects or measures for shedding staff, Clariant had

---

102 "Einbringung von Anteilen an Kapitalgesellschaften. Verhältnis der §§ 20 und 23 UmwStG zu dem sog. Tauschgutachten des BFH vom 16.12.1958," in *Der Betrieb*, 24 Feb. 1995, issue no. 8; see Ekkehard Gross/Jürgen Haun: "Die wichtigsten Steuererleichterungen und Steuerverschärfungen durch das Steuerentlastungsgesetz 1999/2000/2002," in *CH – D Wirtschaft*, no. 5/99, pp. 16–20, p. 18.

to apply to Hoechst AG first of all and convince them of the efficacy of their plans and then they had to obtain Täske's permission.

These repeated negotiations at which Albert Hug[103] was frequently present usually proved to be rather tough as Täske himself was under considerable pressure within the fiscal authority to justify his decisions. However, due to his expertise and his trustworthiness Hug managed to wrest substantial concessions from Täske. Nevertheless, it was just not possible for Clariant to carry out the structuring in Germany the way it wanted. For example, the transfer of a 51 percent share to the Clariant Verwaltungsgesellschaft GmbH was not approved. And so the company was delighted when the mandatory holding period came to an end on 1st January 2004.

Business divisions D and E

Just like Sandoz which provided good reasons for the spin-off of SSC (Sandoz Specialty Chemicals) in the form of Clariant in 1995, Hoechst, too, had solid arguments for the sale of their specialty chemicals business. Marc Moret started the deed with his *Sandoz-90-Reorganisation*; Jürgen Dormann called his measures *Aufbruch '94*. To make the situation more transparent it is better to describe how the Hoechst business divisions D and E became the specialty chemicals business, which was later sold to Clariant. When a successor was required for Wolfgang Hilger's office as Chairman of the Board of Management of Hoechst in 1995, the two 'crown princes' Jürgen Dormann and Karl-Gerhard Seifert were tipped to be the most likely candidates. Ultimately it must be stated that Hilger's unprofessional treatment of the Griesheim incident[104] in 1993 damaged his image both internally and externally, with the result that contrary to tradition he did not become Chairman of the Supervisory Board but stepped down from his post as Chairman of the Board of Management and left the company. Nine months before the actual deadline, Dormann was appointed Chairman in his place.

When in the course of the incipient restructuring measures *Aufbruch '94*, the existing departments were dissolved and several business divisions were amalgamated, there was a discussion in the Managing Board whether Specialty Chemicals, which was divided into various business divisions, should

---

103   Albert Hug, 13 Jan. 2010.
104   Kepplinger, 1994.

be amalgamated into a *single* unit or divided into *two* business divisions. Jürgen Dormann gave Klaus Warning,[105] the former Head of the ZDA and Head of Division E, the task of dealing with the matter and presenting the board with a recommendation. With the support of Hariolf Kottmann and subsequent Degussa manager Bernhard Hofmann, a proposal to create *one* large division of specialty chemicals was drawn up eventually.

After the presentation was favourably received by the Board of Management, Warning assumed that he would be put in charge of the Specialty Chemicals Division. However, things turned out differently, for it soon became known that Reinhard Handte was earmarked for the job. Later Dormann made a deeply disappointed Warning a very attractive offer to go to the USA as Utz-Hellmuth Felcht's successor on the Executive Committee of Hoechst Celanese Corporation. Warning accepted the offer and in his new post was in charge of two fields of activity: Hoechst Celanese Specialty Chemicals and the Advanced Technology Group, the corporate research centre in the USA.

In the course of the next two and a half years Warning flew to Germany at least once a month to take part in meetings of the Specialty Chemicals Division and to exchange information. The frequency of his visits rose drastically when the sale to Clariant became evident during 1996 and Karl-Gerhard Seifert—whom Warning saw as the '*matador*'[106] of the entire deal—asked him to oversee the integration together with former McKinsey employee Joachim Mahler. This task did not just comprise the specialty chemicals business in Germany but also the organisation in North America.

Pulling resources

How did 'old' Clariant and Hoechst actually come together?

In the mid-1980s two people met who got along with each other from the very start and found that almost no words were needed, but they were not able to perfect such an innovative deal—the amalgamation of the dye business of both Sandoz and Hoechst—at such an early stage; the idea of co-operation was born, but the time and the circumstances were not right.[107] However, the

105 Interview with Klaus Warning in Kelkheim on 27 May 2010.
106 Ibid.   ♥
107 The thought of a 'dyes' co-operation could be realized in the modified form of DyStar almost ten years later.

two business economists, Rolf W. Schweizer and Jürgen Dormann, did not lose sight of each other. In the subsequent ten years, the career status of the two differed in that Hilger's one-time 'crown prince' Dormann outstripped his rival and colleague Karl-Gerhard Seifert and became Chairman of the Board of Management of Hoechst in 1994. Similar to Schweizer's career which was advanced by the events in Schweizerhalle in 1986, Dormann benefited from the Griesheim accident of 22nd February 1993.

In 1996, when Clariant had reached the point where it needed to expand and Hoechst had to streamline, Rolf W. Schweizer and Jürgen Dormann did not have to talk long before making a deal which caused a huge but favourable sensation in the industry. The parties to the deal had different motives and targets. Schweizer had to secure Clariant's survival and the coup actually enabled him to occupy a firm place among the economic giants in Switzerland. Dormann, in contrast, sought a solution to secure the finances he needed to realise his other merger plans in order to strengthen his Life-Science Division. *Barolo* was to Dormann what *Junctim* was to Moret: money and the emancipation from traditional products and old sites. Both Moret and Dormann offloaded onto Rolf W. Schweizer's shoulders everything that stood in their path: the two 'grandmothers' along with more than a century of chemicals.

At a different level there was a further constellation which facilitated the merger of 'old' Clariant and the specialty chemicals business of Hoechst: it seemed to Rolf W. Schweizer that he had found support and understanding in the person of his future 'CEO' Karl-Gerhard Seifert because both of them were in dire straits. With his sweeping gestures and his forceful narrative Seifert often gave the impression that carving up Hoechst was absurd and unnecessary and a huge mistake into the bargain. On the other hand, he claimed again and again that he was the driving force behind the brilliant Clariant deal. So what exactly is the truth?

Former head of the ZDA at Hoechst Klaus Warning, who, on the organizational chart[108] of the 'new' Clariant, was earmarked for a fairly important post on the Board of Management, is of the opinion that in 1996 Seifert went all out and did all that was in his power to push the demerger of Hoechst's Specialty Chemicals, i. e. he was definitely an active partner in splitting up Hoechst: "He did more than anyone else to promote the deal with Clariant."[109]

Rolf W. Schweizer had to effect a huge acquisition because otherwise there was a real danger that Clariant would be acquired by Ciba Specialty Chemicals—

108 *Neue Zürcher Zeitung* and *Basler Zeitung*, 12 Mar. 1997; *Palette*, no. 3/1997, p. 1.
109 Klaus Warning, 27 May 2010.

from across the road, so to speak. Hoechst was the ideal partner for the plan and Schweizer knew that there was no better alternative. Seifert, on the other hand, was driven by one thought only: to get away from Hoechst! What may have made the contract with Clariant additionally attractive to Seifert was a personal event in this youth or rather the wishful thinking of his father that one day his son would find his professional destination as a chemist in Switzerland.[110]

Karl-Gerhard Seifert became personally acquainted with Rolf W. Schweizer only a few years after the events in Schweizerhalle. Seifert became a member of the Board of Management of Hoechst in 1988 and was put in charge of operations in Africa. A major topic that had been in his mind for some time was the masterbatch factory in South Africa, in Midrand near Johannesburg, which was managed by Dominik von Bertrab and operated jointly by Sandoz and Hoechst. Every time Seifert stayed in South Africa, he reiterated: "Mr Schweizer, let's resolve the situation here. For heaven's sake, there is no sense in having a fifty-fifty joint venture. One of us, either Sandoz or Hoechst, should take over the majority, preferably Hoechst, of course, as the larger masterbatch manufacturer." But Schweizer would have none of it, because the masterbatch business and South Africa were of the utmost importance as far as he was concerned.

Seifert had a plot of land in Bad Soden near Frankfurt. The land bordered on an old factory, the Eden honey factory which Sandoz had acquired in 1990. When Seifert became aware of this, he phoned Schweizer in Basel. In the course of diversification, Schweizer had advanced to the post of Vice-Chairman of the Board of Management and a member of Sandoz's Board of Directors in the meantime. "Well then, Mr Schweizer, just so that you know: we are now neighbours in Bad Soden. Our plots of land are right beside each other," said Seifert jubilantly and the two of them were pleased to have an excuse to chat.[111] After that there were occasional phone calls but they never actually met. Seifert, who, after the wall fell, had purchased an apartment on Rügen, an island in the Baltic Sea, tried occasionally to persuade Schweizer, who was an enthusiastic yachtsman, to purchase an apartment there, too.

There was still this easy-going contact between the two when Ciba Specialty Chemicals received several billion francs after it was spun-off in March 1996 and it was common knowledge that the next step would be the purchase of little Clariant. It was understandable that Schweizer was in mortal terror of such a thing happening. Therefore, as Seifert reports, it is not surprising that in summer 1996 both Schweizer and he came out in favour of the Clariant-

110 Interviews with Karl-Gerhard Seifert in Frankfurt a. M. on 3 Feb. 2010 and 20 May 2010.
111 Ibid.

Hoechst deal after only two meetings. It was most certainly not the financial aspects which drove Seifert to accept the post of CEO at Clariant for, to all intents and purposes, he had a pension as a member of the Hoechst Board of Management in his pocket. What did motivate him for certain was his enjoyment of conducting business, and 'making and doing'. His hunger for power and a hope of taking over from Rolf W. Schweizer before long are likely to have been a further powerful incentive. In 1997, the year of the Hoechst deal, Schweizer turned 67; under normal circumstances it stands to reason that Seifert could have been his successor at the turn of the century. According to Klaus Warning, the former Head of the ZDA,[112] it is not known whether they had a gentleman's agreement or not.

It can safely be assumed that Schweizer's primary negotiations for Hoechst's Specialty Chemicals were with Dormann. Seifert[113] even thinks he knows how Dormann expressed himself: "Well then, Mr Schweizer, we'll sell it to you. The main thing is that you take Seifert with you, so get on with it."

Thus the deal between Dormann and Schweizer was sealed with a handshake. The many concessions from Switzerland were still to follow. At managerial level it was said: "Rolf W. Schweizer has been at loggerheads with Ciba all his life. Ciba was his arch enemy. And I wanted to get away from Hoechst," Seifert continues. "At that time we two were the best, the right combination. Many Hoechst men who transferred to Clariant later contributed to the fact that Clariant was able to purchase Hoechst cheaply. I am still of the opinion that Hoechst sold their fine chemicals under market value. The cash flow of fine chemicals was substantial; but this was only discovered in Hoechst after it had been sold. The Board of Management of Hoechst was delighted finally to be rid of that terrible man Seifert. That was the reason why they offered such an attractive price."[114]

Cast out by the 'Mothers'

Apart from Clariant there were no other prospective buyers for Hoechst Specialty Chemicals. No bank was involved so that there was no public auction.[115] Talks with Clariant were held only at board level.

---

112   Klaus Warning, 27 May 2010.
113   Karl-Gerhard Seifert, 3 Feb. 2010/20 May 2010.
114   Ibid.
115   Interview with Reinhard Handte in Muttenz on 21 Jan. 2010.

In May/June 1996, shortly after Novartis was founded, Karl-Gerhard Seifert and Reinhard Handte had also discussed a possible merger with the recently spun-off Ciba Specialty Chemicals but they soon broke off the discussions when it became apparent that there would be too many attendant problems. Besides, there were also deliberations about spinning off Specialty Chemicals as an independent company, which would have been a preferable solution for Handte and his colleagues at that time. However, the advantage of a merger with Clariant was the fact that breaking away could be effected very quickly. Negotiations proceeded rapidly even though there were no banks involved. Legal advisors were only called in at a later date.

But Clariant's dyes business was a thorn in the flesh of some Hoechst men. After all, they themselves had just spun off these less profitable products in a very lengthy process to establish DyStar. However, there was one difference: Clariant earned more with its dyes than Hoechst had previously earned. Besides, the men in Muttenz were also better established in the field of textile chemicals so that the companies complemented each other well.

Although some of the employees affected were worried about teaming up with or even being bought up by what was in their eyes a small 'craftsman's workshop' like Clariant, they realized that they had, in fact, some things in common.[116] Just like Hoechst Specialty Chemicals, Clariant, too, had been 'cast off' by its 'mother' Sandoz. Until far into the 1960s the dyes business at both Sandoz and Hoechst had been a cornerstone of each company and it was their profit which had made the expansion of pharmaceuticals possible. Many of the elderly traditionalists in both companies could not understand why they were no longer the favourite 'child'.

On the one hand these parallels produced a certain common bond from the very beginning, on the other hand the different structures and cultures brought considerable potential for conflict in their wake. "Hoechst was actually more technology-driven, more introverted and self-contained," says Reinhard Handte when describing Hoechst. In contrast, the Clariant men who had found themselves thrown into the deep end by Marc Moret were fighters and, what is more, they were thriftier than their Hoechst colleagues.

Even after the acquisition, 'old' Clariant, as purchaser, wanted to call the tune in the company, but the management capacity was inadequate. As a result, very many Hoechst men took over leading positions in the 'new' Clariant. This had the advantage that the two cultures were forced to merge bit by bit, but sometimes that happened voluntarily, too.

---

116   Ibid.

Put in a favourable mood

On 21st February 1997 there was an event in the Arabella Hotel in Frankfurt at which the senior management staff of Hoechst Specialty Chemicals was encouraged to view the transfer to Clariant in a favourable light. It was the first get-together of the main office-holders, of the respective future players: i. e. the potential divisional managers and those immediately under them, between 50 and 60 people, all in all. On this occasion Klaus Warning met Rolf W. Schweizer, the President, and attests that Schweizer possessed considerable charisma. Not only did Schweizer make a speech to perk up the team assembled there but he also met and talked to each of the senior executives personally. Hartmut Wiezer, too, remembers his first talk with Schweizer, who told him: "We assume that you will be running the Fine Chemicals Division."[117]

Schweizer was also keen to take over Warning as a divisional head and member of the Board of Management and his name had already cropped up in the official organisational chart of the 'new' Clariant which has already been mentioned. Warning's enthusiasm was none too great, however, because it was already foreseeable that Karl-Gerhard Seifert would play a major role in the new group. This presented him with quite a problem as his relationship to Seifert was not the best.

In the course of his assistance in the integration project his doubts grew considerably. "Clariant's culture, which was decidedly influenced by Mr Schweizer—it was nearly a one-man show—, was entirely different from the culture which I had become acquainted with at Hoechst Celanese Corporation," Klaus Warning reports. "We had a culture of accountability, i. e. you were given different areas of authority and responsibility for the budget, but then you were accountable; you had to deliver results otherwise you were in trouble."[118]

Trust is good, control is better

When planning the amalgamation of the US subsidiaries[119] with Ken Brewton, his Clariant colleague, Warning made a particularly salient observation: the staff at Clariant had much less freedom. Brewton reported, for example, that as Head of North America he was not allowed to make investments exceeding

---

117 Interview with Hartmut Wiezer in Sulzbach on 24 Feb. 2010.
118 Klaus Warning, 27 May 2010.
119 Ibid.

$ 10,000 unless he obtained permission from Muttenz; that meant that when he wanted to renovate a store or have a new sprinkler system installed, he first had to have the expenditure approved. At Hoechst Celanese, on the other hand, investments of up to $ 1 million could be made at one's discretion without the Board of Management in Germany having to be consulted.

It was no different when it came to staff issues. Warning[120] recalls that Ken Brewton was not in a position to make his own decisions. For example, if a decision had to be made about whether to take the HR manager from Hoechst or from Clariant, there was a discussion and then he would say: "I'll have to ask Muttenz." Unless it concerned business divisions peculiar to Hoechst, the decision from Muttenz was always: "We'll take our own man." Warning was absolutely flabbergasted when he heard the reason—Clariant men earned less, so it saved money to make a Hoechst man redundant. Would it not have been more sensible to reach a decision based on qualifications and performance? That way it might have been possible to learn from the candidate who had been appointed and to see which modus operandi was the best!

CFO Roland Lösser gave him a further impression of the influence exerted by the senior management in Muttenz when the future divisional managers were discussing the organisational structure. Each division had a head, a production manager, a purchasing manager and a controller. The latter was to report not to the head of the division who was his immediate boss but direct to the director of finance. This procedure was nothing new for the 'old' Clariant men, but Warning and his colleagues from Hoechst reacted with a total lack of understanding: "How am I to run a business if my controller is not answerable to me? I need a controller at my side and he needs to report to me." But Lösser argued that Clariant needed to be optimized financially, which was only possible if, as CFO, he had direct access to the controllers. "If somewhere in Latin America some figure or other got out of hand, then Mr Lösser knew about it from the controller before the divisional manager knew about it. The latter, who got a rap over the knuckles from the CEO, didn't even have the figures to be able to explain perhaps or even to understand what the problem was," Warning explains. Thus it was that they tried to control the divisional managers—who as members of the Board of Management were directly responsible to the CEO—through their controllers.

As far as Warning was concerned, this was nothing other than experiencing the extreme form of the old maxim: 'Trust is good, control is better.' This cultural shock, i. e. the fact that Clariant was governed down to the very last detail from Muttenz and first and foremost by Rolf W. Schweizer, was crucial

120   Ibid.

for Warning's decision not to change to Clariant but instead to accept a position with SGL Carbon. Incidentally, the idea that there was someone whose name appeared on the Clariant organisational chart and nevertheless 'struck sail' was considered to be strange indeed.

Warning recalls that Rolf W. Schweizer showed no sympathy for this decision. One day, Schweizer phoned the defector in the USA, accused him of desertion and reprimanded him in no uncertain terms. With no desire to discuss the matter on the phone Warning proposed that they meet in Muttenz—just the two of them. A meeting actually materialized soon afterwards. Schweizer received him coldly and roundly condemned the decision Warning had taken. Warning explained his point of view and criticised Schweizer's managerial style in unequivocal language: "You are like a bottleneck. You have acquired a business worth DM 8 billion. You used to be a firm worth CHF 2 billion. You just can't run this integrated company the way you did in the olden days."[121] At that, Schweizer thawed somewhat and asked Warning to understand his situation. He told him that with the splitting of Sandoz into pharmaceuticals and chemicals all the *good* people went to pharmaceuticals with the result that he had to take charge of and control everything himself. This was also confirmed by Karl-Gerhard Seifert. In the run-up to the negotiations with Hoechst, Rolf W. Schweizer is supposed to have approached him and said: "Karl, if we make this deal, promise me one thing: bring your best people with you. We lost a lot of good people to Novartis."[122]

Here a Chairman justified the radical assertion of his claim to power with the weakness of others, namely of his colleagues and employees. Warning pointed out, however, that with the takeover of Hoechst Specialty Chemicals, Clariant had acquired a group of highly-qualified executives who should simply not be treated as laggards. There is no telling whether Rolf W. Schweizer accepted this but his expression became friendlier and he wished Klaus Warning all the best when they parted.

MS Baslerdybli

The takeover of Hoechst Specialty Chemicals was probably the most important Clariant requisition of all. Both parties' CFOs Roland Lösser[123] and

---

121   Ibid.
122   Karl-Gerhard Seifert, 3 Feb. 2010/20 May 2010.
123   Interview with Roland Lösser in Muttenz, 2 Jan. 2010.

Aboard the MS Baslerdybli, July 1997, Klaus-Jürgen Schmieder, Roland Lösser, Karl-Gerhard Seifert, Rolf W. Schweizer, Martin Syz, Jürgen Dormann (l–r)

Klaus-Jürgen Schmieder and controllers Albert Hug and Peter Jakobsmeier played a decisive role in the negotiations in addition to the two main actors Rolf W. Schweizer and Jürgen Dormann. They were supported by internal and external lawyers during due diligence checks and the drafting of the contract.

As a climax to this ever so important deal, Schweizer had come up with something very special and allegorical. After the contract had been signed officially on 16th June, the protagonists were to meet in Basel some two weeks later to conclude the deal in a symbolic act. Schweizer sent a stretch limousine to fetch Hoechst managers Dormann, Schmieder and Seifert from the airport. The hired car then headed for Birsfeld harbour, just above the lock where the MS *Baslerdybli,* which was the smallest vessel in Basel's passenger shipping and chartered on an hourly basis, was waiting for the guests. Rolf W. Schweizer, Martin Syz, Roland Lösser, Herbert Wohlmann and Urs Schenker from Baker & McKenzie were present.

The signing of the contract was re-enacted and filmed by an advertising agency in the cabin of the *Baslerdybli,* which was a replica of boats from the steamboat era and built in the old-fashioned style. It was anchored in Muttenz, in the middle of the Rhine but level with Clariant, and precisely at this symbolic spot—framed by Switzerland on the one side and Germany on the other—the deal was solemnly 'signed and sealed' for posterity. It was of the utmost importance to Schweizer that this awe-inspiring scene was captured on film but it is fair to assume that the managers from Hoechst who had come all the way to Basel had attended the ceremony out of politeness. The result of the re-enacted scene is a three and a half minute VHS video, with classical music as a background accompaniment.[124]

After champagne and canapés the saloon steamer docked at the *Solbad* in Muttenz, the party disembarked and were taken in the stretch limousine to the group's head office in 61 Rothausstrasse. To Schweizer's great regret, the guests did not stay very long because they had to return to Frankfurt and as the "Art Basel" exhibition was on in the city which was also worth seeing, some of the gentlemen wanted to be sure to to visit it before their departure.

The fountain

In internal talks on the acquisition of Hoechst a proposal was made once or twice that something symbolic[125] should be created in memory of and in view of the historic proportions of the transaction. The re-enacting of the signing of the contract on camera in the cabin of the *Baslerdybli* was quite clearly Schweizer's idea. Martin Syz, on the other hand, thought about having a fountain built in the inner courtyard of the head office; its structure was to be such that it would symbolize the amalgamation of the two companies. He broached the subject to Schweizer but they did not go into details.

The CEO discussed his idea with the then in-house technician Theodor Merz, who was as keen as mustard. Within two weeks a fountain made of Jurassic limestone was erected between Building 906 and Building 907 in Muttenz: two water courses which symbolized old Clariant and Hoechst united in one large basin and from there flowed into another basin lower down.

To create a balance in the top management between 'old' and 'new' Clariant after the acquisition of Hoechst Specialty Chemicals, Martin Syz[126] had to step down from his post as CEO. He relinquished it to Karl-Gerhard Seifert and in the end assumed the post of COO. Syz got on well with Seifert but nevertheless, he felt slighted by Schweizer. As the former Head of the Board of Management he did not want to settle for playing second fiddle during the

---

124   A copy of the video is in the possession of the author.
125   Martin Syz, 10 Dec. 2009.
126   Ibid.

last few years until he retired. Consequently he informed Rolf W. Schweizer of his decision to leave the company early. However, the President of the Board of Directors managed to persuade Syz to remain for another year and to help supervise the integration of Hoechst's activities. However, no sooner had Syz left the company at the end of 1997 than Rolf W. Schweizer had the symbolic fountain removed as it did not fit in with his ideas.

Teasing is a sign of affection

Too big

After the IPO, Clariant was aware that its size was a critical factor and it therefore needed to grow at all costs; this topic was a matter of concern to the staff and occupied their thoughts to a considerable extent.

Even before the takeover of Hoechst Specialty Chemicals was made public—it cannot be ruled out entirely that there were already some premonitions in this respect or that rumours abounded—three members of the global team and the then CEO re-enacted the historic Rütli Oath of 1291 at a big management conference in Weggis at Vierwaldstättersee in 1996, while on an outing to neighbouring Rütliwiese. Hanspeter Knöpfel celebrated the ritual while

On Rütliwiese: Peter Brandenberg, Martin Syz,
Victor Sanahuja and Hanspeter Knöpfel (l–r), 1996.
Double exposed photo.

Rolf W. Schweizer, Karl-Gerhard Seifert, Paul Gemperli and Utz-Hellmuth Felcht (l–r) at the Annual General Meeting in the St. Jakobshalle, Basel in 1997

Peter Brandenberg, CEO Martin Syz and Victor Sanahuja swore the oath which was observed and heard by Rolf W. Schweizer and 40 of his top managers. The oath was in English because it was, after all, a global company. "We solemnly swear that we shall do everything in our power to keep Clariant an independent and Swiss company, so help us God," could be read in a newsletter which was sent to the participants and included photos of the event.

In the event of an essential and therefore unavoidable change, the performers swore, in an allegorical and playful way, to preserve their independence whatever happened. The projection of the current misgivings onto a national event of historic importance may well be seen as a joke but it does underpin the fact that the protagonists knew or guessed that a merger with a foreign enterprise of superior size was imminent.

Several participants at the conference confirm that the atmosphere on the Rütliwiese was absolutely fantastic. Whether this joke became reality later and thus a curb on the integration process or not is not a point of discussion at this point. It only remains to note that with the acquisition of Specialty Chemicals from Hoechst, 'old' Clariant was not inevitably predestined to lose its independence—in point of fact it purchased tangible assets, know-how and human capital, the management of which involved considerable energy, enormous care and great responsibility.

Hoechst was two and a half times larger than Clariant, which meant that from mid-1997 it found itself faced with a new dimension of management overnight.

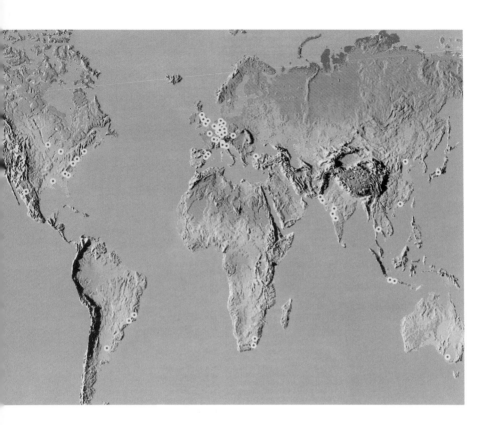

Clariant in 1997 had over 130 production sites all over the world.
ost important ones were:

tina: Buenos Aires

alia: Altona

¨a: Vienna-Floridsdorf

¨m: Louvain-la-Neuve

: Suzano, Resende

¨: Guangzhou, Tianjin

e: Cuise-Lamotte, Huningue

any: Ahrensburg, Frankfurt/Höchst/
heim, Cassella-Offenbach, Gendorf,
hofen, Knapsack, Lahnstein, Leinfelden,
oaden

¨ Kolshet, Thane, Roha

¨esia: Cilegon, Tangerang

Italy: Merate, Lomaga, Palazzolo

Japan: Shizuoka

Mexico: Santa Clara

Pakistan: Jamshoro, Karachi

Switzerland: Muttenz

Spain: Prat, Tarragona

South Africa: Chamdor, Randburg

Thailand: Bangkok

Turkey: Topkapi/Istanbul

UK: Horsforth, Stainland, Watford, Wigan

USA: Albion, Branchburg, Coventry, Clear Lake,
Holden, Martin, Minneapolis, Mount Holly

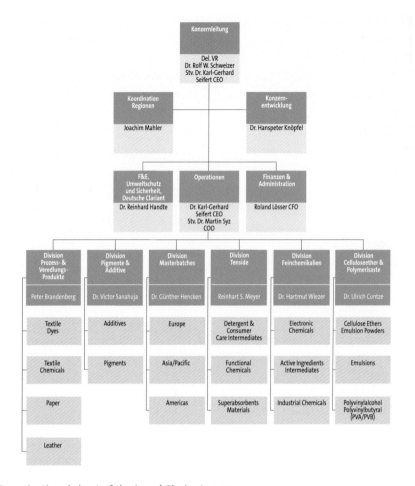

Organisational chart of the 'new' Clariant 1997

Most of the Sandoz people were neither mentally nor de facto prepared for this event and without delicate professional guidance, of which there was inevitably a considerable shortage, they were scarcely in a position to adapt immediately. It is true that there was an integration team under the leadership of Hanspeter Knöpfel or rather Ralph Rutte and Joachim Mahler. It was equipped with a substantial budget but it could not be effective from the very first moment. It could not always be in place to give first aid in everyday management and certainly not at the initial meetings when one party, due to the location, always had home advantage. The same applied to issues of authority or when lightning decisions had to be made out on the market

Paul Gemperli, a retired member of the National Council and the Council of States and an army colonel from St. Gallen, who was a member of the

Clariant Board of Directors between mid-1995 and mid-1999, puts the former constellation and the inherent problems in a nut shell: the two words "too big"[127] say it all.

Those directly affected found the situation even more extreme. The founder members still recall their impression at that time in amazement and consternation. "Just imagine! There we were—a small company with three men at its head—and opposite us stood an entire force—an incredible number of people!" says Controller Albert Hug in an interview.[128] But in a way the Clariant employees were also dismayed: "Never had Sandoz had anything like the technology Hoechst enjoyed. Those were pearls, genuine pearls we saw there," former member of the Board of Management, Doctor of Chemistry Hanspeter Knöpfel relates.[129]

It cannot be denied that the conditions which prevailed were different and various forces clashed head on. Three events should exemplify the encounters between ca. 8,000 Clariant men and approx. 23,000 Hoechst men. They really happened but through time have diminished into anecdotes which make people grin in relief nowadays or even roar with laughter. At the time, however, they made blood boil. To a certain extent it was a sudden, forced marriage with numerous and large sources of friction; it was only after some ups and even more downs, and after innumerable conflicting experiences that those concerned learned to deal with, to accept and to cooperate with each other, and finally—after many years of conflict—to act in concert.

Giraffe

Sometimes it is the small things in life which give pleasure. This is evident in the example of the Clariant giraffe, a simple toy which became the mascot of the North American pigments industry.[130]

In 1969 William Goulden, General Manager of the Dyes and Pigments Division of American Hoechst, was searching for a gimmick[131] to draw the attention of the visitors to the Plastics and Coatings Fair to the relatively small

127 Interview with Paul Gemperli in St. Gallen, 24 Jun. 2010.
128 Albert Hug, 13 Jan. 2010.
129 Talk with Hanspeter Knöpfel in Pratteln, 22 Nov. 2010; see "Ein Querdenker blickt zurück," in *Palette*, No. 4/1998, p. 6.
130 Interview with Norbert Merklein in Muttenz, 1 Feb. 2010.
131 Chuck Jones/Andy Zonoyski: "The Giraffe Turns Forty!" in *Clariant Compact*, no. Oct. 2010, p. 22.

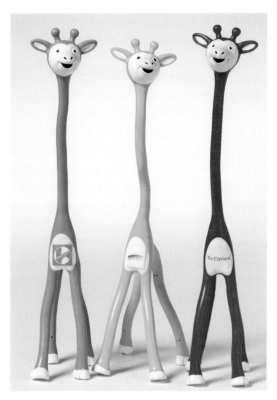

Colourful advertising media: the giraffe mascots of
1996, 1997 and 1998

dyes business of Hoechst's US subsidiary. On a visit to Germany he saw a
promotional toy, which Hoechst had ordered from a Heidelberg manufacturer
of plastic goods. He took a shine to the giraffe which was coloured with carbazole violet pigment 23—also known as Carbazole Violet[132] and still in the
portfolio today—, and so he ordered 20,000 units without further ado. In fact
the plastic animals were even more popular than Goulden had ever dreamt
of. More than 100,000 were sold over the counter in the first eighteen months.

In Frankfurt, the giraffe era drew to a close at the end of 1970, but Goulden
held on to the idea and wondered how the advertising product could be made
more varied. He came up with the idea of giving the figurine a different colour
every year thereby focussing on new pigments.

In the years the followed the customers waited with bated breath for the
new giraffe, which was introduced at the RETEC Fair every autumn and soon

132   "Das Pigment Violett 23 wird 50 Jahre. Ein farbechter Dauerbrenner," in *chemie.de*, 21 Jul.
      2003.

became a collector's item. One of the most memorable is the 1976 giraffe, which was the only one ever to have three colours and which was patriotically presented in blue, white and red—the national colours—in honour of the 200th anniversary of the Declaration of Independence. The 1980 model was also out of the ordinary because of its brown metallic surface.

After the last giraffe with the Hoechst logo had been manufactured in 1996, Frank Kochendörfer, the executive in charge of sales and distribution in the USA, faced a problem in 1997, when at the beginning of the year the giraffe had to be ordered for the fair in autumn. Clariant's acquisition of Hoechst Specialty Chemicals had been announced but the contracts were not yet signed, sealed and delivered. By the time the fair took place, the Hoechst logo would no longer be valid and using the Clariant logo seemed to be somewhat premature at that point, which is why he decided to forego the company emblem. As an interim solution he chose instead the so-called colour mop, an internal trademark of the Pigments Division. At that time he could not foresee that this decision would call down the ire of the new marketing management on his head

When Clariant's new head of marketing attended the fair in the USA for the first time that autumn and saw the giraffes with the mop, there was a fierce exchange of words in the Marriott Hotel in Atlanta where Kochendörfer was standing with his back to an open balustrade on an upper floor. The manager shouted at him and wanted to know why he had used a logo which had nothing to do with the new company. Thus the tiny toy became a bone of contention in the merging of the two pigment departments of Clariant and Hoechst. These initial irritations did not prevent the giraffe from continuing its triumph under the Clariant flag. The coloured animal even attained honour as a poster entitled 'The Pigment Hall of Fame'. The Pigment & Additive Division even brought out a special edition to launch Licocene waxes in 2005. Since it was the new family of waxes and not pigments that was to be promoted, this giraffe was made of transparent plastic. It remains to be seen many more giraffes we may look forward to.

The customers are not amused[133]

Due to the acquisition the former Hoechst men experienced various changes. Many retained their familiar surroundings and their previous areas of re-

---

133 Norbert Merklein, 1 Feb. 2010.

sponsibility, but there were also new staff constellations with new teams and new responsibilities. This is also confirmed by Norbert Merklein, who at the time was Marketing Manager in the Pigments Division. He continued with his usual assignments and looked after the usual customers but he had a new boss with whom he had controversial discussions occasionally, which could be attributed to the fact that the pigments business of Hoechst was considerably larger than that of old Sandoz-Clariant.

Out on the market there were also debates and speculations because some of Hoechst's customers reacted sceptically to Clariant taking over the Frankfurt specialty chemicals business. This was Merklein's experience, too, when for the first time he went with his new marketing manager on a business trip to visit customers. On the schedule was among other things a visit to ICI Paints in London. ICI was a major pigment customer with whom Hoechst had always maintained very good business relations but Richard Woodrow, the International Purchasing Officer there, did not seem to have a very high opinion of Sandoz and Clariant. Nor did he make any secret of his antipathy when he greeted his visitors with the comment that he would never have had talks with 'old' Clariant at this level. He went even further when he turned to Merklein's boss and said: "As 'new' Clariant you will need to make a huge effort if you are going to achieve the level of confidence that Hoechst placed in me!"

It seems likely that Woodrow's earlier experiences with Sandoz had been less than happy. At least it was evident in this case that Hoechst enjoyed a considerably better reputation in the pigments sector than Sandoz did. For that reason many customers feared that the company could adopt a different focus due to the merger with Clariant, which in turn could have an adverse effect on the quality of the products, the service and co-operation. Hoechst was highly regarded as a valued supplier and Clariant would have to meet the same standards if they wished to gain the same reputation.

Although the new marketing manager reacted to this awkward situation in a professional and business-like manner, he preferred in the end to leave any contact to this British customer to Norbert Merklein in future. In the years following, relations between Clariant and ICI developed so well that, according to Merklein, Richard Woodrow eventually admitted some years later: "Indeed, I can now see in 'new' Clariant the qualities and performance to which I was accustomed with 'old' Hoechst."

"K"—The plastics trade fair[134]

The integration of many of Hoechst AG's activities into Clariant did not always go smoothly, as becomes apparent in the example of the participation in 'K'—the leading European trade fair for anything to do with plastics. The event which took place in Düsseldorf every three years was, in Hoechst's eyes, one of the most important to its business. Hoechst, along with BASF and Bayer, was one of the three major exhibitors and it vividly presented the entire portfolio it had to offer to the plastics industry on a stand and floor space of about 1,000 square metres.

The plastics trade fair at which the new company was to be present for the first time was to take place in 1998. Ingrid Reusch in Pigments and Additives—at that time located in today's Industrial Park in Höchst—was put in charge of the preparations for the exhibition. Reusch is one of the employees who have shared the fortunes and borne the changes in the company for more than 30 years. She joined the Communications Department of Hoechst in 1980 and after the merger in 1997 worked as a communications management expert at Clariant.

Before the 'K' trade fair in 1998 Ingrid Reusch had first of all to sort out with the Communications Department of 'old' Clariant in Muttenz whether the exhibition stand for her sector had to be booked separately or whether there were perhaps other Clariant divisions represented at the fair, too. She learned from a colleague in the team of Walter Vaterlaus, the Head of Communications at that time, that a Clariant exhibition stand had already been booked with the organisers in Düsseldorf. In reply to her question how large the stand was she received a reply which reassured her for the moment: "Well, the stand which has been booked is our part, the 'old' Clariant/former Sandoz part for the Masterbatches Division, and in addition there is the former Hoechst part for Pigments and Additives."

The former Hoechst employee was absolutely flabbergasted when she talked with the organiser and learned that merely a corner stand with an exhibition area of 198 square metres was reserved for the Masterbatches Division of 'new' Clariant. When she complained to the colleague in charge in Muttenz, the latter declared that he had assumed that when the stand had been reserved they would naturally be given the area Sandoz had always had and that the organiser would automatically add the area Hoechst always had because after all they were now one company. The mistake had, therefore, been made by the

134   Interview with Ingrid Reusch in Sulzbach, 22 Feb. 2010.

person whom he had contacted at the Düsseldorf trade fair and whom he apparently notified accordingly.

Unfortunately several attempts to obtain a larger stand for Clariant were to no avail. The only alternative the organisers could offer so that the Pigments and Additives of the former Hoechst AG and consequently a sector of 'new' Clariant could be presented at the 'K' was a 120 square metre linear booth—some distance away from the masterbatch stand of 'new' Clariant. All the other exhibition stands had been allocated and there was absolutely nothing to be done.

So they just had to grin and bear it and make do with a relatively poor stand that year. Unlike the generously proportioned, free-standing island booths at which Hoechst had been presented up until then, this stand, which was closed on three sides, was comparable in size to a 'rabbit hutch.' The organisation of it proved to be particularly challenging. However, with the help of an accomplished booth builder it was possible in the end to put up a stand which nonetheless looked attractive.

Attempts to rent adequate stand and floor space at the 2001 and 2004 'K' trade fairs failed, too. It was not until 2007 that Clariant was able to present its Masterbatches Division and its Pigments and Additives Division to the trade professionals in a total area of 400 square metres and thus underpin its leading position on the market. For a long time relations with the organiser were not the best.

'Mergeritis'

Dreaming of the largest specialty chemicals company

In conversations with Rolf W. Schweizer in the early 1990s, Martin Syz[135] frequently talked of his dream. Syz had good contacts to former fellow students
at Ciba-Geigy and when he met up with them, the same topic cropped up time
and again: a merger of Sandoz Chemicals with Ciba-Geigy Chemicals. They
dreamed of the largest specialty chemicals company in the world under the
Swiss flag… Certainly at that time the division was not experienced enough
and was still too completely embedded in Sandoz or Ciba, but the vision was
there and Schweizer advised Syz every time to stop raving let alone start
something; he would only annoy Marc Moret with the very thought because
the case of Toms River was still a latent problem in the relationship between
the two companies.

After the Second World War, vat and anthracene dyes in particular recorded
the largest growth on the American dye market. These dyes were principally
used for dyeing various textiles and in the printing industry. The capacity at
the plant in Cincinnati which had been established by the partner companies
of Ciba, Geigy and Sandoz within the framework of the Basel Syndicate was
not adequate to keep pace with this trend.

That was why a joint venture was established in Toms River in New Jersey
in 1952. Ciba had a 52 percent share and Geigy and Sandoz each had a 24 percent share. In the 1980s the plant fell into disrepute on account of pollution
which meant extra expenditure on reconstruction and clearing up and the
payment of fines. On account of its more aggressive sales strategy, for which it
was famous in the industry, Sandoz took far more than the 24 percent capacity amount to which it was actually entitled and so the joint-venture partners

---

135   Martin Syz, 10 Dec. 2009.

thought it only appropriate that Sandoz assume a share of the environmental compensation not according to their 24 percent participation but according to the actual amount it had taken delivery of.

As this demand was not legally tenable, Sandoz did not comply with the request and dropped out of the Toms River joint venture by setting up its own dye factory in Martin, South Carolina, which caused very icy relations between Sandoz and Ciba-Geigy that lasted long after Toms River was closed in 1988.

More than ten years after these events it seemed that finally Martin Syz's one-time dream might still come true, for Rolf W. Schweizer started to seriously entertain the idea of merging with DyStar or Ciba Specialty Chemicals.

DyStar

Jürgen Dormann describes, from his point of view, the formation of DyStar and the envisaged co-operation with Clariant as follows:[136] In January 1984 Dormann was appointed a deputy member of the Board of Management of Hoechst. Rolf Sammet assigned North America and Division D to him; his field of responsibility, where traditionally only chemists were in charge, included dyes, pigments and late-stage intermediates. Did this assignment happen on account of potential necessary changes?

Three years later, in 1987, Sammet approached Dormann and asked him whether he wished to succeed Hans Reintges as the Head of Finance at Hoechst. Dormann had actually studied finance and accountancy at university but he had never actually worked in that department. 'I do not have the necessary expertise at present,' he must have thought that weekend, which was all the time Sammet had granted him to reach a decision.

It goes without saying, however, that Dormann assumed the post of Head of Finance. One of his first tasks was to explore the opportunities for improving the competitive position of textile dyes. He was assisted by chemist Karl Holoubek, who as his successor assumed responsibility for dyes, pigments and late-stage intermediates. It was a stroke of luck that Holoubek's former fellow student Udo Oels was Deputy Chairman of the Board of Management in Leverkusen and consequently it was possible to enter into more intensive talks with Bayer. A factor which they both had in common was a respect-

---

136   Jürgen Dormann, 3 May 2010.

ful and trustworthy manner which is crucial in business because it is always people who make it happen. Nevertheless, the negotiations were tough, the asking price slowed down the decision-making process and the historical significance of dyes which was firmly established in many heads was again an obstacle in the struggle for sensible co-operation.

Arduous in-house talks at Hoechst with such vetoes as: "We cannot give up the dye business; if we only hold 50 percent, we won't be in charge anymore!" and still more arduous talks with Bayer finally led to the foundation of a joint dye company called DyStar in 1995. Rolf W. Schweizer, who at that time was still employed at Sandoz, had already been informed by Jürgen Dormann about the idea of uniting 'dyes' in Germany.

On account of the situation resulting from the transfer of Specialty Chemicals from Hoechst to Clariant, Rolf W. Schweizer no longer attached the same importance to his textile dye business—which had come entirely from Sandoz originally—as part of the 'new' Clariant portfolio and therefore he intended to disinvest[137] the division. Schweizer saw a potential purchaser in DyStar and the very first talks between the two parties took place in December 1996, at the time when the Hoechst deal was announced. Six months later, when Hoechst's share actually went to Clariant via Virteon, DyStar resumed talks with its partners Bayer and Hoechst and with Clariant and in October 1997, after repeated negotiations, agreement was reached on a purchase price of DM 800 million; the original price envisaged by Schweizer had been DM 1.4 billion.

In the course of time Clariant's[138] objective changed: even if the sale of textile dyes was originally to the fore, a participating interest in DyStar gradually became the focus of attention so that this also became part of the discussions. In this case, according to DyStar's offer which remained unchanged, Clariant was to receive a cash payment of DM 400 million and a 25 percent interest in the new joint venture. Alternatively, Clariant would agree to the above-mentioned cash payment and a stake of only 20 percent, contingent on the guarantee by existing DyStar shareholders of DM 450 million in the event of the sale of these shares within the framework of a later IPO.

In December 1997, it was put about that, in the next stage,[139] anti-trust approval was to be applied for in Brussels and a revision of the partnership agreement between Bayer and Hoechst was to be negotiated. According to Schweizer's plan, Clariant's activities in the field of textile dyes was to be transferred to DyStar at the end of June 1998 but in principle he had no objec-

137 Protocol of the Board of Management of Hoechst AG, 7 Jan. 1997, 2 May 1997 and 15 Oct. 1997.
138 Protocol of Board of Management of Hoechst AG, 4 Dec. 1997.
139 Protocol of Board of Management of Hoechst AG, 16 Dec. 1997.

tions to an earlier date. The Deutsche Bank, which was brought in to objectify the valuation issue, analysed the situation with regard to a possible IPO and decided in favour of the mandate to negotiate in addition to a 20 percent interest. A meeting took place to this effect in Frankfurt[140] in the presence of the Deutsche Bank on 25th March 1998. It was attended by Clariant-CFO Roland Lösser, DyStar-CEO Alfred Rad, his deputy Elmar Stachels and Richard Pott, a member of the Bayer staff department.

DyStar closed the fiscal year 1997 with an EBIT of DM 81 million; Clariant in comparison achieved an EBIT of DM 130 million. The difference in the earning situation of the previous and the current business year was one of the principal reasons why the negotiations were virtually at a standstill until midsummer 1998. Schweizer by no means pressed for the transfer of his textile dyes because the division had 'taken off like a rocket in the first quarter' as the *Neue Zürcher Zeitung* put it when commenting on the situation.[141]

A further complication was the circumstance that Bayer and Clariant wished to include further activities such as leather dyes and textile auxiliary agents as the 'big solution'. The progress of this enlarged deal was interrupted for the first time by a telephone conversation Rolf W. Schweizer had with Manfred Schneider on 26th August 1998, in which he informed the latter that the leather colorants and textile dyes business was not to be included within the framework of DyStar but, analogous to the huge Hoechst deal, against the disposal of shares. This would have meant a stake of between 20 and 30 percent for Bayer, whereas the company in Leverkusen would only have accepted an interest of at least 50 percent.[142]

As far as Clariant was concerned, the issue threatened not only to escalate but through time it also turned into an obstacle because what Rolf W. Schweizer definitely did not want in the 'new' Clariant's future portfolio at the end of December 1996 and wished to sell in good time, was still being carried around as a dead weight until mid-1998. With all the to-ing and fro-ing the right moment, *the momentum,* was lost because with the passing of time the textile dye business had forfeited some of its profitability. There had been a considerable deterioration in market opportunities and potential. Even at that time this business sector was still only an inconvenient marginal operation which, due to the relocation of the European textile industry abroad and the

---

140 Letter from Manfred Schneider to Rolf W. Schweizer, 3 Jul. 1998.
141 Daniel M. Hofmann: "Glänzende Clariant will Chancen nutzen," in Neue *Zürcher Zeitung,* 16 May 1998, p. 25.
142 Memorandum to Hoechst AG's Board of Management: DyStar/Takeover of Clariant's Textile Dyes, 27 Aug.1998.

growing competition from the Far East, no longer offered the chemicals giants any perspectives. Nevertheless, in autumn 1998 Clariant continued to lay emphasis on the 'excellent performance' and the synergies of its textile chemicals business, which had exceeded expectations in the first six months.[143]

When requested to furnish particulars on DyStar, Karl-Gerhard Seifert reflects: after the idea of a potential co-operation with Sandoz was no longer on the cards on account of the events in Schweizerhalle in 1986 and the opposition of the Cassella Board of Management, Dormann and Seifert conceived the plan at some time in 1992/1993 to merge the 'dyes' of Hoechst with those of Bayer. "We managed to do with Bayer what did not work with Sandoz," Seifert relates.

Later, when Seifert and Hoechst Specialty Chemicals were 'at home' in Muttenz, he remained strictly neutral during the negotiations between Clariant and DyStar. He deliberately kept out of the transaction to avoid any conflict because at Hoechst he had assisted in the founding of DyStar in 1994/1995 and was later on the DyStar Advisory Board.[144]

When asked what might have happened at the negotiations between Clariant and DyStar, Seifert replies succinctly: "Rolf W. Schweizer suddenly began to have his doubts. Remember, he grew up in dyes and he had worked very successfully in the branch for many years. When the rumour went the rounds in Basel that 'old' Sandoz was selling its dyes to this German company, DyStar, people phoned Schweizer and appealed to his conscience: "Rolf, you can't do this, those are our dyes!" Under this public pressure 'Mr Clariant' gradually broke off the negotiations with DyStar for it almost looked as though 'Grandmother' was to be sold once again, was to be thrown out once more…

The writing on the wall

In spring 1998 'new' Clariant had only been in existence for nine months and while fledgling CEO Karl-Gerhard Seifert was away on holiday in April, Rolf W. Schweizer was already having merger talks with the Alusuisse-Lonza Group, a company steeped in tradition, which had been bought up by Martin Ebner and Christoph Blocher in 1997.[145] The group had a staff of 31,000 em-

143 "Clariant holds on to textile dyes," in *Chemical Week*, 9 Sept 1998.
144 Karl-Gerhard Seifert, 3 Feb. 2010/20 May 2010.
145 Albert Steck: "Der standhafte Patriarch. Rolf W. Schweizer," in *Facts*, 9/2003, p. 70; Adrian

ployees, of whom 5,800 were employed in Switzerland. Its three divisions—Packaging, Aluminium and Chemicals—generated turnover of CHF 8.87 billion and a net profit of CHF 466 million.

Seifert remembers that when he returned to his office after his holiday, his President reported that he had tried to reach him in Mexico on the phone, but in vain. The CEO at Alusuisse-Lonza, Sergio Marchionne, had been to Muttenz and Schweizer wanted to know whether Seifert got along with the Italian because there would be another meeting soon.

There is proof that talks did in fact take place between Clariant and Alusuisse-Lonza in spring 1998. Roland Lösser remembers two or three visits by Theodor Tschopp, the President there, and his CEO. At this point Schweizer had also activated his contacts on the investor side; for example to Martin Ebner. The idea was, Seifert continues, to merge Alusuisse-Lonza with Clariant, then demerge Lonza, transfer it to Clariant and finally split up the group. Schweizer would have liked to close the deal but negotiations were broken off and Alusuisse later struck another deal in quite a different way: they took on the name of Algroup and in 2000 merged with the Canadian company Alcan, which merged into Rio Tinto Alcan in 2007.

If the merger with Alusuisse-Lonza had materialised, Seifert's position would have been at risk. He could not fail to be aware of that! "If I had been smart, I ought to have left Clariant there and then, when they got up to such little games behind my back… And I'm still annoyed with myself that I did nothing about it at the time, but everything went so fast and besides, that month, I had just bought a house in Lörrach which cost a small fortune", Seifert remembers nostalgically.[146] But he obviously realized that Schweizer must also have talked with Theodor Tschopp and Sergio Marchionne about the post of CEO.

After the planned merger with Alusuisse "did not go through due to insuperable differences in structural, cultural and strategical thinking",[147] day-to-day business was so amazing that it outshone Schweizer's tactics and anyway Seifert was busy moving his family to their new home in the tri-border region. Spirits were high. For many it was like a dream: Clariant soared higher and higher in the wake of acquiring Hoechst. The share price rose to a record high, which has never been surpassed since. Nothing could dampen the high spirits.

Knoepfli: *Im Zeichen der Sonne. Licht und Schatten über der Alusuisse 1930–2010*, Baden 2010, p. 237.

146   Karl-Gerhard Seifert, 3 Feb. 2010/20 May 2010.

147   Knoepfli 2010, p. 263.

Rolf W. Schweizer and the members of the Board of Management with their wives on the Rigi, June 1998.
Karl-Gerhard Seifert, Edda Seifert, Michaela Meyer, Reinhart S. Meyer, Sigrid Brandenberg, Inge Schweizer, Victor Sanahuja, Carmen Sanahuja, Peter Brandenberg, Rolf W. Schweizer, Gaby Lösser, Ulrich Cuntze, Roland Lösser, Hannelore Cuntze, Joachim Mahler, Elisabeth Wiezer, Regina Maria Titzrath-Mahler, Hartmut Wiezer, Günther Hencken, Heidi Hencken, Reinhard Handte, Gisela Handte (l–r)

In June Rolf W. Schweizer went on a wonderful trip to Engelberg with the members[148] of his Board of Management, who were accompanied by their wives. In accordance with the wishes of the team, the colonel and ex-commanding officer of the 21st Infantry Regiment asked Werner Flükiger, his 'right-hand man', to prepare a suitable programme with culture, entertainment, culinary delights and an 'obstacle course'. As in military exercises, the participants had to cover a certain course, during which they had to carry out various tasks: finding their bearings in unknown terrain, exercises in skill such as crossing a torrent by rope, finding objects or sewing in the woods. For the group photo on Mount Rigi, Schweizer—just like in the group of Sandoz's international dyes representatives on the Bürgenstock 30 years earlier—placed himself once more in the middle of the group. It was an unforgettable event and the participants still rave about it today.

---

148   Only François Dennefeld from the Board of Management is missing.

While Clariant was busy working on the merger of Hoechst Specialty Chemicals, negotiating with DyStar, toying with the idea of Alusuisse-Lonza and seeking unsuccessfully to take over the Fine Chemicals Division of Ems-Chemie owned by Christoph Blocher, Ciba pulled off a major deal. Allied Colloids Group plc, the water-processing company located in Bradford, England, was being courted by Hercules, an America company. It was to be a hostile takeover but it failed due to the intervention of the British authorities. When things calmed down, Ciba from Muttenz made a play for Allied Colloids and in the role of a 'white knight' out-priced those acting in the hostile merger.

In March 1998—at the time when Clariant was having talks with DyStar which involved Deutsche Bank in Frankfurt—the deal with Allied Colloids was settled but the price of CHF 3.6 billion paid by Ciba Chairman Rolf A. Meyer was three times what that notorious American company Hercules had offered for the package only a few months earlier. Weakened by its seven-figure acquisition but enlarged by one more business field, in which no one else at the 'Rhine's Knee' was engaged, Ciba, an object of loathing for ages, presented a totally acceptable picture to Rolf W. Schweizer, who saw that his hour of glory had come and so the merger talks between the neighbours on Rothausstrasse in Muttenz got underway.

Philipp Hammel, the then Head of Investor Relations, regards the Asian crisis[149] as one of the main reasons for the merger. The crisis, which loomed as early as 1997, hit the sector in late summer/early autumn 1998. Turnover decreased sharply; in some cases it slumped dramatically, triggered by large idle facility costs in particular—and both Ciba and Clariant had to deal with this situation.

On 18 June 1998 Clariant's shares peaked at CHF 93.60. The macroeconomic conditions led in succession to a weakening of the stock market worldwide; Clariant, as a cyclical share which always showed above-average volatility, mostly lost more than the market did in the same period.

"In 1998 the share reached an all-time peak and even Ciba's share tended to be rather high-flying, but since then a comparable level has never been reached ever again. It was from a relatively strong position but already weakened by the Asian crisis that we talked to each other," Philipp Hammel reports.

Hammel thinks that approaching each other cannot have been easy for either of them. "Rolf W. Schweizer would have had better reasons for approach-

---

149   Interview with Philipp Hammel in Pratteln, 8 Sept. 2010.

ing Rolf Meyer positively and self-confidently because there was this 'fire' burning throughout Clariant; this was due among other things to the takeover of Hoechst Specialty Chemicals, which had saved Clariant so to speak from the clutches of Ciba Specialties. You see, the over-priced acquisition of Allied Colloids in Britain in January 1998 had put a damper on Ciba both financially and mood-wise. Moreover, Schweizer was of the opinion that expenditure was still much too high and that we were still lugging around far too many unwished for dyes. This way we could now really tackle the combined pools of costs—by eliminating duplication, i. e. any overlap—and do things better together. In other words he thought we should combine our strengths and get rid of the unloved parts so to speak or if necessary sell them off to reduce the volume." [150]

Hammel also thinks that another reason for Schweizer's merger plans was the fact that after the takeover of Hoechst Specialty Chemicals he was keen to secure another spectacular deal as a crowning conclusion to his career before retiring from his post. "And it must be said that he put the deal before everything, before absolutely everything else. All the Clariant and the ex-Sandoz managers in particular were 'chucked' out so-to-speak and were scarcely to be found on the organisational chart because practically none of them was earmarked for one of the top, really important posts such as CFO, COO or divisional manager. And what was actually even worse was the fact that the whole thing was a 'drawing board manoeuvre' by Rolf W. Schweizer. Yes, indeed. The whole thing was primarily devised by him alone on the drawing board in his office and with an exchange ratio moreover that amounted to nothing more than a cheap sell-out. The exchange ratio, when merger plans were announced in a press release, stood at 1 to 5.35. This ratio attracted such unfavourable attention that the Clariant shareholders must have been shocked or even incensed. All the advantages were entirely on the Ciba side, but naturally he, I mean Rolf W. Schweizer, still had his post. He would still have been President of the Board of Directors for a certain period. But after that we would all have been virtually taken over by Ciba! This imbalance caused considerable embarrassment, especially in the relevant management positions at Clariant. As a result, Clariant took a particularly close look at things during the ensuing due-diligence phase and found many appropriate grounds for breaking off the negotiations or for adjusting essential merger parameters."[151]

150   Ibid.
151   Ibid.

There is a little anecdote, with an undertone that tries to play the incident down, about how the two Presidents might have found a way to reach an agreement in the end; it is said that one of the two, either Rolf A. Meyer or Rolf W. Schweizer, described the background history as follows: some two weeks before the merger was announced they had talked to each on the phone; at first they had merely discussed corporate matters but then all of a sudden one of them proposed that they merge after all.[152] This phone call marks the inception of *Project Ohio*.

As a result of these moves the unsuspecting Seifert noticed one day that, despite the good relationship with his boss, "Rolf W. Schweizer and his secretary would suddenly act very furtively when I came into the office and the transparency on the desk would quickly disappear." Every attempt was made to hide the preparations for and the documents pertaining to the merger from Seifert. Two or three weeks after all this secretiveness, that was in October 1998, the amalgamation seemed to be a foregone conclusion because Schweizer entered Seifert's office and told the then 52-year-old that Clariant was going to merge with Ciba. He, Schweizer, would become President, Rolf A. Meyer would acquire the post of CEO in the new company and the present CEOs of the two companies would have to step down. Seifert relates that at the same time Schweizer reminded the former Hoechst man that he had frequently talked of not intending to work all that long and pointed out that he had a good contract anyway. Hermann Wodicka, CEO at Ciba nearby, was simultaneously given the same news by Rolf A. Meyer, whereupon he handed in his resignation immediately.

Outwardly Seifert received the bad tidings rather calmly and without moving a muscle but inwardly he was immeasurably disappointed that Schweizer had gone behind his back and had negotiated the whole merger with Rolf A. Meyer entirely on his own. The idea of amalgamating the two Swiss chemicals groups was not new; the dream of being the biggest specialty chemicals company was almost a legend, which not only Martin Syz and his former fellow students at Ciba-Geigy desired, but Schweizer and Seifert, too, had often spoken of wanting to amalgamate with Ciba.[153] Therefore Seifert found Schweizer's going it alone for a second time all the more incomprehensible.

The divergence of their views lay in the way they perceived the merger. Seifert's credo was: We acquire our neighbour and using our management skills take over Ciba, which has been weakened financially because of Allied Col-

152   Ruedi Mäder: "Es war wieder mal Zeit, anzurufen," in *Aargauer Zeitung*, 10 Nov. 1998; *Die Zeit*, 12 Nov. 1998, p. 37.
153   Karl-Gerhard Seifert, 3 Feb. 2010/20 May 2010.

loids. Schweizer, in contrast, agreed to certain concessions with Ciba, agreed to *fifty-fifty*, took on board the model of an amalgamation among equals and accepted the fact that the Clariant CEO would see his head roll.

Was Seifert's departure one of Ciba's conditions and therefore a concession Schweizer had to carry out unconditionally? Or was it Schweizer himself who hit on the idea and used the merger as a welcome opportunity to rid himself of Seifert? Was Seifert's disappearance from the scene—as a rather unmanageable central figure—to accelerate the integration of the Hoechst team or even to crush their pride?

In that bitter hour, when Schweizer told him that his job was over, Seifert was firmly convinced that he would have been the only one—and he was extremely proud of the fact—with the necessary experience to merge Clariant with Ciba and to run the huge company of Clariant and its 'butterfly.' Ultimately, "I thought that if the powers that be are of the opinion that Rolf Meyer is better than I, then it's better for me to go," Seifert comments.[154] Consequently he drove to Frankfurt next day- that was in October 1998 and the only people to know of the imminent merger with Ciba apart from Schweizer were at best Roland Lösser, Reinhard Handte, Herbert Wohlmann and the secretary Doris Hufschmid—and there he negotiated a job in the Private Equity Division of Deutsche Bank. Agreement was reached quickly so that Seifert came out of the bank with the option of a new job. After that he went on holiday for a week and used the time to mull over everything in peace. After careful consideration he decided once and for all to leave Clariant. "Clariant had been my life up to that point," Seifert says about his decision. "I fought all I could for the 28,000 people under me, I wanted to lead them into a better future, but the fact that he had done such a thing behind my back and did not even consult me was a great disappointment to me. I knew you shouldn't start a war you cannot possibly win. And I knew that as Clariant CEO I could not possibly win this fight with the Swiss Board of Directors."[155]

The Presidents of the Boards of Directors of Clariant and Ciba Specialty Chemicals announced the signing of an agreement in principle at a press conference on 9 November 1998.[156] With the merger of two equal partners both companies wanted to become the largest company for specialty chemicals in the world with an annual turnover of approx. CHF 18 billion. It was their aim

---

154 Ibid.
155 Ibid.
156 Clariant *Aktionärsinfo*, 9 Nov. 1998; Birgit Voigt: "Basler Chemie überflügelt alle" in *Tages-Anzeiger*, 10 Nov. 1998, front page; Claudia H. Deutsch: "Ciba Is Set for a Merger with Clariant" in *New York Times*, 10 Nov. 1998.

Press conference held by Clariant and Ciba on the occasion of the
announcement of the merger plan on 9th Nov. 1998

to expand their leading position in core businesses with their impressive product portfolio and to create a strong growth platform. The merger was to take
place in accordance with the Swiss Code of Obligations as a so-called pure
dual annexation merger whereby both companies would have been absorbed
into a new company whose organisational chart had already been decided.
The company was to be called Clariant but the name was to be combined with
Ciba Specialty Chemicals' distinctive symbol of the butterfly and it would retain its head office in Basel. According to the plan, the final agreement on the
merger was to be approved in December 1998 after the extended process of due
diligence had ended. The merger required the consent of the shareholders of
both companies and of the authorities. Warburg Dillon Read acted as advisers
for Clariant and Credit Suisse First Boston as advisers for Ciba.

At the time of the announcement the two negotiating partners recorded
the following operating figures: in 1997 Clariant generated turnover worth
just under CHF 10.2 billion. In the same period Ciba had a turnover of CHF
7.8 billion i. e. a pro-forma turnover amounting to CHF 9 billion allowing
for the result of Allied Colloids which had been acquired in March 1998. In
an exchange of shares Clariant shareholders were to receive approximately 54
percent and Ciba shareholders about 46 percent of the registered shares of the
new company. Accounting planned according to US GAAP was to leave open
the option of a future IPO on the US stock markets. The 45 percent participa-

tion of Hoechst AG in Clariant would presumably remain unchanged until completion of the merger. After that Hoechst's stake in the new company was to be reduced proportionally.

The merger was to increase earnings as from 2000 and it was hoped to meet medium-term strategic targets more quickly. As expected, cost saving due to improvements in efficiency was to rise annually to more than CHF 600 million until 2001. The shedding of 3,000 jobs worldwide had been calculated, but there were to be no additional significant redundancies in Switzerland. The amalgamated company was to offer jobs to a total of 52,000 employees.

Voices of dissent

The merger plans were received with mixed feelings. Even Head of Communications Walter Vaterlaus only learned of the planned 'marriage' a few days before the public announcement was made and wondered whether it might not have been better to make a declaration of intent first and then to take time—two or three months—to examine the books very thoroughly instead of prematurely announcing the deal as 'ready-made.'[157]

Suddenly there were reservations about whether the deal could even be pulled off as planned, for anti-trust issues materialized on account of the huge share of the future company on the pigments market. Seifert relented at this stage and offered Schweizer his help. The idea cropped up that, within the framework of the merger, a part of Pigments should be spun off into a new company with Seifert as its CEO. The company was then to be sold or floated on the Stock Exchange. Some Clariant men who had been slighted in the Clariant-Butterfly organisational chart felt themselves acknowledged—albeit temporarily—in this new pigments company.

Upon closer examination of the terms of contract Walter Vaterlaus and Philipp Hammel, his colleague who was in charge of Investor Relations, began to query the correctness of the exchange ratio. The impression was gained that the Clariant shareholders would find themselves at a decided disadvantage. Furthermore, Vaterlaus felt that the Chief Communication Officer at Ciba at the time, the Australian Kirsten Gallagher, was trying to pull a fast one on him. They had agreed jointly on a new logo, in which the Clariant name and the Ciba butterfly stood in proportion to their individual size. However, Va-

---

157   Walter Vaterlaus, 25 May 2010.

terlaus learned later that the lady had presented the Ciba management not with the joint design but with something entirely different.[158]

Walter Vaterlaus and Philipp Hammel[159] expressed their doubts to their CFO Roland Lösser, who would have lost his post as Head of Finance to Michael Jacobi from Ciba in the amalgamated company. In a lengthy meeting, the three of them came to the conclusion that if the deal went through, Clariant's shareholders would get the short end of the stick and the former Ciba management would gain the upper hand when it came to running the company. They decided to prepare themselves well and inform Rolf W. Schweizer of their findings. At first he reacted somewhat brusquely to the arguments they presented but in the course of their remarks became more and more thoughtful.

But there was not only criticism from senior staff. Both the media and analysts from the financial sector and the stock exchange were mainly critical of the envisaged merger between Clariant and Ciba, which was even judged by some to be an admission of weakness. Economic journalist Daniel M. Hofmann expressed his opinion on the eventual risks and reservations[160] in the weekend edition of the *Neue Zürcher Zeitung*, 5th/6th December 1998.

As both companies no longer had the best balance sheet ratios due to their acquisitions in the recent past and the cyclical situation was making it difficult to achieve the earnings target, analysts tended to see defensive reasons for the merger. Moreover, they were not inclined to believe in the supposed economies of scale to be gained by the merger of two market leaders. Apart from the restrictions imposed by the cartel authorities, the critics feared a cannibalization of sales because many purchasers do not like to be dependent on only one supplier and consequently would look around for new sources of supply.[161]

Consequently there was no reason to expect that the market share of the two amalgamating companies could be improved in any way. There was just as much scepticism about the significance of fine and electronic chemicals and water treatment, which were presented as having a promising future. As these only accounted for 14 percent of sales revenue, old products would continue to account for most of the turnover. Moreover, the analysts rated the predicted synergy profits of CHF 400 million as comparatively low and their trend in the future as rather unstable in view of the economic situation. Be-

---

158 Ibid.
159 Philipp Hammel, 8 Sept. 2010.
160 Daniel M. Hofmann: "Die neue Clariant will (noch) nicht glänzen. Weitverbreitete Skepsis in der Analytiker-Gemeinde," in Neue *Zürcher Zeitung*, 5–6 Dec. 1998, p. 27.
161 Ibid.

sides, there were already indications shortly before the merger was due to take place that the 'brand-new' Clariant would record a huge deficit in its first fiscal year 1999, as goodwill would also accrue in addition to the merger costs of CHF 800 million. The shareholders' reaction to the announcement was extremely restrained. It was merely on the day of the announcement that the share price rose slightly but returned to the old trend next day and even continued to drop thereafter. Roland Lösser stresses that it was the analysis of the planned merger by economic journalist Daniel M. Hofmann in the weekend issue of the *Neue Zürcher Zeitung* that contributed substantially to the change in mood, for on the following working day Rolf W. Schweizer addressed the issue in a decidedly objective and critical manner. Indeed, after the talk with Lösser, Vaterlaus and Hammel it was noticeable that the wind had changed direction and Schweizer, for his part, was now beginning to impose conditions on Ciba. But these were no longer acceptable to Ciba so that the proposed 'marriage of the two companies' was finally called off exactly one month after it had been announced.

Talks discontinued

On 9th December 1998, Clariant announced the decision by the Board of Directors not to finalize the proposed merger agreement with Ciba Specialty Chemicals,[162] whereupon the talks with Ciba were called off. This decision by the Board was reached after a comprehensive process of due diligence had been completed. This process revealed commercial and financial risks, legal and regulatory risks and constraints relating to the execution of the planned transaction and the future of the amalgamated companies. In the opinion of the Board of Directors these risks were so significant as to undermine the future benefits and synergies which were to be achieved by the proposed merger announced on November 1998. Furthermore, the Board of Directors was persuaded that under these circumstances it was in the interest of the Clariant shareholders that the enterprise remained independent. It was deeply regretted that after very constructive and open negotiations with Ciba the merger had to be abandoned. In the end, Clariant and Ciba agreed not to make public any confidential information or to publish any additional reports on this topic.

---

162   Clariant *Press Release*, 9 Dec. 1998.

When asked for more information Rolf A. Meyer[163] referred to the above-mentioned agreement not to reveal any confidential information. However, he did mention a publication by himself which appeared in a Festschrift of the University of St. Gallen in 1998. This 16-page essay by Rolf A. Meyer on the "structural transformation in the chemicals and pharmaceuticals industry" depicts the developments of the previous ten years and summarizes the trends in the sector but the article contains no specific statements on the failed merger between Clariant and Ciba, since the paper had been published prior to the merger plans.

On 9th December 1998 the media announced that the merger talks had been called off. Seifert heard the news on the radio while he was driving along the motorway from Frankfurt to Basel. Upon his arrival in Muttenz he found an atmosphere of elation and the champagne was bubbling: "Thank God all that nonsense with Ciba is over and Seifert will be staying," all his closest colleagues who were present that evening rejoiced.[164]

It was only natural that Ulrich Cuntze, Günther Hencken, Reinhart S. Meyer, Victor Sanahuja and Hartmut Wiezer, whose names had no longer appeared on the Clariant-Ciba organisational chart,[165] experienced the greatest satisfaction. Of the former eleven members of the Board of Management only four would have remained in office after the merger with Ciba: Peter Brandenberg, Reinhard Handte, Roland Lösser and Joachim Mahler, and all four of them would have had different, less important positions than they had held since the company went public in 1995 or since the merger in 1997.

Despite the jubilant mood, Seifert could not relax; he still felt hurt to the core and even today he still feels annoyed that Schweizer negotiated with Alusuisse-Lonza without his knowledge. The writing had already been on the wall then, but he was incapable of interpreting it and intervening in time.

Be that as is may, the storm had passed and Seifert could have continued at Clariant as CEO because he had not been dismissed, and in contrast to Hermann Wodicka who had resigned voluntarily, Seifert had kept his head at the critical moment. He had even looked for a job in the private equity sector quickly and on the quiet and then he waited to see what would happen. But

---

163 E-mail from Rolf A. Meyer to the author, 3 Aug. 2010; Rolf A.Meyer: "Strukturwandel in der chemischen und pharmazeutischen Industrie. Neue Chancen für die Spezialitätenchemie" in Sascha Spoun/Ernst Müller-Möhl/Roger Jann (Ed.): *Universität und Praxis, Tendenzen und Perspektiven wissenschaftlicher Verantwortung für Wirtschaft und Gesellschaft. Festschrift*, Zurich 1998, pp. 273–288.

164 Karl-Gerhard Seifert, 3 Feb. 2010/20 May 2010.

165 See the Clariant-Ciba organization chart in Markus Sutter: "Zwei starke Firmen werden zu zweit noch starker," in *Basler Zeitung*, 10 Nov. 1998.

nothing did happen, as Seifert relates, for the subject remained taboo between the Chairman and his CEO after the merger had fallen through. Schweizer and he continued to work next door to each other but they never mentioned what had happened—two heads that could not settle a matter that had gone awry the way two adults should.

The barbed pen

Man always searches for the truth or at least an explanation of things. Public opinion is an expression of a yearning for a meaningful interpretation and is also an outlet for prevailing prejudices about facts and circumstances. A person in the public eye can scarcely escape public notice. Anyone not wanting to be lumped with the rank and file, holding a prominent position into the bargain, even achieving top performances or stumbling in his eagerness must expect to be always under observation and to be a target of the pen wielded by sharp-tongued journalists and cartoonists. It was no different when attempts were made to forge a merger with Ciba.

Naturally, the editorial in the Zurich *Tages-Anzeiger* on 10 November 1998, like most of the media at that point, concentrated on the merger that had been announced.[166] On the front page there was also a cartoon by Nico, a cartoonist from Solothurn, who had taken up the motif of the 'Basel Marriage' by Hans Geisen in the 1970s when Geisen had interpreted the earlier merger of Ciba and Geigy as a safe amalgamation and a major step forward of two strong types. Nico, however, depicts a situation which is by no means happy because he shows two figures who are sitting side by side but who give the impression of being unrelated and with whom a doctor is having an serious word: i. e. the relationship not only requires medical advice but a remedy into the bargain— a remedy called 'merger.'

The topic of the merger was a godsend to the cartoonists and it was Ciba's mascot, the butterfly, which was particularly suitable for allegories of very different kinds. Someone in the senior management is supposed to have pinned a cartoon on the notice board in one of the Clariant offices; it showed a figure chasing a moth with a butterfly net and the connotation was understood by one and all even though the picture had no title.

166   Birgit Voigt: "Basler Chemie überflügelt alle," on the front page of the *Tages-Anzeiger,* 10 Nov. 1998.

«Wenn Sie sich daran halten, wird Ihre Chemie stimmen, und Sie werden sich gesundstossen.»

Merger, Cartoon by Nico, in the *Tages-Anzeiger*, 10th November 1998

Ernst Feurer, a cartoonist from around Basel whose pseudonym was Efeu, took the allegory one step further in the weekend issue of the *Sonntagsblick* on 15 November 1998. In it he linked the metamorphosis of the caterpillar into a butterfly and Novartis, the example par excellence of a merger, with the current events. The cartoon by Feurer depicts a caterpillar on a platform; the caterpillar has Rolf W. Schweizer's face and bears the inscription 1995; from its body a butterfly is emerging which has the same face but its wings are the dotted wings of Ciba and it is dated 1998. The text in Schweizer's speech bubble—"I, too, am turning into one of the merger greats"—is directed towards the easily recognizable figure of a well-known personality in Basel chemicals, who is standing in front of the platform looking up at the monumental metamorphosis in astonishment.

The illusion of a miraculous metamorphosis and of flying in the guise of a colourful butterfly was of short duration.

Emil

It was at a Clariant Christmas celebration in Alsace at the end of 1998, just after the merger had failed, that a member of the management who was a

gifted comedian gave an imitation of the well-known Swiss comic Emil Stein-
berger and did a sketch on the failed merger with Ciba. The alleged Emil took
a telephone, put a hat on his head and pretended to hold a conversation in
which Rolf W. Schweizer and Rolf A. Meyer, the two initiators of the Clariant/
Ciba deal, talk about the point of the merger and the distribution of roles in it.
"You know, Rolf," the longest-serving of the two is supposed to have said to his
neighbour from across the road, "I'm building a monument to myself and you
can manage it for me!"[167] Those present were convulsed with laughter. Rolf W.
Schweizer, too, was present. It was the presentation of an opinion which was
strictly taboo and in which people were openly criticized, but the joke in this
context did serve to defuse the situation.

Carnival in Basel

The failed merger between Clariant and Ciba also found its way onto the floats
in the carnival processions in Basel in 1999. This event always begins at four
o'clock on the Monday after Ash Wednesday, lasts exactly 72 hours and is considered to be 'the finest three days.' During this period the centre of Basel is
taken over by the so-called 'carnival cliques' in their multi-coloured costumes.
During the processions, which are more or less the equivalent of the carnival
processions in Germany, the carnival cliques weave their way through the city
centre on their decorated floats; aboard are groups playing music, and clubs
or associations who take serious events in contemporary history or currents
issues as their themes and satirize them. This also finds expression in the costumes, the props and the painted lanterns, which have been especially geared
to the themes. In addition, leaflets—called 'Schnitzelbängg'—with humorous
verses are distributed and visitors can admire the artistically designed and
illuminated lanterns on display in front of the Basel Minster and study the
verses at leisure.

In February 1999 one of the lanterns centred on the two Rolfs—Rolf W.
Schweizer and Rolf A. Meyer—and visually made fun of the plans to merge
Clariant and Ciba. A carnival poet alias Fäärimaa, a name derived from the
word 'ferryman', was also inspired by the 'mergeritis'. He wrote the following

---

167 A really great business deal before retirement is regarded in the economy as the equivalent
     of a monument. See Judith Raupp: "Nach mir die Fusion. Was alternde Firmenchefs mit un-
     ternehmerischer Logik begründen, dient oft nur der eigenen Denkmalpflege," in *Cash*, 13 Nov.
     1998, no. 46, p. 11.

verse and recited it, as is the custom in Basel, in various pubs and inns during the three days of carnival. Moreover, the 'Schnitzelbängg'[168] clearly draws upon memories of the consequences of the fire in 1986—the mass death of fish. Two other Ciba objects, the butterfly as their logo and adhesive as a showcase product of the one-time Ciba found their way into the satirical song.

In the Birs, such a thing has ne'er been seen,
The fish've been stuck to the water with glue.
And CIBA, of course, was hopeful and keen
To stick, with glue, the butterfly to Clariant, too.

(The Swiss-German original reads:
In dr Birs, ych ha's no nie erläbt
hän sie d'Fisch mit Lyym ans Wasser kläbt
und by dr CIBA hett d'Hoffnig scho afo kyyme
me kennt dr Schmätterling au an d'Clariant lyyme.)

Rolf W. Schweizer, who insisted on attending the procession despite the frosty weather, took the satire in his stride. In reply to a question by journalists from *Cash* he said that he did not regard the failed merger as a loss of face and added: "Both parties ascertained during the process of due diligence that their expectations could not be fulfilled."[169]

Ciba survived these events for almost ten years until, from 2008 onwards, it became increasingly drawn into BASF's orbit. Ciba's name was removed from the Swiss trade register on 1st March 2009.[170]

The secret telephone number

After the negotiations with Alusuisse-Lonza which had been called off, the unsuccessful talks with DyStar and the plans for a merger with Ciba which had fallen through, Clariant faced huge economic problems in various regions in 1998. In the wake of the crisis in Asia, momentum collapsed to such an extent that the downturn could not be offset by the favourable trend in Europe. That year, the company generated a turnover of CHF 9.5 billion; EBIT

---

168 Markus Vogt: "Dr Christo paggt y – und d Bänggler sinn derby" in *Basellandschaftliche Zeitung*, 22 Feb. 1999.
169 Judith Raupp/Victor Weber: "Die Mitarbeiter haben mittlerweile eine dicke Haut" in *Cash*, 5 Mar. 1999.
170 See Sergio Aiolfi: "Ciba zum Letzten. Das Verschwinden einer 125 Jahre alten Industrie-Ikone," in Neue *Zürcher Zeitung*, 6 Apr. 2009.

amounted to CHF 833 million and the operating cash flow fell to CHF 712 million. At the Annual General Meeting in Basel on 12 June 1999, a 1:2 share split was approved. At the same time agreement was reached on a contingent capital increase from CHF 40 million to CHF 80 million and the introduction of an authorised capital of CHF 40 million so that capital could be raised, but only in the case of an acquisition, at short notice.

In 1998 Clariant concentrated investments primarily on growth areas. The largest single project was the erection of manufacturing facilities for photo resists and electronic chemicals in Ansung, Korea and in Branchburg, USA and the expansion of production facilities for printing pastes and the reconstruction of the AZO-II pigments plant in Frankfurt-Höchst.

On the day after Clariant announced that the proposed merger with Ciba had been aborted, Rolf W. Schweizer disclosed an alteration in his strategy. This new strategic plan becomes clearest in the combination of the numbers *2–15–20–20*, a combination which was known by heart by everyone at Clariant.[171] This secret telephone number united all of Rolf W. Schweizer's visions because these numbers represented the most important targets of the company. The 2 stood for the envisaged growth, which was to be 2 percent higher than growth in the industry. The 15 stood for operating profits (EBIT), which were to reach 15 percent of turnover; 20 represented the target for the operating profits margin before amortization (EBITDA in percent of the turnover) and profitability related to the net assets (non-interest bearing assets minus non-interest bearing liabilities). Clariant wanted to reach this performance level by 2003, not just in peak years but permanently. The management was told: "Always remember the magic figures: 2–15–20–20."

Size and life science

When the deal with Ciba failed to come off, Schweizer focussed more vigorously on strategic issues: What could a consolidation in the future look like, who and with whom, and what was going to happen next? He held numerous talks with members of the Board of Directors on consolidation momentum in the industry. He was convinced that he had to play an active part in this process and that size would be a major feature of survival, i. e. the quality of the future.

---

171 Ulrich Schäfer/Andreas Meier: "Wir setzen alles dran, die Gewinnzahlen zu erreichen," in *Finanz und Wirtschaft*, 16 Jan. 1999, p. 15; "2–15–20–20" in *Clariant Direkt* 3/99d, 15 Feb. 1999.

The widely-held view that life-science groups[172] would be content to obtain their late-stage intermediates from other chemical manufacturers was hype[173] and was fed by analysts, the trade press and assumptions in the industry. This opinion unleashed a new movement in the chemicals industry, whereupon there were visions of a new economic growth market and considerable earnings. In expectation of significant benefits a gold rush feeling crept in and the grossly exaggerated reports caused the number of active market participants to rise perceptibly. Was it merely a trend or really an option for the future? The fact that this was a hype was not known and besides, no one was aware that hypes are cyclical.

Clariant, just like its competitors, had long toyed with the idea of an acquisition in the fine chemicals sector in order to gain a foothold in the field of pharmaceutical late-stage intermediates, which were generally held to have a very promising future. With this in mind, Rolf W. Schweizer began to negotiate with Laporte, a British company, early in 1999. Seifert, who remained at Clariant until the 1998 Annual General Meeting, i. e. until June 1999, fought this decision tooth and nail, reiterating incessantly: "As long as I'm here, we will not buy a British company. British fine chemicals companies are the worst chemicals companies in the world."[174] Unlike Schweizer, Seifert intended to acquire the American company of Great Lakes. He met Mark Burliss, the chairman of the company, several times and got on very well with him. Both of them were convinced that their businesses would complement each other extremely well.

According to his former CEO, however, Rolf W. Schweizer did not want to enter into any business with an American company for two reasons: Schweizer liked American as a country but he sometimes had problems getting along with Americans. The second reason why he refrained from acquiring an American company was a historical one and astonished Seifert considerably. "You know, Karl, as Swiss, we have a special relationship to the English. It was they who helped us so much during the war," the Clariant President disclosed to his CEO on the eve of talks with Laporte.[175]

Schweizer figured that taking over Laporte could consolidate his position as one of the world's largest specialists in fine chemicals[176] and that he would

172 See Juan Enriquez/Ray A. Goldberg: "Transforming Life, Transforming Business: The Life-Science Revolution," in *Harvard Business Review*, vol. 78, no. 2, Mar.-Apr. 2000, pp. 94–104.
173 Georg Honsel: "Die Hype-Zyklen neuer Technologien," in *Spiegel Online*, 21 Oct. 2006.
174 Karl-Gerhard Seifert, 3 Feb. 2010/20 May 2010.
175 Ibid.
176 Michael Roberts: "Laporte travels the long, hard road from commodities to specialties," in *Chemical Week*, 18 Aug. 1993.

have all the factors of success on his side to take over as the leading manufacturer of fine chemicals and thus set the pace in the life science sector. Wanting to be the industry's major player is a tempting idea but getting there is extremely hard work.

Veto

On 12th April 1999 Laporte plc, which was based in the English town of Luton, announced that it had entered into sales negotiations.[177] On the same day, its share price soared by almost 30 percent and analysts were convinced that Clariant had practically taken over the British fine chemicals manufacturer already, even though both Clariant and Laporte denied having negotiations at all. In reality, the negotiations were already far advanced. Agreement had been reached on a purchasing price of £2.1 billion, i.e. US$3.4 billion, and the assumption of liabilities amounting to £550 million. Moreover, in the City (London's financial centre), it was considered certain that Clariant would pay as much as 850 pence per share for the prestigious specialty chemicals company. In 1998 Ciba had paid 13.3 times its gross profit (EBITA) for Allied Colloids; Clariant hoped to acquire Laporte for ten or eleven times its profit for the year.

Scarcely had the news of the plans for an acquisition leaked than Laporte announced next day that "the other party" had been unable to continue the talks. This unexpected turnaround was not due to the price or the process of due diligence of the finances nor was it a matter of personalities, for President George Duncan and his CEO Jim Leng got on well with Clariant. By all accounts Clariant ended the talks because it could no longer rely on the support of Hoechst, its main shareholder. Michael Kayser, the Financial Director at Laporte, reported in retrospect that both parties had been willing to sign the contract but "at the '59th second of the 59th minute of the 11th hour' the other party had suddenly asked for more time. It could not say whether it would need one day or several months and Laporte pulled the plug. We couldn't sit around in limbo."[178]

177 Francesco Guerrera: "Laporte's pounds 1.5bn deal founders on Hoechst veto," in *The Independent*, 14 Apr. 1999; Claudia Hume: "Clariant's Laporte Acquisition is off," in *Chemical Week*, 21 Apr. 1999.
178 Sean Milmo: "Hoechst Forces Clariant to End Possible Takeover of Laporte," in *Chemical Markets Reporter*, 19 Apr. 1999; "Laporte breaks silence over merger failure," in *Chemistry and Industry*, 16 Aug. 1999.

Analysts see the more definite reason in the fact that the purchasing price for Laporte would have amounted to almost CHF 6 billion, which in view of Clariant's liquid assets of ca. CHF 600 million at the time would have had to be financed with outside capital. As the Hoechst management itself was just on the verge of a merger with Rhône-Poulenc and, if anything, intended to sell Clariant shares to finance the deal, a drop in the price of the share would have been inconvenient, to say the least. Consequently Clariant was, without further ado, obliged by its major shareholder to 'pull back'. [179]

A journalist picturesquely described the failure of the talks with Laporte as the "the renewed closing of a door,"[180] and the press broached the subject of Rolf W. Schweizer's dwindling reputation in professional circles and the declining motivation among his staff. All the same, they waited for the next step, for the President made no secret of his intention of making some acquisition or other. Schweizer had a 'watch list' comprised allegedly of no less than 20 companies and 'the next drawer was just waiting to be opened.'[181] With his numerous drawers and 20 candidates for a takeover, Rolf W. Schweizer was, to a certain degree, even under duress to implement his plans. First of all there had been the failure to merge with Ciba in December 1998 and then in April 1999 the acquisition of Laporte was thwarted by Hoechst. As all good things come in threes, a third attempt by Clariant was expected…

Secondary offering

The smooth transition to further acquisition negotiations was postponed, however, on account of the secondary offering. Hoechst AG announced in June 1999 that it wanted to reduce its 45 percent stake in Clariant substantially because Clariant products no longer fitted into the group's strategy which was directed towards life sciences.[182] In this project which had been given the name of Condor, Hoechst bore the code name Hector and Clariant was termed Crown. Via a secondary public offering both institutional and private investors in Germany and in Switzerland were offered around 4.11 million shares at a price of CHF 645 each. Further, a four-year convertible bond was

---

179   Dieter Claassen: "Clariant von Großaktionär zurückgepfiffen," in *Tages-Anzeiger*, 14 Apr. 1999.
180   Peter Knechtli: "Schweizer unter Erfolgsdruck: Letzter Streich darf kein Flop werden," in *Online-Reports*, 2 Apr. 1999.
181   Felix Erbacher: "Clariant zieht bald die nächste Schublade," in *Basler Zeitung*, 17 Apr. 1999.
182   "Beteiligung schnell loswerden," in *Manager Magazin*, 1 Jun. 1999

issued with a coupon of 2.75 percent which could be converted into 1.58 million Clariant shares. The Clariant shares were in great demand and went like 'hotcakes'.[183] In July 1999, thanks to the huge demand, Hoechst even managed to sell all its shares for a total of € 2.8 billion. Both companies appeared very satisfied with the proceeds. Clariant gained a significantly broader base of investors and in the end the secondary offering gave Hoechst € 5.5 billion which was a substantial profit, as Hoechst-CFO Klaus-Jürgen Schmieder confirmed at the time.

183   "Wie warme 'Weggli'," in *Finanz und Wirtschaft*, 10 Jul. 1999.

BTP and the consequences

A capital blunder

Clariant, just like its competitors, had been toying with the idea of an acquisition in fine chemicals for some time in order to gain a foothold in the sector of pharmaceutical late-stage intermediates, which were generally held to be particularly promising. After the takeover of Laporte had foundered at the last minute—due to the veto by Hoechst, the major shareholder—Schweizer began negotiations with another British company.

During the *CPhI*, the International Trade Fair for Pharmaceutical Ingredients and Intermediates, François Darrort, Clariant's Divisional Manager for Life Sciences appeared at the stand of British Tar Products plc on the first day of the fair and announced that his President Rolf W. Schweizer and COO Reinhard Handte would be visiting the booth next day. That was the first time that Schweizer and Steve Hannam, CEO at BTP, met. Hannam recalls[184] that Schweizer, while looking round the stand,

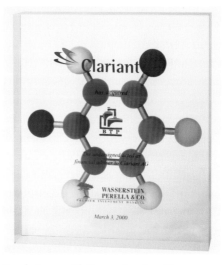

Tombstone with the molecule 5-Fluorouracil: Clariant acquired BTP on 3 March 2000

---

184 Steve Hannam agreed to answer in writing the author's questions on the topic and this resulted in correspondence consisting of ten to twelve e-mails at the end of 2010 and the beginning of 2011.

remarked: "You have done a good job building BTP, ready for Clariant to acquire!"

BTP[185] was 30 to 50 years younger than either Sandoz or Hoechst. It had been established as a chemicals plant in Cadishhead near Manchester in 1915, during the First World War; its main focus was on dye distillation; at that time its logo was the distinctive old-fashioned tar boiler. What distinguished BTP from the mainstream just before the turn of the century and made it of interest was its speedy reaction to development trends in the sector. From the mid-1990s on, the company, under the management of Steve Hannam, began to acquire life science companies in a big way. As a result it had a range of products which appeared to be a useful and effective complement and expansion to the portfolio of many pharmaceutical companies and aspiring pharmaceutical suppliers, such as Clariant wished to become. BTP had about 2,800 employees worldwide and in its Fine Chemicals Division manufactured intermediates and ingredients for pharmaceuticals and agrochemicals, and specialty chemicals for the electronics industry and personal care. Biocide, leather chemicals and various other products were produced in the Performance Chemicals Division. In the fiscal year 1998, BTP had generated turnover of £ 374 million sterling and an operating profit of £ 58 million.[186]

The company held a major position on the growing fine chemicals market. A number of companies in Europe and the USA had already expressed interest in it but until then there had been no official approach; however, in view of the situation, BTP with its adviser UBS Warburg had drafted a *teaser*—as was common practice with mergers & acquisitions—giving a short outline of the business on offer so that it would be in a position to react properly in the event of a takeover bid. In actual fact Schweizer broached the subject at the *CPhI* in Frankfurt but was informed by Hannam that if Clariant were interested, it would have to write to BTP's Board of Management.

Hannam took to Schweizer immediately and liked the special twinkle in his eyes. He thought that the Clariant President had a good head on his shoulders and seemed to be 'upfront.' He did not really know the company in Muttenz but he had always kept an eye on Sandoz, for he had regularly temped in the dye research laboratory at Sandoz in Leeds-Horsforth in the school holidays and then as a chemistry student during holidays. He had later followed the fortunes of Moret's group out of personal curiosity. As far as the young company of Clariant was concerned, he knew that there were a few overlaps

185   David Hunter:"BTP hard at work behind the scenes. BTP plc Company Profile" in *Chemical Week*, 1 Apr. 1996.
186   Reto Schlatter: "Auf Shoppingtour," in *Handelszeitung*, 26 Jan. 2000.

in leather chemicals with BTP subsidiary Hodgson Chemical, which had a strong position in wet end Chemicals whereas the company in Muttenz was better positioned in Leather Finishing.

After the first meeting at the stand at the Frankfurt fair, BTP received several phone calls from Schweizer and Handte whereupon President John Ketteley and his CEO Hannam were invited to Basel. According to Hannam, this was probably the only time the two Presidents, Ketteley and Schweizer, met. The meeting was very businesslike and an offer without engagement was handed to Ketteley to take to his Board of Management in Manchester. After that BTP included UBS Warburg in the negotiations. The latter informed Clariant that without a suitable advisory bank the Swiss company was not allowed to make an offer for a British stock corporation. Consequently Schweizer commissioned Wasserstein Perella & Co., which was based in New York, for he already knew Joe Perella through Raymund Breu from Sandoz times. From then on the transaction was supervised by the banks. The negotiations were well advanced when BTP discovered that UBS was also advising Clariant about credit facilities for financing the acquisition. As a result, BTP felt at a disadvantage and replaced UBS Warburg with Merrill Lynch.

The talks were resumed after Christmas and culminated in a weekend meeting in London, at which Roland Lösser and Reinhard Handte acted for their company. Clariant put the pressure on. BTP attributed this to the fact that only a few months earlier, in April 1999, the Muttenz executives had been unsuccessful in their attempt to acquire Laporte, another a British fine chemicals company, and were determined to strike a bargain this time—which meant that BTP clearly had an advantage.

There was a further considerable disadvantage for Clariant: whereas both partners in the negotiations for the takeover of Hoechst Specialty Chemicals had looked closely at each other beforehand, inspected the figures going back over a period of years and had checked the patents, there was no process of due diligence prior to the potential acquisition of BTP. "Everyone wants to know why we did not carry out due diligence at BTP but we were not able to do so because that is just not possible if you make a public offer. We made a public offer on the Stock Exchange and BTP said: 'If we grant you a due diligence, then we have to do that with every other applicant'," Herbert Wohlmann,[187] the then Head of the Legal Department and Secretary to the Board of Directors explained.

---

187   Herbert Wohlmann, 9 Feb. 2010.

"The business with BTP was a purchase of shares which was why, in principle, you only had recourse to publically accessible data and could not carry out a due diligence. It is a completely different approach if a company buys on the stock exchange," Herbert Link,[188] a former member of the Board of Management and Head of Clariant Germany from 2003 confirms. In a so-called *share deal* there are several prospective buyers as a rule. If only a chosen few among the applicants had been shown all the books, the entire research and development pipeline and every factory, for example, other potential buyers would have been at a disadvantage.

Hannam reports, however, that Clariant took the opportunity to obtain additional information in a 'question and answer session'. For this purpose Clariant, represented by Reinhard Handte and Roland Lösser, met with the BTP team and their respective advisers from UBS Warburg. The meeting lasted an entire afternoon and was recorded so that, if necessary, other bidders could later obtain exactly the same information.

Agreement was reached therefore—but without the traditional process of due diligence—that BTP's Supervisory Board would recommend that its shareholders accept the deal. In a friendly takeover bid by Clariant on 24 January 2000, BIP shareholders were offered 600p per share in cash. This offer corresponded to an evaluation of BTP share capital of approx. £ 1.08 billion sterling, which convinced the majority of the shareholders. Consequently the deal was settled only six weeks later in early March 2000 and the takeover reached a successful conclusion. Clariant paid CHF 3.4 billion to BTP i. e. a price of CHF 2.7 billion and an additional CHF 700 million for liabilities.[189]

The purchase price was generally criticized but the acquisition itself was quite favourably received. Analysts and economic journalists[190] even assumed that due to the acquisition Clariant could soar to first place in the ranking list of suppliers to the pharmaceutical and agrochemical industries, in front of the Dutch DSM Group and the Lonza Group. In the fine chemicals sector Clariant expected the comparatively highest profit margin and started out from a considerable potential for expansion. As 40 percent of BTP's turnover was accounted for by the USA, Clariant thought that the takeover would afford it an opportunity to expand its position on this major market. Both portfolios complemented each other well, which simply meant that there were few overlaps. In the leather chemicals sector, the existing range of products was comple-

---

188   Herbert Link, 13 Apr. 2010.
189   Philipp Hammel, 8 Sept. 2010.
190   Daniel M. Hofmann: "Clariant positioniert für Margenverbesserung," in Neue *Zürcher Zeitung*, 22 Mar. 2000, no. 69.

mented by BTP's wet end chemicals. Clariant wanted to tap an attractive growth market with the newly-added products from the life sciences sector—the resulting additional turnover potential was put at more than CHF 500 million.

The BTP tombstone shows the familiar Clariant logo and the BTP trademark—the traditional tar distillation boiler from Manchester—, the fatal date on which the deal was concluded and the logo of Wasserstein Perella & Co., the company which supervised the deal for Clariant in an advisory capacity. The acrylic block of

Steve Hannam, former CEO at BTP

the tombstone appears to encase the three-dimensional molecular display of a chemical formula.[191] It is that of 5-Fluorouracil, which is manufactured on an industrial scale by Archimica, a BTP subsidiary in Puerto Rico. The material forms the base for cytostatic drugs which have a retarding effect on the growth and separation of cells and are therefore used in the treatment of cancer. At the time the deal was concluded, the substance was no longer in the pipeline but was sold commercially and distributed by Archimica. That means that with the change of ownership Clariant gained access as a supplier to the main pharmaceuticals industry. It is not known any more who originally had the idea of using 5-Fluorouracil as the symbol of the deal but the programmatic motive speaks volumes: Life science. And, of course, that was to be the name of a new division at Clariant!

The acquisition of BTP meant that there was an enlargement of the Board of Management in the person of Steve Hannam from Great Britain. After graduating from Manchester University with a degree in chemistry, Hannam began his career at Warwick International Ltd, a manufacturer of detergent components in Yorkshire and there he was appointed Director and General Manager in 1979. In 1987 he moved to BTP in Manchester as Head of the Chemicals Division and rose to the position of CEO of the entire group in 1994. In the period following he distinguished himself by being very active in the field

191 The definition of the formula was supplied by Ralph Rutte on 7 Jun. 2010 in congenial cooperation with chemicals colleagues Angelica Marson, Reida Noëmi Rutte, Hans Bohnen, Hans Dümpelmann and Detlef Wehle.

of global acquisition. This created strangely critical reactions but also amazing appreciation in the industry, as a report in *The Independent* shows: "BTP, which makes ingredients for Viagra, is transforming itself from an unfocused chemicals group to a lean specialty chemicals machine. In the past two years it has forged 20 separate deals." [192]

At the time when Rolf W. Schweizer invited his group managers and their wives to Rigi in summer 1998, Hannam already had Hexachimie in France in his portfolio and a share in Chemstar in India, and he was in the process of acquiring Archimica in Italy.[193] In retrospect these activities were called 'building a collection' at Clariant.

A direct shot to the heart

In the intoxication felt at the newly forged deal, the coup of the year 2000 was described as a 'direct shot to the heart,'[194] which in hunting language means an unqualitied success. The reality and the events which followed show a completely different picture, because the bullet was to ricochet and in the end hit the gunman himself.

In his written interview, Hannam reports that the sale of BTP had made him financially secure for the rest of his life. At the same time he was on Clariant's payroll, but he resigned in May 2000, two months after his appointment. However, Rolf W. Schweizer persuaded him to remain with the company for another year. As a result of this intervention, Hannam was put in charge of the Fine Chemicals Division, which was then renamed *Life Science & Electronic Chemicals*. In this way Hannam became acquainted with the everyday business at Clariant, learned how the company worked, familiarized himself with the sites in Germany and elsewhere and was involved in the integration of the new company. His observations confirm those criticisms no one dared to put into words under the presidency of Rolf W. Schweizer.

The Board of Management was dominated by managers from Hoechst and Clariant was still a long way from integrating the German business, despite what was stated officially.[195] The ex-Hoechst men acted in the manner to which they had been accustomed at Hoechst AG, and now Hoechst, which had still not

---

192 "The Investment Column: BTP," in *The Independent*, 9 Jun. 1999.
193 Alex Scott: "BTP Buys Italy's Archimica," in *Chemical Week*, 15 Jul. 1998.
194 Hofmann 2000.
195 Clariant *Annual Report* 1998, p. 7 and 1999, p. 39.

been integrated, and the new company of Clariant, which still had not fused, were joined by BTP. Hannam found less synergy than expected and experienced three different culture although in his eyes the former Sandoz employees and those of BTP appeared to have more in common. The Hoechst men stood apart and kept themselves aloof—the situation was difficult at the time.

Hannam was rather astonished at "how little of the Sandoz service ethic remained".[196] Moreover, there was an extremely complex matrix structure with constant quarrels between the divisions and the countries. Hannam reports that it was not easy and was very time-consuming for the management to integrate the BIP structure, which had strongly entrepreneurial characteristics. Upon examining the Clariant portfolio more closely he was surprised to find that there did not seem to be much of a fine chemicals business. He was highly critical. As far as he could see, the business consisted of intermediates which were manufactured in large loss-making sites. Even worse, the former Hoechst men at Clariant hadn't much of a clue about fine chemicals and cooperation with the customers was largely lacking in concept.

These observations correspond to the status quo: Hoechst had brought the problem of the intermediates with them to Clariant, and Reinhard Handte knew all about the causes, namely that Hoechst had invested far too little in this sector for decades. A good example was Griesheim. Handte, too, had hoped to cut this Gordian knot by means of a huge acquisition and like no other in the company had supported Rolf W. Schweizer in the purchase of BTP. But the desired result failed to materialise because a proper concept, strategical leadership, organised sites and disciplined staff were all missing.

Like every business, that of fine chemicals has its pitfalls. It is highly likely that the dangers—the probable drop in demand, the performance curve of the various products, the behaviour of the purchasers and the pricing pressure from the life science groups—were well known in the sector. It was also no secret that BTP had lost an outsourcing order just before the deal with Clariant due to the fact that the potential purchaser began to manufacture the product himself because his own capacities were not being utilized.[197] An order from a pharmaceuticals manufacturer had also dissolved into thin air after the substance in question did not meet the customer's expectations in the last phase of development.

In reality, the problem was that after the acquisition of BTP the pharmaceuticals industry had come to a standstill—a phenomenon which hit the en-

---

196 'Service ethic': Steve Hannam means what is understood by 'the spirit of entrepreneurship'. See the chapter on "Company Culture".

197 Andreas Meier: "Britische BTP wäre ein guter Fang für Clariant," in *Finanz und Wirtschaft*, 22 Jan. 2000, no. 6.

tire fine chemicals sector. A number of products had failed just after being launched on the market and the approval procedures on the part of the Food and Drug Administration in the United States were exceedingly slow. Contrary to all beliefs, pharmaceuticals and agrochemicals did not flourish as was hoped for. What was more, the competition, which needed to be taken seriously, was gaining a foothold in Asia, in India and China in particular.

Then again, major projects, especially at Clariant, were delayed or cancelled by customers. Moreover, Hannam believed he had noticed a change in the relationship to existing customers since BTP had become part of a larger group of companies. All this happened at a time when the Clariant management had to invest a considerable amount of time on internal quarrels and integration, which in turn led to a decrease in efficiency. There was a downward trend in business and Clariant was especially susceptible because it had paid a very high price for BTP and financed the deal with borrowed funds. "Clariant had paid a very high price," Hannam stresses categorically. Incidentally, the project to acquire BTP was called *Joy & Fun*.

Sponsoring

In many respects the millennium was a special time. That year Rolf W. Schweizer celebrated his 70th birthday. In addition to the CHF 3.4 billion acquisition, Clariant, which was known for its great thriftiness, spent money on sponsoring several projects including an exhibition at the Fondation Beyeler in Riehen, three mountain farming families and Kisoro, the silverback gorilla in Zolli Zoo in Basel. It is unclear what reasons the President had for this spate of donations in his last year of office. Schweizer was not the type to blow his own trumpet or try to enhance his image with generous gestures. It is only possible to speculate on his motives.[198]

Felix Erbacher[199] ascertains that Clariant took practically no part in the cultural life of Basel; it was as if there were no such things as culture or sport.[200]

---

198 Lilly Sulzbacher: "Unterstützung für drei Bergbauernfamilien," in *Presseinformation* Winterhilfe, 31 Jul. 2000; (cf.) "Clariant wird Götti," in *Palette* 1/2000, p. 11; Katalin Vereb: "Welttiertag. Ein Tier als Göttikind," in *Coopzeitung*, 3 Oct. 2006, no. 40, pp. 8–9, 11, 13.
199 Felix Erbacher, 26 Feb. 2010.
200 Clariant did occasionally make funds available for sponsoring. Some people remember seats reserved for customers at tennis tournaments in Basel or donations to the mountain village aid which was probably initiated by Markus Kündig, a politician interested in social affairs and Deputy President of the Board of Directors. Now and again Reinhard Handte supported

Every year, for example, Ciba sponsored young artists in a concert in the casino. Roche lives in and fosters a family culture which is passed from generation to generation. Novartis built a campus and is firmly rooted in Basel. And in Muttenz a new company developed, which was always on the outside. There was never any contact between the people of Basel and Clariant; they lived completely separate lives. "It was as if there was a huge hedge between them," says Felix Erbacher, just like a frontier.

If you didn't happen to be a shareholder of the company, there was absolute disinterest on both sides. This, too, was mostly due to Rolf W. Schweizer's character for he rarely appeared in public. He may well have been sociable in private but otherwise gregariousness was not second nature to him. According to Erbacher, the 'Daig', the upper echelon of Basel society, never accepted him. For example, the *Basler Zeitung* has, for years, had a gossip column called *tout Bâle*. Schweizer was never mentioned once. Most journalists could not relate to him. Astonishingly it was only Felix Erbacher who had a good rapport with Schweizer and yet it this very Erbacher who, in interviews, frequently stamps Rolf W. Schweizer as a technocrat.

The Chairman's reserve towards the public suddenly disappeared in his last year of office. At Clariant it is not known precisely where Rolf W. Schweizer and Ernst Beyeler, the gallery owner and founder of the art museum Fondation Beyeler in Riehen, met and what the reason was for the unprecedented sponsoring.[201] One thing is certain: neither of the two men belonged to the 'Daig'; i. e. they were not members of the long-established Basel families with their long-standing traditions but were to a certain extent newcomers. Their success was based on individual achievement.

Head of Communications Walter Vaterlaus, who was in charge of the sponsoring, makes an attempt at giving a plausible summary of the events as he remembers them. He believes that the two men may have known each other from Sandoz times and the creator of the foundation took the opportunity to ask if Clariant might be prepared to sponsor an exhibition. The theme *Colour > Light* was well suited to a manufacturer of textile dyes and pigments[202] and thus may well have provided the opportunity to make good on the promise.

The President's family and Vaterlaus relate that it was actually Schweizer who is supposed to have given Beyeler the idea of the colours exhibition. There is an old video entitled *Colours* made by the French cineaste François

the Football Club Basel with small donations.
201 Report by Ulf Küster, Fondation Beyeler Riehen, on the sponsoring and on the exhibition he staged.
202 Textile dyes were mainly manufactured in Muttenz at that time.

Ernst Beyeler and Rolf W. Schweizer outside the Fondation
Beyeler in Riehen, 2000

Reichenbach, who was involved in making the documentary film, the *History of Switzerland,* on the occasion of the 700th anniversary celebrations of the Swiss Confederation in 1991. The rather worn video cassette bears a Sandoz inventory number and contains the same film three times in a row. It lasts a total of 75 minutes and features impressions of colours which are enhanced by literary and biblical quotations and classical music. From a present-day perspective, the film seems more like a commercial or a visual background at an exhibition stand. It is hard to imagine that this video could have inspired one of the greatest gallery owners of our time to mount the *Colour > Light* exhibition.

Originally Beyeler intended to acquire a *Fauve* exhibition from Paris which had already been assembled.[203] The exponents of *Fauve*—which means something like 'wild beasts'—attributed an autonomous character to colour and chose it as an individual characteristic; their works stem from the period between 1900 and 1910. For a number of reasons it was not possible to obtain the exhibition from Paris and as it was 'a hard nut he had to crack' Beyeler tried to solve it 'via the back door.' He mounted an analogue show in double-quick time by rounding up a number of suitable works himself and developing the theme right up to the present day. The gallery owner united works of classical modern art by William Turner or Claude Monet for example with objects by Joseph Beuys or with light installations especially created by Michel Verjux

---

203 Beyeler: "Basel wird eine Stadt des Lichts sein," in *Basler Zeitung,* 17 Apr. 2000.

Factory Buildings 938 and 939 in Muttenz

for the exhibition, which was why the exhibition in Riehen was given the title *Colour > Light*.

Vaterlaus wondered how the topic could be presented within the company to create acceptance among the employees. He wished to avoid the tricky situation where there could be accusations that Clariant was spending money on something which, in many eyes, was considered to be an elite occasion. As an incentive to approach the exposition with an open mind, employees were given two tickets free of charge, a free catalogue, a lunch voucher worth CHF 40 for the Berower Park Restaurant in the museum and an order form for two further tickets—which was really overdoing things. There was even an appeal by the President in the company magazine *Palette*,[204] in which the favourable terms for a museum visit were announced.

Everyone was surprised at such a generous gesture and said: "I don't believe it! It's impossible!" Nevertheless, they all flocked to Riehen to the museum, and the exhibition, which was staged from 16th April to 30 July 2000, was a phenomenal success. This co-operation with Ernst Beyeler made a substantial contribution to improving Rolf W. Schweizer's image (he celebrated his 70th birthday on 6 August 2000).

Clariant was mentioned in the catalogue[205] in three languages but only in one sentence. That may appear somewhat meagre but was well in keeping with

---

204 *Palette*, no. 3/2000, p. 16.
205 Fondation Beyeler (Ed.): *Ausstellungskatalog Farbe › Licht*, Riehen, 16 Apr. – 30 Jul. 2000, Ostfildern-Ruit, 2000, pp. 7, 137, 149.

Schweizer's style, who wanted to do good but did not necessarily want to talk about it. As far as the size of the donation is concerned, there are a number of rumours but Beat Privat, the accountant in charge of the Fondation Beyeler at the time, confirms that it amounted to CHF 700,000.[206]

Was it possible that at 70 Schweizer had acquired a certain mellowing which sometimes comes with old age and which prompted him to do something good quite independent of the business? Or did the emotions aroused by the turn of the century move him to do something special? Was sponsoring to be a farewell present because the President originally intended to step down? In actual fact, his retirement was delayed because no provision had been made for a successor.

Age limit

It is only natural and very human that one would like to remain as long as possible. Letting go is difficult and that applies both to one's private and professional life. Understandably, every entrepreneur keeps a firm hold of the reins as long as he or she can. However, there can be no objections to pursuing a rational development of potential senior executives parallel to that. Arranging for a successor poses one of the greatest challenges in business and is a delicate matter into the bargain. However, it frequently happens that it is suppressed and put on the back burner because everyday business appears to be much more urgent. Yet, if there is no forward-looking planning, many things come unstuck and this circumstance can cause untold harm.

Certainly, no one is accustomed to placing his or her own company in someone else's hands—normally such a thing only happens once in a lifetime—and it is also very difficult to find the right candidate, for one always applies oneself as the yardstick.

In the case of Clariant the following considerations may have been of importance when someone from outside the company was appointed in 2000: Schweizer was very well known in *Vorort*, the Swiss Association of Industry and Commerce. Moreover, he was Chairman of the Swiss Society of the Chemicals Industry (SGCI). Was there no one in the industry or among the 'Big Linkers' with whom he had been associated for decades whom he regarded as worthy and who would have been prepared to assume a mandate at

---

206 Report by Beat Privat, Basel.

Clariant? How stringent were the requirements he imposed during his search for a suitable successor? Just how choosy was he? How much interest was there withinin Clariant? Were Schweizer's footsteps too big for any successor? Or was the company in dire straits even then? Had Schweizer started to look in time or had he missed the right moment to attend to arrangements for a successor and to take care of the future of the company?

"You'll get my job"

It was an unwritten rule both at Sandoz and at Hoechst that longstanding service in the company automatically led to promotion and especially gradual promotion towards the top of the hierarchy. But Schweizer seemed to have turned his back on this procedure—which he himself had gone through—and ignored his top managers when he considered looking for a suitable successor out on the market. Roland Lösser reports that Schweizer hoped to be able to solve this problem through an acquisition. "If I promise 'you'll get my job,' I'll have solved the problem of who will succeed me and at the same time I will have created an added incentive to agree to the deal."[207]

Born in 1930, Rolf W. Schweizer regarded his advanced age as a great advantage. His thinking was that the prospect of acquiring the post of CEO and of President of the Board of Directors at Clariant ought to be an additional incentive for the negotiating partner in a potential merger or a planned acquisition to agree to the deal. Consequently, according to this logic, Karl-Gerhard Seifert from Hoechst became CEO at Clariant from mid-1997 and he really could have been Rolf W. Schweizer's successor if there had been no further acquisitions. If the merger with Ciba had succeeded, Rolf A. Meyer was definitely to have become CEO in 1998 and President of Clariant at the end of the fiscal year 2000. Schweizer's plan, therefore—the enticement of 'You'll get my job'—would have panned out absolutely and been entirely practicable.

As the case of Seifert had taken care of itself as a result of the merger talks with Ciba and the fact that due to the failed merger there could be no successor in the person of Rolf A. Meyer, the question arose whether Steve Hannam, who had also appeared on the scene through an acquisition, might be a potential successor.

207 Roland Lösser, 2 Jan. 2010.

It is very unusual that at Schweizer's request Hannam, who had hitherto held office as CEO of BTP in Britain, withdrew his resignation from Clariant, allowed himself to be persuaded to remain in the company and even assumed a lower position, i. e. of a divisional manager. Why did Schweizer not let Hannam, who was 20 years younger, go? Did the two of them have an understanding? How important was the role which Hannam occupied in Rolf W. Schweizer's theoretical strategy?

To all appearances the formula of 'you'll get my job' just refused to work. Another, far more practicable solution would have been to choose the successor from his own team. In 2000 Clariant had 31,546 employees worldwide[208] so justifiably the question arises as to just how professionally the order of succession was planned by the company in the first place. Was there no capable group of talented managers in the two long-standing predecessors Sandoz and Hoechst which came to constitute Clariant in 1995 and 1997 respectively? Did Clariant have no pool of up-and-coming talented young people in its own ranks who were being groomed and nurtured?

It is well known that after the oil crisis Sandoz's Chemicals Division had never generated the revenue aimed at by the group. As a consequence, there had been continuous efforts since 1973 to cut costs, including among other things several recruitment freezes. This resulted in an age gap in the cadres—the term used in Switzerland to describe the members of the management—that in turn had led to a high percentage of older staff in the cadre hierarchy.[209] Schweizer's comrades have often mentioned his comments that the qualifications of his staff did not meet his expectations. However, when new opportunities presented themselves to the former Sandoz Chemicals Division through the brilliant action of 'going public' in 1995, Clariant would certainly have had the chance to fill the age gap by means of corresponding investments in human resources, training personnel and acquiring good people.

Rather slow-moving

Pierre Borgeaud,[210] a member of the Presidium in Muttenz and former President of Sulzer AG in Winterthur, gives reasons why Clariant was unable to produce an heir to the throne in 2000: On the one hand, the plans for a suc-

208   Clariant *Annual report 2000*, p. 56.
209   Hanspeter Knöpfel, 22 Nov. 2010.
210   Pierre Borgeaud, 28 Jul. 2010.

cessor and promotion programmes could not take effect in such a short period after the foundation of the new company in 1995 because these had to be re-implemented and that took time. On the other hand, it was unfortunately not possible to keep the good people who, from the point of view of the Presidium, might have been suitable as they would not have had the patience to wait.

Could it be that their impatience had something to do with the financial conditions? Was it perhaps fuelled by the pecuniary conditions which determined the salaries? Pierre Borgeaud admits that at that time remuneration in Basel was not exactly over the top; there were no unusually high payments and possibly it was here that an incentive might have been created. "We did discuss it, but then it would have had to apply to everyone and not just a few, otherwise, as I see it, it wouldn't have been fair. So, planning a successor at Clariant was rather slow-moving," Borgeaud says and nods.

Irrespective of how the promotion of young staff may or may not have been carried out at Clariant, there was a considerable scramble for the job of successor within the company. At least two mature Sandoz men and at least two younger Hoechst men aspired to the post and were secretly tipped among the colleagues as potential candidates.

These questions are likely to have been the main preoccupation of Clariant when three different events happened at the end of 2000, which from a present-day perspective vaguely anticipated a future radical upheaval and to a certain extent are to be understood as harbingers of the changes which followed. Clariant received an application, a resignation and an acquisition enquiry. The applicant was Hariolf Kottmann, the resignation was handed in by Roland Lösser, and Karl-Gerhard Seifert was vying for a sale.

Invitation to Muttenz

Having decided in autumn 2000 to leave Celanese in Dallas, Texas, where he had been employed for some years, and to return to Europe, Hariolf Kottmann[211] got in touch with a number of companies: He approached Utz-Hellmuth Felcht at Degussa, Robert Köhler at SGL Carbon, as well as Wacker, the Dow Chemical Company and BASF. In this context and at the invitation of Reinhard Handte, who had learned that Kottmann was looking for a new

---

211   Interview with Hariolf Kottmann in Wiesbaden on 1 Sept. 2010.

position, he also travelled to Muttenz on two occasions to have talks with Clariant.

Handte and Kottmann, both former employees at Hoechst, had known each other since 1992/1993. At that time the younger of the two was in the ZDA and Handte had taken over the management of Business Division D. Their relationship was that of friendly colleagues. After the accident in Griesheim in 1993, they had worked together in the crisis management group for months.

When the two Hoechst men met in Muttenz in November/December 2000, the venerable Hoechst AG no longer existed and the constellation was a different one: COO Handte hoped or knew that in a few months he would be appointed to a higher position at the Annual General Meeting on 16th May. On behalf of his president, he offered Kottmann membership on Clariant's Board of Management. There were two possibilities: either the position as the Head of the Pigments Division, since Victor Sanahuja the longstanding manager was due to retire shortly or as Manager of the Functional Chemicals Division, which later became Industrial & Consumer Specialties. At that time Reinhard Meyer, nicknamed Sack-Meyer, was Head of FUN and also about to retire.

The initial talk went well for both parties and after exchanging views they agreed on a further meeting. When Kottmann visited Handte in Muttenz for the second time, financial conditions were also discussed. Afterwards, the applicant had an interview with Rolf W. Schweizer in that very room in Building 907 which was later to be his office in the period between 2008 and 2010. In the course of their discussion Schweizer indicated to Kottmann that they had other plans for him than just the post on the Board of Management and the head of a division because both Handte and he were convinced that Kottmann also had the qualities to run a company. It is likely that Handte as CEO in spe wanted to appoint Kottmann as his successor in 2001 because he himself hoped for the post of Chairman of the Board of Directors. How Schweizer planned to place the figures on his chess board, on the other hand, is not known.

Kottmann would have simply loved to join Clariant for he knew the business inside out. Both divisions in question came from Hoechst which was after all where he had once worked as Head of Production and Technology in the Fine Chemicals Unit. The positive arguments on Kottmann's list of pros and cons were twofold:—it was not only the professional challenge which attracted him but there was an important private reason, too: his son was to attend a boarding school at Lake Constance to take his 'A' levels there. However, what Clariant was offering as a basic salary and bonuses to someone with a doctorate in chemistry and with experience abroad was simply not competitive when compared with the rest of the market and therefore a definite counter-argu-

Reinhard Handte and the Board of Management, 2001: Nico Gontha, Peter Brandenberg, Joachim Mahler, François Note, François Dennefeld, Reinhard Handte, Hartmut Wiezer, Reinhart S. Meyer, François Darrort, Günther Hencken (l–r)

ment. He would have earned considerably less than he had earned at Celanese in the USA and probably substantially less than a member of the managing board of a MDAX-company in Germany. The remunerations were simply not comparable; 'rather slow moving' in fact, as Pierre Borgeaud, the Big Linker and member of the Presidium at Clariant, also confirmed.

A further reason for Kottmann's scepticism was his realization that the scope for organization and management on the Board of Management of a very traditionally-run Swiss company was considerably more restricted than on the board of a German stock corporation. Furthermore, Kottmann could not get rid of the odd feeling that at that time—in 2000—Clariant had developed less towards the future but rather had lost its track and stagnated on the sidelines.

The Chairman and his COO were very pleased with the candidate— Schweizer is said to have even found him 'very suitable'—and were very keen to woo him over to Clariant.[212]

Retirement at 60

Roland Lösser[213] considered his special field to be finance and administration and felt quite comfortable there. He believes that it was never one of his

212   Reinhard Handte, 21 Jan. 2010.
213   Roland Lösser, 2 Jan. 2010.

aims in life to climb the highest rungs of the career ladder. He felt it was more important to get things done. Earlier he would never have thought of becoming the Head of Finance in such a large company listed on the stock market. The idea of carving out a career for himself at the age of 60 was alien to him because, unlike many others, he was of the opinion that it was better for managers to stop at 60 and to forego taking on new challenges or desiring to set up a monument to themselves.

Lösser's resignation, which was due to his reservations about the purchase of BTP in Britain and the deterioration in his working relationship with Rolf W. Schweizer, was announced in December 2000 but he stayed on until the Annual General Meeting because he considered this to be his responsibility— "that is my year-end." Lösser was the first ever since the IPO to resign voluntarily from the Board of Management.

Cassella

Schweizer had deeply hurt his CEO Seifert when he attempted to merge with Ciba and later failed to clear the air by having a talk with him. When Seifert stepped down officially at the Annual General Meeting in April 1999, it was said that he went quite happily because his task, the integration of Hoechst, had been completed. This account must, however, be refuted, for the integration of two global groups cannot be accomplished in a mere 21 months. An acquisition of this size needs a much longer integration process.[214] The success or failure of a merger can only be ascertained after several years at the earliest.

No matter what reasons Seifert and Clariant gave for his departure, it does not alter the fact that afterwards Seifert took the opportunity to return to Muttenz on a number of occasions or at least to remain in the vicinity of where the action was.

Having read in the newspaper in November 2000 that Clariant intended to sell off part of the plant in Gersthofen, Seifert[215] drove to Muttenz to see Rolf W. Schweizer and made him an offer—the acquisition of the entire site in Gersthofen with its then approx. 800—today about 1,000—employees. The Presi-

---

214 Jürgen Dormann: "Akquisition und Desinvestition als Mittel der Strukturanpassung bei Hoechst," in the special edition of *Zeitschrift für Betriebswirtschaft* (Sonderheft: Globalisierung und Wettbewerb), 2/1992, pp. 51–68.

215 Karl-Gerhard Seifert, 3 Feb. 2010/20 May 2010; see Thorsten Winter: "Wir standen vor zwei Jahren vor dem Abgrund," in *Frankfurter Allgemeine Zeitung*, 28 Jun. 2011.

dent of Clariant was not averse to the idea but the plan met with considerable opposition from Reinhard Handte, the then COO. As a young chemist Handte had first started work at Hoechst in Gersthofen, where he still possessed the house he had bought there. Moreover, he was friendly with the mayor. Parting with this plant was out of the question as far as he was concerned.

But Seifert did not abandon the revival of his contact to Clariant and the dream of his own chemicals plant so quickly and made a different proposition to his friend Rolf: "If Gersthofen won't work, why not sell me a plant in the Rhine-Main region? You've already got Wiesbaden, Höchst, Griesheim, Offenbach and Fechenheim. That's five plants in the Rhine-Main region and now with the acquisition of BTP you've got hundreds of other plants all over the world."

Schweizer was prepared to negotiate. Among the companies in question was Cassella[216] in Fechenheim where simple late-stage intermediates for the further refining of Clariant products were manufactured. Such a location, where the same old but essential products had been made for 30 to 40 years, was considered to be ballast for a company that wanted to move forwards. The arrangement between Schweizer and Seifert was to lead to the foundation of Allessa,[217] to whom Clariant would have to pay considerable subsidies in the future.

All in all, things happened in late 2000 which were to be repeated in the period which followed. According to Walter Vaterlaus, an external candidate, who was considered to be eminently suitable and who was to be appointed, backed down at the last moment and soon there was to be another deserter. A senior manager handed in his resignation and a short time later dozens turned their backs on the company. A disinvestment, whereby benefits were granted to the purchaser, was approved, which in turn heralded the start of an era of costly sales. Within the group the age of compromise and mayhem had dawned.

Schweizer succeeds Schweizer

Traditionally, the Chairman of the Managing Board at Hoechst retired at 65 and was automatically appointed Chairman of the Supervisory Board. This

216 Claudia Hume: "Clariant Sells Intermediates Unit to Former CEO," in *Chemical Week*, 28 Mar. 2001; Andreas Meier: "Clariant speckt ab. Werk Cassella ausgegliedert," in *Finanz und Wirtschaft*, 11 Jul. 2001, no. 54, p. 20.
217 Jürgen Salz: "Glut bewahren," in *Wirtschaftswoche*, 5 Jul. 2001.

also applied to Karl Winnacker and Rolf Sammet, but not to Wolfgang Hilger, whose retirement had been prompted to a significant extent by the events in Griesheim in 1993. Jürgen Dormann, who had grown up in this tradition, broke with it and rewrote the rules.

In Switzerland, retirement age for the Chairman of a Board of Directors is 70, but it is well know that the exception proves the rule. Maurice Jacottet was 72 when he stepped down from his post at Sandoz, his successor Yves Dunant took over the post of Chairman Emeritus at the age of 73 and Marc Moret was likewise an exception. He remained in office until he could eventually 'light his biggest firework' i. e. when he merged Sandoz with Ciba to create Novartis; at that time he was approaching 73 years of age.

In the case of Clariant the fireworks failed to materialize with the sensational acquisition of BTP and after Rolf W. Schweizer had celebrated his 70th birthday in August 2000, industry and his family waited for him to step down from his post. His elder son Juerg[218] relates that his father had had every intention of spending more time with friends and family at long last and of devoting time to yachting with the family. There were plans to purchase a mooring on the Mediterranean and a boat to go with it and to spend a whole year yachting.

The first official statement[219] about Schweizer's successor was made just before Christmas Eve 2000 when the identity of the future CEO was revealed: in future the office was to be shared. "Handte for Schweizer, that was no surprise," said Philippe Rohner, an analyst at Pictet & Cie. in Geneva.[220] This decision in favour of Handte was not unexpected because only a few days after the takeover of BTP had been concluded in March 2000, the *Aargauer Zeitung*[221] had already begun to speculate about who could succeed President and Chief Executive Officer Rolf W. Schweizer, who would be retiring on grounds of age in early 2001. The paper encouraged its readers to 'hand(te)-tight,' firm conjectures thus suggesting that the successor in Muttenz might well be Handte. The periodical *Finanz und Wirtschaft*[222] considered both Handte and Roland Lösser as potential successors.

Handte fitted the bill but the *division* of the existing double function of CEO and Chairman of the Board of Directors was unexpected. In truth, the fact that Handte was *only* appointed CEO raises several questions but at the

218　Telephone conversation with Juerg Schweizer on 2 Mar. 2011.
219　*Handelsblatt*, 20 Dec.2000, No. 246, p. 28; *Finanz und Wirtschaft*, 20 Dec. 2000, No. 101, p. 24.
220　Jan Kirchhofer: "Clariant: 'Keine Doppelfunktion mehr'" in *Basler Zeitung*, 20 Dec. 2000, p. 18.
221　*Aargauer Zeitung*, 22 Mar. 2000.
222　Andreas Meier: "Schwierige Nachfolgeregelung," in *Finanz und Wirtschaft*, 22 Mar. 2000.

same time gives some answers, too. We are talking about management style, timing and esteem.

It is very likely that the management constellation which had proved so successful at Clariant over the years ended for a number of reasons. It would appear that the office was divided up because in Schweizer's eyes the in-house candidate was not the right person for a double mandate. Schweizer had other notions about the person to take over the presidium. The decision to split up the double function which he had held until then into a president of the Board of Directors and a head of the Board of Management i. e. CEO was announced as a resolution by the Board of Directors just before Christmas 2000, when Schweizer's resignation was disclosed.

It was with this in mind that Walter Vaterlaus approached his boss in spring 2001: "We have been fighting side by side for the best part of six years. It is time for you to stop. Then I, too, would like to do something else,"[223] he said because he thought the time had come for him to look around for a new assignment. Since the acquisition of BTP, Vaterlaus had had the impression that he had had to gloss over things in his communications now and again which made him feel increasingly uneasy in his decidedly responsible job.

Indeed the following sentence in a press release[224] in early 2000 sounds decidedly euphemistic and grotesque—especially from today's perspective when it is known that almost all the sites which were acquired with BTP have meanwhile been shed with difficulty: "The expanded business has at its command an infrastructure with state-of-the-art manufacturing facilities in four continents." Note that the emphasis is on 'state of the art'.

An additional argument why Vaterlaus wanted to retire from office is that Rolf W. Schweizer was actually supposed to step down because he had reached retirement age. With an offer from an investment company coming at an opportune moment, the Head of Communications put his intention into practice and handed in his resignation at Clariant. He proposed Philipp Hammel, who up to that time was in charge of Investor Relations, to succeed him.

A few weeks after handing in his resignation, the Chief Communications Officer was approached by Schweizer, who asked if he could not withdraw his resignation because he himself was going to stay another year. He added that as they had always worked well together, it would be nice if they could also spend the last year together. But as far as Walter Vaterlaus was concerned, it was out of the question. Schweizer stated that the reason for the extension

---

223 Walter Vaterlaus, 25 May 2010.
224 Clariant *Press Release,* 21 Mar. 2000.

of his term of office was that the candidate he had designated as President of the Board of Directors had backed out at the last minute and that he had no alternative such a short time before the next Annual General Meeting but to extend his mandate beyond the statutory age limit of 70.

Walter Vaterlaus has never discovered who the person was that Schweizer originally intended to propose as his successor. He was left with the odd feeling that the refusal did not come amiss because it gave Schweizer an opportunity to possibly compensate the unsuccessful BTP deal with more successful transactions and to bow out as the winner after all. But fortune clearly turned its back on Rolf W. Schweizer with the result that there could be no more talk of profitable activities.

The time was ripe for him to go but although there had been notification in the Annual Report 2000 that Rolf W. Schweizer was to resign on the day of the Annual General Meeting on 16 May 2001, Markus Kündig,[225] the Vice President of the Board of Directors, suggested to the shareholders at the meeting— a point which was not on the agenda- that Schweizer, the former President, should be re-elected for another year. Thus Schweizer succeeded Schweizer as President of the Board of Directors. Kündig backed up his proposal by saying that it was sensible for Schweizer to follow current projects through.[226]

Whether the decision at the Annual General Meeting 2000 to extend Schweizer's period of office was indeed unanimous is debatable. Many managerial staff, who felt they had been passed over in the BTP deal and found themselves confronted with the disastrous aftermath, did not agree with the acclaim, actually feared legal steps and hoped very much that Clariant could, if the worst came to the worst, sit out the possible consequences according to the principle: Where there is no plaintiff there is no judge.

Pierre Borgeaud justifies Rolf W. Schweizer's extended period of office as follows: "Well, it was also a period when there were still some things pending, in the sense that we were no longer on the some marvellous course as in the initial years. And I believed that in this situation we could not afford to do without the experience and knowledge of someone like Mr Schweizer."[227]

In reply to the question whether there had ever actually been a successor who had backed out, which was the explanation Schweizer had given to Va-

225 Article "Markus Kündig," in *Historisches Lexikon der Schweiz*; Roland, Heinz: "Ein Tausch-handel," in Clariant *Clartext*, 1 Jul. 2007.

226 *Neue Zürcher Zeitung*, 17 May 2001; *Finanz und Wirtschaft*, 19 May 2001, p. 24; Felix Erbacher: "Auf Schweizer folgt Schweizer," in *Basler Zeitung*, 17 May 2001, p. 19; Bolke Behrens: "Absturz vom Himmel," in *Wirtschaftswoche*, 24 May 2001; Heiner Hiltermann: "Aus der Traum: Scheitern gehört zum Geschäft. Do it again Sam," in *Basler Zeitung*, 28 Dec. 2001.

227 Pierre Borgeaud, 28 Jul. 2010.

terlaus, Zug-born Markus Kündig, Clariant's long-time Vice-President of the Board of Directors, owner of a printing works, former CVP (Christian Democratic) member of the Council of States and media baron, answers as follows: "I can safely say that we did think about a successor but it simply was not possible to find or to appoint a person who could have stepped into the breach at that time. After all, it had to be someone who could have held a candle to Mr Schweizer. I cannot recall names, nor can I remember discussing potential successors who had backed out. I mean, I don't know, I really don't. The only thing I can say is this: we tried to win over the 2000 Annual General Meeting—which took place in May 2001—and get an extension for a year so that there would be another 12 months in which to settle the issue of a successor. The task of the future president was certainly not going to be an easy one. Clariant was a young company, which required stability in its structures and we firmly believed that it would be best if Mr Schweizer still had a year to get this organization on its feet and that is why it was definitely made clear: one year, but no longer than that."[228]

During Schweizer's extended period of office, there was the transaction with Seifert concerning Cassella, the retreat of a US partner and a last attempt at a merger, which went pear-shaped.

Clariant was prepared to sell Cassella to Seifert, who had been Chairman of the Supervisory Board there at one time, but attached three conditions to the sale: The site in Offenbach was to be acquired, too, Seifert was to be Managing Director for two to three years and both Dirk Thomas, Head of the Specialty Intermediates Business Unit and Frank Schmidt, Head of the Pigments Technology Business Unit, were to be incorporated into the new company.

And so AllessaChemie—the name is an ananym of Cassella, i. e. it is written back to front—came into being on 1th July 2001. In the course of the negotiations, agreement was reached on a so-called *take-or-pay* contract. This meant that Clariant undertook to purchase a certain production volume annually, which initially constituted about 80 percent of Allessa's turnover and which was to be reduced gradually over the years. To compensate this reduction later on, Allessa wanted to make use of the good facilities and technology which were available to add new products to their production programme. But the terrorist attack on the World Trade Center and the Pentagon on 11th September 2001 and the ensuing recession meant that in the first few years Clariant was not in a position to purchase the amount stipulated and had to pay subsidies to Allessa instead.

---

228 Report by Markus Kündig on the Annual General Meeting in 2000.

Procter & Gamble

In 2000, Procter and Gamble, a bulk buyer in the USA, placed an order with Clariant for a raw material for detergents. Clariant had a new state-of-the-art plant worth CHF 100 million specially built for the production of this ingredient in Muttenz. The project went by the name of *Pick*.[229] Building 933/934 in Rothausstrasse was ready to be used and staff had been recruited when the customer unexpectedly cancelled the order in July 2001.[230] As they had decided in the end not to add the product to their range, the raw material which Clariant was to supply exclusively was no longer required.

The approx. 40 metre-high building with an area of 58,000 square metres has remained unused to date for it was purpose-built for the manufacture of this one product. Although Clariant did not suffer any financial damage because the customer was bound by contract to assume the investment costs, there was nobody to reimburse Clariant for the money spent on research and personnel resources, let alone the profits it missed out on.

It was also a particularly serious matter that the 57 employees who had been hired to work in the new plant were now no longer required. Although Clariant did its utmost to support the staff concerned with a redundancy package and help them find a job within the company or on the open market, redundancies were unavoidable.[231]

A letter from Rügen

On 15th August 2001 Clariant published a press release on the course of business in the first half of the fiscal year: the group recorded a net loss of CHF 1.3 billion on account of non-recurring effects; ten sites were to be closed and 1,000 jobs were to be shed.

A day later, Karl-Gerhard Seifert, who was on holiday on the island of Rügen at the time, read several press articles and commentaries on the Internet.[232] On the same day he sat down and wrote a letter to Rolf W. Schweizer:

---

229 Clariant *Palette*, 6/2000, pp. 3, 7.
230 "P&G withdraws order for Clariant with the loss of SFR 100 M," in *Chemical Business Newsbase*, 1 Aug. 2001.
231 Felix Erbacher: "Nagelneue Clariant-Fabrik wird nicht gebraucht," in *Basler Zeitung*, 29 Jun. 2001.
232 Daniel Hug: "Nachwehen einer überbezahlten Übernahme," in *Tages-Anzeiger*, 16 Aug. 2001; "Clariant Opfer des Eifers," in *Handelsblatt*, 16. Aug. 2001, no. 157, p. 18; Thorsten Fischer: "Einkaufslast erdrückt Clariant," in *St. Galler Tagblatt*, 16 Aug. 2001.

"I wrote," Seifert relates,[233] 'Dear Rolf … If you like, I would be more than happy to help you reorganise Clariant … I'm planning to take up residence in Frankfurt again in the next few weeks. If Clariant and you wish, I would be prepared to postpone moving house until spring and to work with you at Clariant over the next few months. A company like AllessaChemie can only thrive if Clariant is thriving.'

Seifert received no reply in writing but about a week later Schweizer phoned him on his mobile and left him a voicemail. "Dear Karl, many thanks for your letter but we don't have a problem. We only have a communication problem," Seifert[234] recalls, reflecting on Schweizer's reaction. Schweizer presumably meant that there had merely been an external communication problem and that externally the acquisition of BTP ought to have been put across much better.

Rhodia

Schweizer's voicemail made it clear that as far as he was concerned Seifert's offer and the disinvested Cassella were water under the bridge. At that time he had other things to think about for he had begun merger talks with Rhodia,[235] a French company. Jean-Pierre Tirouflet was both President and CEO of Rhodia and had succeeded Jürgen Dormann as chairman of CEFIC, the European Chemicals Association. The French company of Rhodia was formed in 1998, the result of the amalgamation of the Chemicals, Fibres and Polymers Divisions of Rhône-Poulenc, which continued to hold an interest in the demerged company. After Rhône-Poulenc's remaining business divisions were merged with Hoechst AG to form Aventis at the end of 1999, the holding in Rhodia was transferred to Aventis. Two members of the Aventis board, namely Jean-René Fourtou and Igor Landau, were also on Rhodia's Board of Directors. When Rhodia's economic situation deteriorated at the turn of the millennium, these two together with Tirouflet looked for opportunities to reinvent the company.

Although well aware that the British acquisition was a grossly overpriced mistake, that he had failed to train a successor and that he had to step down before long, Rolf W. Schweizer still held talks at the last minute with the

233 Karl-Gerhard Seifert, 3 Feb. 2010/20 May 2010.
234 Ibid.
235 Jürgen Dormann, 17. Feb. 2010/3 May 2010.

20 years younger Tirouflet in summer/autumn 2001. Initially two meetings took place between Clariant and Rhodia in Strasbourg, at which Schweizer and Tirouflet appeared without advisers. Aventis CEO Jürgen Dormann chaired the talks. The project went by the code-name *Lake*, whereby Clariant and Rhodia assumed the names of rivers which were to unite in the lake through the merger. The management presentations in which the respective Divisional Managers introduced their business divisions took place in Zurich.

However, the two parties were unable to reach an agreement. On the one hand, the project failed due to the fact that Schweizer and Tirouflet found themselves unable to relate at a personal level and there was also little rapport between Clariant's CEO Reinhard Handte and the President, Director General Jean-Pierre Tirouflet. Witnesses report, however, that it was not simply a matter of the huge differences between the Swiss-German and French cultures but in the attempts to find common ground other irreconcilabilities became apparent.

In *Chemical Week,* 5th December 2001, Rhodia confirmed that there had been merger talks with Clariant but added that these had already been discontinued in November: "Clariant took the initiative to stop the talks over disagreement over the scale of restructuring needed as a result of a merger."[236]

On 18th December 2001 the media announced that Clariant's President Rolf W. Schweizer had finally found a successor in the person of a member of the Clariant Board of Directors, Robert Raeber from Nestlé[237]—apparently just in time to end the negotiations with Rhodia.

Referring to the topic of Rhodia, Raeber raises his voice perceptibly: "We, the members of the Board of Directors, managed to put a timely end to these discussions, which were supposed to lead to a potential merger."[238] It was because of his intervention that the negotiations were ultimately stopped. Both the French company of Rhodia and the company in Muttenz, which was encumbered by the acquisition of BTP, found themselves in a similar situation: Rhodia, spun off by the pharmaceuticals and chemicals group Rhône-Poulenc in 1998, went public furnished with only very modest funding. Afterwards, the parent company had withdrawn completely from the newly established business. A merger with Rhodia would have been a threat to Clariant's very

---

236 "Rhodia ends talks with Clariant" in *Chemical Week,* 5 Dec. 2001; see *Finanz und Wirtschaft,* 3 Nov. 2001, issue 86, p. 3; "No Chemistry between Clariant and Rhodia?" in *Swissinfo.ch,* 22 Nov. 2001; Ian Young: "Rhodia's Tirouflet Sticks to his Guns," in *Chemical Week,* 19 Feb. 2003.
237 *Finanz und Wirtschaft,* 19 Nov. 2001, issue 99, p. 16.
238 Interview with Robert Raeber in Frankfurt a. M. on 12 May 2010.

Robert Raeber, President of Clariant from May 2002 to May 2006

existence, weakened as it was by the acquisition of BTP and needing to do its own homework, Raeber elucidates.

How Robert Raeber came to be at Clariant[239]

At the 2001 Annual General Meeting held in May 2002, Steve Hannam, Dieter Seebach and Robert Raeber were elected to the Board of Directors of Clariant. When and where Raeber, Executive Vice Chairman of Nestlé SA, met Rolf W. Schweizer for the first time has slipped his memory. Probably he ran across him at a conference of entrepreneurs or within the framework of one of the various committees of which Raeber as Head of European Operations at Nestlé was a member. Raeber thinks that "Switzerland is a relatively small market," so that as a rule leading entrepreneurs know each other. It was on one such occasion that Schweizer had eventually asked him if he would be interested in assuming a mandate on Clariant's Board of Directors.

Robert Raeber found Rolf W. Schweizer to be a very likeable person, "who had had an interesting and successful career at Sandoz before they sent him over to Clariant after the business was split up." Raeber is convinced that Schweizer always wanted the best for his company, even in the case of the acquisition of BTP, which in retrospect proved to be an enormous mistake.

---

239   Ibid.

It was after his search for a successor had again proved unsuccessful in 2001 that Schweizer approached Robert Raeber and begged him to take over the office of president as his successor. Raeber hesitated, for he had made it clear when he joined the Board of Directors that he had no ambitions to become president. But Schweizer practically pleaded with his colleague from the food industry to help him. In the end Raeber allowed himself to be persuaded and accepted the mandate. Consequently he took over from Rolf W. Schweizer as Chairman of the Clariant Board of Directors in May 2002.

Serious blows

At the last Annual General Meeting chaired by Rolf W. Schweizer, the main business concerned the change of president and the restructuring of Clariant.[240] The event where the 71-year-old finally stepped down from office took place in the Congress Centre of the Trade Fair in Basel on 7th May 2002. At that point in time Schweizer could look back on a career of 44-years in industry and it is highly likely that he did not find it easy, especially at his farewell, to have to talk about the failures of the previous few years, the plant closures, relocations and reductions in staff. Getting started in the Life Science Unit in 2000 had taken a heavy toll.

Schweizer had to face many a criticism from the shareholders during the meeting. Above all, there were bitter complaints about the expensive takeover of BTP, which had brought write-offs amounting to billions in its wake. The fact that contrary to the normal custom the unfavourable price trend of the Clariant share had not been mentioned in the annual report also attracted awkward attention. In addition, the advanced age of the Board of Directors was censured severely. Thereupon, it was pointed out that the remuneration of the President and CEO had been ploughed back into the company and not paid out.

After an extraordinary write-down of goodwill on the BTP business had to be made in the financial statements for 2001, Clariant wrote off the entire goodwill remaining in the Life Science & Electronic Chemicals business amounting to CHF 790 million and made an additional asset write-off of CHF 100 million from the balance sheet. The goodwill write-down led to a consolidated loss of CHF 648 million which consequently did not permit a dividend payment for the fiscal year 2002.

---

240 Felix Erbacher: "Einige Kritik auf der Clariant-GV," in *Basler Zeitung* , 8 May 2002, p. 18.

Clariant suffered a further grave setback when there were unexpected technical problems in a new plant for detergent raw materials in the USA, which required additional investments and caused considerable expenditure. It involved the project called *Pluto*,[241] a further deal with Procter & Gamble in the Mount Holly West plant in Charlotte, North Carolina, where bleach activators were to be produced for the successful *Tide* laundry detergent. *Pluto* was to a certain extent *Pick*'s successor and the undertaking itself would actually have been lucrative if its inferior implementation had not put paid to a favourable result. The former Sandoz men take the view that the reason for the negative result may be attributable to the fact that *Pluto* was possibly implemented at the insistence of former Hoechst men; the 'old' Clariant had absolutely no experience in this field and as a consequence the procedure was completely new to them. These are serious accusations, which once again illustrate how responsibility and liability can be laid at someone else's door.

The product was developed in the laboratory on the Höchst Industrial Estate. As part of the scale-up the product normally goes from the laboratory where it is manufactured in quantities of one kilo to a pilot production plant where hundreds of kilos are produced and from there to a large-scale plant where thousands of tonnes are manufactured. An appropriate pilot production plant costs CHF 5 to 7 million as a rule, but in the case of *Pluto* the pilot plant was omitted for financial reasons: i. e. they went straight from a kilo to a ton.

Several sources also confirm that *Pluto* had not even been approved by the Board of Directors although photos of the excavation pit in Mount Holly were already being shown around. Moreover, the local engineers, who built the plant facilities without any backup from Germany, were out of their depth as far as German high technology was concerned. Consequently, some of the materials used were the wrong ones and that resulted in the equipment being prone to corrosion.

Start-up operations were delayed several times and by 2002 overspend had soared to CHF 50 million. In the end Clariant was not in a position to supply the quantities desired within the periods stipulated in the contract so that it had to pay a penalty for breach of contract and the project was finally abandoned in summer 2003.[242] This had a negative effect on the result of the group and the Functional Chemicals Division.

241   Ken Elkins: "Clariant adding two plants in $ 50 M Gaston expansion," in *Charlotte Business Journal*, 7 Dec. 2001.
242   Victor Weber: "Pluto macht Clariant ärmer und ärmer," in *Cash,* 23 May 2003, no. 21, 5; "Clariant mit hoher Sonderabschreibung," in *Handelsblatt,* 17 Jun. 2003, no. 114, p.15; Knight Ridder: "Mount Holly, N. C., Clariant Plant Loses Detergent Additive Deal," in *Tribune Business News,* 17 Jul. 2003.

In the fiscal year 2002 Clariant sold several business sectors: the global emulsion-powder business as well as the European emulsions business to Celanese AG, in Kronberg, Germany, and the hydrosulphite business, which was part of the Textile, Leather & Paper Chemicals Division in North America, to Chemtrade Logistics Inc., in Ontario. Over and above that, the former minority shareholder Socer acquired the Portuguese Clariant subsidiary *Resiquímicas*, which was responsible for the emulsion business on the Portuguese market. Individually, these were peripheral businesses, which generated around 7 percent of turnover at the time, which were sold. Parallel to these disinvestments six plants were shut down.

Case study for students

Requested to describe the BTP deal, Pierre Borgeaud replies without any resentment: the motive for the acquisition was that the company wanted an addition to its portfolio. They examined the British company by studying its figures and visiting the various sites. BTP had a fairly good reputation but when they looked at it more closely, they noticed that there was not much substance and above all, many of the plants were very old. "Not every acquisition can be a success but this deal was painful. Yes, it went pear-shaped and in retrospect it proved to be the wrong decision."[243]

Naturally, the highly over-priced purchase of BTP is frequently regarded in the media as a serious management mistake.[244] But these reports were not instances of journalistic fervour as is also proved by INSEAD, where the case of the Clariant-BTP deal has been part of the syllabus in the Strategy Department since 2006. This private business school was established in Fontainebleau in 1957 and in addition to Stanford and Harvard has meanwhile become one of the leading educational establishments of its kind worldwide. Many members of Sandoz's managerial staff have received further education and training there since Yves Dunant's time. Some of the younger economic elite set great store by INSEAD and Patrick Jany, who has been CFO at Clariant since 2006, also studied there in the 1990s.

Term for term, Laurence Capron, Professor of the Strategic Department,

---

243 Pierre Borgeaud, 28 Jul. 2010.
244 Thomas Hengartner: "Clariant braucht härtere Korrekturen. Auslastung zu tief, Kosten zu hoch. Potenzial von BTP falsch eingeschätzt," in *Finanz und Wirtschaft*, 18 Aug. 2001, no. 64, p 23.

deals with the steps taken by Clariant at the time and examines the following three questions with successive economics students in Fontainebleau: "Does the acquisition of BTP by Clariant make strategic sense? To what extent is the price paid for BTP comparable with earlier deals? What advice would you give Rolf W. Schweizer, if he were to pursue this deal?" The 20-page-long paper can be downloaded from the Internet as teaching material and is available to anyone.

In answer to the question by the author as to the purpose of her seminar, Laurence Capron[245] points to the significant impact of the Clariant case as it is an excellent illustration of the 'hype' that infected several companies and caused them to overpay their acquisitions. A more thorough process of due diligence along with stricter governance mechanisms on the part of the Board of Directors would have helped to prevent the transaction.

In retrospect we know very well that by buying up a number of companies BTP had succeeded in becoming the kind of enticing proposal the analysts liked. It was managed as a *patchwork company* and everything was done to increase profit margins in the short term. Hannam and Ketteley prepared it for a willing purchaser, who could not see behind the scenes of this mirage on account of the technical and competitive regulations of the stock exchange, but who was prepared to pay a huge sum for it because he was longing for a growth spurt and wished to outperform the traditional cyclical business as quickly as possible. There was no opportunity to apply for exclusivity because then the same right would have had to be extended to anyone else interested in the company, which would have hiked up the share price considerably.

Herbert Wohlmann[246] qualifies the opinion that Clariant bought a pig in a poke when they purchased BTP. The lawyer believes the mistake was not so much in the rating of BTP but rather that it can be attributed to the fact that the concept of selling pharmaceutical late-stage intermediates and ingredients—all the big chemicals companies were pursuing this policy at the time—was not sustainable because the pharmaceutical companies were only selling off excess capacities or old products and only on condition that old locations were also included in the acquisition. Furthermore, Wohlmann stresses, the modus operandi of the analysts can be held against them: "If you follow the analysts' reports from that time, then it could be said that the management—

---

245 E-mail from Laurence Capron, 10 Dec. 2010: "Dear Anna, The Clariant case is used to show the 'hype' that the chemicals industry faced in 2000 where several companies overpaid their acquisitions … A more disciplined process of due diligence along with stronger governance mechanisms could have helped. Regards, Laurence Capron."
246 Herbert Wohlmann, 9 Feb. 2010.

Mr Schweizer and Mr Handte—was practically pushed into purchasing a company like BTP. That is not an excuse, merely an explanation."[247]

When asked about due diligence, Siegfried Fischer's reply is similarly matter-of-fact and certainly not to be ignored. After graduating as a doctor of mechanical and process engineering, Fischer, who started his professional career at Hoechst in 1984, spent four years as Head of the Engineering Department in Brazil, came to Clariant as a result of the merger and was Reinhard Meyer's successor as Head of the Functional Chemicals Division and a member of the Board of Management between 2003 and 2009. He believes: "The English locations certainly did not display the standards which were usual at Hoechst or Sandoz but they did meet the legal requirements; they all possessed a valid operating licence."[248]

A sly fox

The acquisition of BTP caused Clariant unforeseen major problems, but for Steve Hannam it was certainly a good deal. While many of the Clariant staff are extremely critical of him, there are definitely others who confirm that he made a clever move. Unlike many of his then colleagues Robert Raeber has no difficulty in finding words of appreciation and recognition for Steve Hannam, with whom he enjoyed the occasional chat. In his eyes, the former CEO of British Tar Products plc was a clever fellow and one could still learn something from him: "After all, he did make the best deal. Why should he be blamed for that? He is a cunning fox, a great guy." [249]

247 Ibid.
248 Telephone conversation with Siegfried Fischer, 9 Mar. 2011.
249 Robert Raeber, 12 May 2010.

Vital changes

Digestive problems

In February 2003 an article entitled "Digestive Problems" appeared in the trade journal *ICIS Chemical Business*. It was a long interview that Frankfurt economic journalist Dede Williams conducted with Joachim Mahler.[250] After studying physics and engineering management, Meyer worked as a consultant for McKinsey, moved to Hoechst in 1985, then to Clariant and succeeded Steve Hannam as Head of the Life Science and Electronic Chemicals Division in March 2002.

Mahler spoke openly on some matters: The Fine Chemicals Division which was transferred from Hoechst to Clariant in 1997 had mainly manufactured raw materials and building blocks for use in other Hoechst products so that business was almost exclusively internally focused. The employees in this business unit had a lot of expertise in complex research and manufacturing processes but not enough in marketing. Thus Mahler's statement confirms a fundamental observation also made by Steve Hannam.

Moreover, Mahler stressed that it was time—it was four years after the acquisition of BTP—to point out that Clariant is one of the pharmaceutical industry's major suppliers.[251] It is incomprehensible really—as if one had not already effected enough write-offs, which made it more than clear what value the acquired assets actually presented. What was also questionable was the time chosen to become a successful supplier[252] to the major life-science companies, because the right time was already past. Consequently it really makes

250 Dede Williams: "Digestive problems", in *ICIS Chemical Business*, 27 Feb. 2003.
251 "Now the job is to spread the word that Clariant is one of the pharmaceutical industry's major suppliers," in: ibid.
252 Jörg Fröndhoff: "Krise in der Pharmabranche erfasst Zulieferer," in Handels*blatt*, 4 Dec. 2002, no. 234, p. 14.

you think when you see how much Clariant still clung to outdated ideas and to illusory bygone ideals at the beginning of 2003. In this difficult phase, in which Clariant had only just started to digest the acquisition of BTP, Reinhard Handte was CEO and Robert Raeber was Chairman of the Board of Directors.

Fetched from the flower garden

Born in 1943, Roland Lösser tendered his resignation to Clariant in December 2000, because, as he stated clearly, a manager ought to step down from office at the age of 60. A further reason for his retirement was his deteriorating relationship with Rolf W. Schweizer. At that time both colleagues and employees tended to be divided in their attitude towards Lösser. Some even saw his resignation as open opposition to Schweizer and regarded it favourably. Others thought that his resignation was only belated remorse because of BTP.

In 2003, not so very long after Roland Lösser's[253] resignation, the CEO also stepped down. The reason for this was that Reinhard Handte had come increasingly under pressure both inside and outside the company after he had touched upon the subject of a capital increase at the press conference on financial statements on 25 February. He did so without the backing of the Board of Directors and his remarks aroused considerable ire among the shareholders.[254] The share price also suffered due to the confused communications and the share lost no less than 40 percent of its value within a week. A fundamental problem was also the fact that Handte had clung too long to the life-science strategy. To contain the damage, the Board of Directors reacted with great speed and only two weeks later there was a change at the head of the Board of Management.[255] It was in the end the unfortunate announcement[256] which caused Handte's downfall and the fact that neither were mistakes admitted nor solutions made public.

A former Director believes that they should have started looking for an external candidate at that point but everything had to happen quickly so that

253 Roland Lösser, 2 Jan. 2010.
254 "Clariant hinterlässt ein ungutes Gefühl: Kapitalerhöhung angekündigt," in *Finanz und Wirtschaft*, 26 Feb. 2003, no. 16, p. 21; *Cash*, 7 Mar. 2003.
255 Klaus Max Smolka: "Nach zwei Verlustjahren tauscht Clariant Vorstandschef aus," in *Financial Times Deutschland*, 13 Mar. 2003, p. 10; Ruedi Mäder: "Clariant-Chef wirft das Handtuch" in *Aargauer Zeitung*, 13 Mar. 2003.
256 Nina Streeck: "Falsche Formel," in *Bilanz*, 1 Apr. 2003; Wolfgang Strasser: *Erfolgsfaktoren für die Unternehmensführung*, Wiesbaden 2004, pp. 126, 158.

virtually acting out of necessity they hit on the idea of bringing Lösser out of retirement. One thing was certain: the former CFO knew the company and the staff, and he had a solid and well-qualified background due to his long years at Sandoz. No one else knew the business as well as Roland Lösser and an experienced financial expert was what was needed and so the Board of Directors decided to ask him whether he would be prepared to take over as CEO.

According to a legend in the company, Lösser, who was a hobby gardener, is said to have been literally fetched from his flower garden in Lörrach to the telephone when Clariant asked him for help and advice. In fact it did not happen like that at all. During a meeting of the Board of Directors on 11 March when the unfortunate remarks made by Hundte at the aforementioned press conference on financial statements were being discussed, Lösser, who was a member of the Board of Directors, was asked to step outside. Lösser had a good idea what was in store for him but he did not see it as the climax to his career for he knew that the issue was financially orientated and would mean a stupendous amount of work.

In fact the fledgling CEO had no time to catch his breath, because the next day, at Robert Raeber's behest, he had to take charge of all the press meetings which had been arranged beforehand. Afterwards, finding a solution to the financial problems had absolute priority. Clariant was deeply in debt which was in infringement of the credit agreements. At first Lösser thought that the banks were only 'making a fuss' about the credits. It was only in later talks that he realized: what the banks had actually said signalized that the company was doomed sooner rather than later.

Lösser's target was to step in at short notice to save Clariant and set the financial situation to rights. He braced himself for two rather than three years but by no means the six months conjectured by the press. During his period of office, he also considered it to be his responsibility to groom a successor.

The actual problem and what could be done[257]

In the 1980s Roland Lösser had worked for Sandoz Germany in Nuremberg and there he had met Thomas Wellauer, who was carrying out a pro-

257 Interview with Thomas Wellauer in Zurich on 17 Sept. 2010.

ject as part of a McKinsey team. When Lösser was elected CEO and took over from Reinhard Handte in 2003, he spoke to Wellauer and the two of them sat down with Robert Raeber, the Chairman of the Board of Directors, to discuss the Clariant problem. In the beginning the task was not clear cut. Raeber outlined the actual problem resulting from the inheritance of BTP, referred to the relative weakness of the management bench and asked Wellauer if he would be interested in helping on a mandate basis. The latter was not only interested but he also had time and so in May 2003 he joined Clariant "without", as he expressed it, "any clear idea of what the assignment was" and worked out a comprehensive programme to increase Clariant's profitability.

Wellauer conducted an analysis based on facts, figures and numerous talks with staff from the whole company and in summer 2003 presented Lösser and Raeber with a programme for improving the difficult situation in which Clariant found itself. Logically Wellauer saw the cause of the unfortunate situation in the poor results but also in the fact that the company was running at an absolute limit with regard to the balance sheet and liquidity. This fact had a direct bearing on their plans because they could hardly afford any restructuring costs. Closing plants and large-scale redundancies etc. were just not possible. Firstly, the programme needed to cost little and free up cash as quickly as possible, so that more costly measures could then be realized in a second step. It was entirely a matter of survival. It was uncertain just how long Clariant could hold out and avoid liquidation. According to in-house assessments, which were only expressed among a very few, Clariant would not survive the summer of 2004. The second point was to plan and document the programme in such detail that a capital increase would be an option. This was discussed and approved, Wellauer relates.

From the very beginning, he was of the opinion that Clariant could not possibly implement the programme under its own steam; it needed intensive support from advisors who, if possible, knew the company already. There were two companies worth considering: Accenture, who had been working for Clariant in the Process and Computer Science Unit for years and McKinsey, who had been working on the strategy since Lösser took office as CEO. That meant there was one team of advisors who knew the company from the ground upwards and there was one who knew it from the top. Wellauer described the main features of his programme to the two companies and gave them six weeks to present detailed proposals for implementing the programme. In the end McKinsey was chosen unanimously by the entire Board of Management in August 2003 because they had presented the better plan.

CPIP[258]

On the occasion of the semi-annual conference in August 2003 Clariant announced the implementation of a so-called transformation programme called *Clariant Performance Improvement Program*, CPIP for short. It consisted of two main projects with a total of nine different individual projects, to which sponsors from the Board of Management were assigned who bore responsibility for each project and supported the project team. The first main project was comprised of five 'operational improvements projects,' whose target it was to increase profitability in the short term. They had in common the fact that they achieved sustainable results quickly, were not expensive, and did not require any major changes in the organisation of the company. First results were envisaged for 2004 and total success was anticipated two years later. The heads of the projects were engaged on the job full time and had to give up their previous work. This involved the following persons, whose names are given with their field of responsibility along with the name of their respective sponsor (in brackets) from the Management Board: Oliver Kinkel/Logistics Network (Joachim Mahler), Lukas Kreienbühl/Purchasing (Nico Gontha), Vincent Liu/Marketing (Dominik von Bertrab), Ulrich Kussmaul/Production (Uwe Nickel), Karl-Heinz Schönwälder/Current Assets (Siegfried Fischer).

The four remaining projects, the 'structural improvements projects', constituted the second main project in the transformation programme. Their target, too, was the sustainable increase in profitability but they were concerned with the organisation of the company. Their task was to make structures and processes simpler and more effective. These projects were set up in the medium term and were to result in restructuring. With one exception the heads of these projects worked on the assignment but kept their previous jobs: Walter Kindler/Legal Design (François Note), Norbert Wester/Production Site Design (Hartmut Wiezer), Klaus Unterharnscheidt/Supply Chain Design (Joachim Mahler), Pierre Wüst/Finance & Administration Design (Peter Brandenberg).

Wellauer reports that first of all they worked on reducing the current assets because that would free up cash most quickly. Parallel to that an unusually detailed controlling was set up. Every measure worked out was marked with milestones, recorded electronically and subjected to a close examination at monthly intervals whereby it was ascertained that the figures available

258 Ibid.; see Clariant *Management Report 2003*, pp. 9, 30–31; Hans-Georg Klose: "Alles CPIP oder was?" in *Clartext* 4/2004, p. 7; *Management Report 2004*, pp. 4, 20–21; *Chemietechnik Online*, 22 Aug. 2005; *Clartext* 1/2006.

Some members of the CPIP Project, 2003: Pierre Wüst, Thomas Wellauer, Lukas Kreienbühl, Ulrich Kussmaul, Vincent Liu, Klaus Unterharnscheidt, Michael Farrensteiner, Oliver Kinkel (l–r)

were frequently incorrect. This applied, above all, to the number of employees. The figures differed according to whether they came from the financial or from the personnel system! As the programme involved, among other things, a considerable reduction in staff, all the employees were recorded by name in one large data bank. From that point on, not only the implementation of the measures was tracked and the figures checked in order to cut costs but a name check of the employees was also carried out. If personnel was to be shed somewhere, the employees who would be affected by the measures needed to be identified by name so that a check could be carried out as to whether these names were no longer on the list or whether they cropped up again somewhere else.

CPIP pervaded every department of the company, austerity measures were to be identified everywhere. However Wellauer soon discovered that initially motivation among the employees to cooperate in the project tended to be rather slight because a certain resignation had developed. From the various restructuring measures in the past they had gained the impression that huge plans were only ever outlined but never implemented. Then, moving into 2004, the mood changed suddenly. Of course there were people who were simply unable to change or were resistant to change but many at Clariant sensed that this time things were really happening and this gave rise to a certain enthusiasm. It might even have been that the employees understood better than many a superior that something drastic had to happen if the company were to survive. People started to become actively involved and had no inhibitions about getting rid of dead wood or tackling topics which might affect them negatively. Consequently, good proposals were put forward and in the end many targets were even exceeded.

The pick of the bunch

In the meantime, Lösser became something of a hero. Unlike the occasion of his resignation in 2000, many in the company gave him credit in 2003 for the fact that—when Clariant was faced with bankruptcy on account of BTP—he was instrumental in saving the company.[259] When he took over the active role of CEO, one of the principal reasons for choosing him was his experience and his contacts to the financial sector. Thus, the company found the financial basis to remove itself from the immediate danger zone and was even able to carry out restructuring measures by selling off parts of the company. The disinvestment did not affect parts of BTP; some of the best parts of Clariant, very profitable business units were sold, for it is easier to sell anything of value: that can be sold extremely quickly.

Three months after CPIP was introduced, Clariant announced, as a first step in the process, the sale of its Cellulose Ether[260] Business Unit for € 241 million to the globally active Japanese company Shin-Etsu Chemicals. The business unit, which was part of the Functional Chemicals Division and generated turnover of € 187 million in the fiscal year 2002, held a strong position on the market and incorporated both the modern manufacturing plant at the Wiesbaden location and the Tylose brand which had grown to be a globally recognized industrial standard. The 500 employees in the unit were kept on, which provided them with new prospects for the future.

After Clariant had sold the Construction Chemicals Unit to Celanese and two further units, which produced chemicals for manufacturing textiles and adhesives, were bought by the Japanese group Kuraray, AP Chemicals, a company in England which was part of the Life Science & Electronic Chemicals Division, was also disposed of. There the last remaining hydrosulphite production plant was also closed.

The disinvestments went hand in hand with Clariant's own acquisitions

---

259 Interview with Alexander Sieber in Muttenz, 22 Dec. 2009.
260 Thorsten Winter: "Mitarbeiter helfen Clariant in Höchst beim Sparen," in *Frankfurter Allgemeine Zeitung*, 22 Nov. 2005.

and investments. The purchase of Quality Colour, a supplier of dye and additive concentrates in Canada, ensured the expansion of the presence of the Masterbatches Division on the North American market. In addition, a new plant was opened in the emerging Vietnamese market.

The company turned its attention particularly to service-orientated businesses. These included the Clariant Oilfield Service, an analytical laboratory developed by the Functional Chemicals Division; with its help crude oil samples could be analysed directly at the oil field, which meant that problems could be solved considerably faster. With the integrated ColorWorks Service, the Masterbatches Division gained access to the design processes of manufacturers of branded products. In the ColorWorks Design Centres in New York, Taipei and Frankfurt, product designers now had the chance to transfer their ideas for the colour of packaging, camera cases and other synthetic articles directly onto the monitor in three dimensions. With Archroma Global Services the Textile, Leather & Paper Chemicals Division developed a service which enabled textile manufacturers to establish colour standards, impart them worldwide and to implement them uniformly, with computer-aided processes, in their plants all over the world.

The measures work

The envisaged capital increase, which had been preceded by in-depth talks between Thomas Wellauer, Robert Raeber and Roland Lösser, took place around January 2004. Initially Lösser had grave doubts because on taking up his post as CEO he had said in an effort to reassure investors that there would be *no* increase in capital.[261] Eventually he realized that they had no choice in the matter. The banks, too, reacted sceptically at first, but a detailed presentation of the programme planned soon convinced them. The increase in capital provided the company with a breathing space, the sword of Damocles, as Wellauer put it, no longer hung over Clariant's head and the measures continued as planned.

In 2004 CPIP reached an important milestone when the project phase was completed, i. e. the improvement measures had been worked out. Potential cuts of more than CHF 800 million were the result. A third had already been implemented and came into play in Clariant's performance. In the two pre-

---

261 Christoph Eisenring: "Clariant im strategischen Vakuum. Neuer Konzernchef – keine Kapitalerhöhung," in Neue *Zürcher Zeitung*, 13 Mar. 2003; "Clariant. Die Chemie stimmt nicht," in *Manager Magazin*, 13 Mar. 2003.

ceding years approximately, the project teams had worked out more than 5,500 measures for improving performance by means of definite implementation plans and precisely scheduled milestones. The improvements in performance were soundly underpinned by adjustments to the structure of the organisation, its processes and its systems within the framework of the new 'Clariant Operating Model'. Besides, as part of their project work, the project teams had created a multitude of new 'tools' which were widely used and ensured the sustainability of the envisaged improvements.

The huge efforts were already making an impact and in 2004 Clariant's balance sheet became structurally sound again. The net debt dropped by CHF 1.8 billion from CHF 2.9 billion to around CHF 1.1 billion. In the calendar year there was an improvement in the share price by 13.2 percent which was considerably higher than the 2 percent increase recorded by the Swiss Market Index (SMI). The market capitalisation of the company rose by around CHF 1.4 billion. The shareholders received a payout of CHF 0.25 per share in cash in the form of a par value reduction. Of the 4,000 redundancies announced in February 2004, 1,000 jobs had been shed in the year under review.

The disinvestment begun in 2003 continued in 2004. Lancaster Synthesis went to the chemicals company Johnson Matthey and the Japanese subsidiary Clariant Polymers K. K. was taken over by Nippon Synthetic Chemical Industry. Moreover, Clariant relinquished its minority stake in SF-Chem to Swiss private-equity company Capvis.

In July 2004 the company also parted with its subsidiary AZ Electronic Materials in Wiesbaden. The transaction value of CHF 518 million included a vendor loan granted by Clariant amounting to CHF 40 million. AZ was a global supplier to manufacturers of semiconductors and flat screens and the business unit, with about 800 employees worldwide, 169 of them in Germany, generated turnover of € 288 million in 2003—a profitable and promising field of activity which, however, required considerable investment and Clariant just did not have the necessary financial resources.

AZ was purchased by the American Carlyle Group, an investment company which had, due to various takeovers, special know-how in the semi-conductor industry at its disposal. After the acquisition by the American company a familiar name was to be found on the Board of Directors in addition to Denys Henderson, former Chairman of ICI: It was Steve Hannam, who was all too well known at Clariant.

When asked to assess the course of Clariant's business, Hannam was emphatic: "For me it was very interesting seeing one business (BTP) go into the Clariant matrix and be negatively affected and another business (AZ) liberated from Clariant and succeed! There is probably a management text book to be written on the subject!"[262]

Parallel to the disinvestments there was a personal contribution which could be celebrated as a counterpoint: the Pigments & Additive Division laid the foundation stone at its site in Höchst for the first plant in the world where waxes would be produced by metallocene catalysis.[263] Behind the name of the product—Licocene—was a trend-setting technology. Due to the innovative manufacturing process it was possible to design with absolute precision the important properties of the waxes such as the hardness, the melting behaviour and the viscosity and to adjust the application properties precisely to match the wishes of the customers. A distinguishing feature of metallocene waxes is their cost-benefit ratio. They are used in such products as dispersing agents, adhesives and sealants, as release agents for black toners in photocopiers and in glass- and natural fibre-reinforced compounds.

Apart from 'hard' measures Lösser also introduced 'soft' human resource measures: at the behest of Roland Lösser, Clariant introduced the Regional Management Program (RMP) in cooperation with the University of St. Gallen and the Ross School of Business at the University of Michigan in 2004. He closed the gap between training courses for future senior management staff and those for the upper management. Thanks to the regional focus of the programme, which was carried out in Europe, Asia and America, the cultural and business peculiarities of the respective countries could be taken into consideration.

Movement in the Board of Directors

In many respects 2004 was a dynamic year. Apart from Wellauer's and Lösser's efforts, Chairman Robert Raeber also effected some changes in his sphere of competence: the Board of Directors.

Even under Schweizer, it had struck Raeber[264] that the Chairman had already agreed in advance with his CEO on many of the issues which were raised at the meetings of the Board of Directors with the result that they only had to be presented at the meetings and let through on the nod. "I'm sorry,

---

262 E-mail from Steve Hannam, 31 Jan. 2011.
263 Clariant *Press Release*, 2 Sept. 2004; Thorsten Winter: "Clariant baut in Höchst eine Produktionsanlage für Spezialwachse," in *Frankfurter Allgemeine Zeitung*, 9 Sept. 2004.
264 Rober Raeber, 12 May 2010.

but that shouldn't be," Raeber reports in a matter-of-fact way. He insists that the Board of Directors "must not be a rubber-stamping committee but must be a genuine committee that discusses and reaches decisions independent of the management." He assumes that the acquisition of BTP would never have been made if the Board of Management and the Board of Directors had discussed and checked the project in an open, unbiased and decisive way. Raeber endeavoured, if nothing else but for that reason, to implement the decision-finding in the committees in terms of a clearly defined corporate governance.

Until the 1990s little notice was paid to this matter in Swiss companies. The attitude that the shareholders are the owners of a group only developed when shareholders became active and gave impulses towards improving their position.

The legal foundations for a responsible corporate management were laid by the reform of the law on stock companies in 1991. The reform was intended to strengthen the protection of the shareholders, to increase transparency, to improve the structure and function of the various executive bodies, to make capital procurement easier, and to prevent abuse. However, these framework conditions were inadequate with the result that many regulations continued to be merely on paper.

On the basis of the codes which had been mainly developed in Anglo-Saxon countries the Economiesuisse (the Federation of Associations of Swiss industry) produced a Swiss Code of Best Practice for Corporate Governance. This came into effect in 2002 and was updated again in 2007 but it merely makes recommendations. Only the corporate-governance directive issued by the SIX Swiss Exchange in 2002 contains more binding regulations.

After Robert Raeber assumed office on 7th May 2002, this subject became a focal point at Clariant. In the Annual Report 2002 there was, for the first time, a chapter dedicated solely to corporate governance entitled "Modern Corporate Management at Clariant."[265] In this section of eight pages there was a description, in detail such as had never been seen before, of corporate structure and shareholders, capital structure, the Board of Directors, the Board of Management, compensation, interests and loans, shareholders' rights of participation, auditing, change of control and blocking mechanisms and disclosure policy.

Spurred on by the Swiss Code it was now necessary—as was the case in many Swiss companies at that time—to effect a change in culture and to put good corporate governance into practice. In that respect Raeber wished for

---

265 Clariant *Annual Report 2002*, pp. 12–20.

a younger member, who was still actively engaged in business and above all impartial, to succeed Pierre Borgeaud on the Board of Directors.[266] It seemed to him that Kajo Neukirchen was the right candidate. He was a successful German entrepreneur renowned for calling a spade a spade even if it did not always make him friends. Raeber also brought onto the Board Peter Isler, an excellent lawyer who was highly conversant with corporate governance. Neukirchen and Isler joined the Board of Directors in 2004.

The mandate of Heinrich Bossard who died tragically in a plane crash in 2004 was assumed by Klaus Jenny, a former banker with Credit Suisse.

'Prinzipal'

The seven-year holding period, which in his time Albert Hug had termed the drawback because it not only restricted Clariant to a considerable extent but downright oppressed it, expired in January 2004. The time for a belated restructuring had come and, in addition, the conflagration lit by BTP still had to be extinguished further.

CPIP and 'Prinzipal' were different measures which were carried out parallel to each other.[267] CPIP which began in 2003 was to aid cost cutting and cash management. Prinzipal, on the other hand, was a process and cost-optimizing project which altered the legal structures in Clariant's European companies. As the focus was on processes, the term CPR, *Core Process Redesign*, was applied.

The core of the 'Prinzipal' model which was introduced early in 2005 was the *Prinzipal*, the head of the new organisation, who had the power to direct and manage and who was the pivotal point where all business processes converged. Accordingly, the divisions were responsible for business at global level. Activities spanning various divisions were integrated in Service Units at regional and country level, which was meant to decrease complexity and cut costs.

First of all, the 'Prinzipal' project meant that the business model changed so that there were three companies in each country—a holding with service functions, a manufacturing company and a distribution company—and each business basically sold everything to Switzerland and from there it was resold

---

266 Robert Raeber, 12 May 2010.
267 Gion Job explained 'Prinzipal' to the author and on 28 Mar. 2011 released the background information, as given here, for publication.

direct. That meant that the business processes were reorganised in such a way that in the case of a good transaction an appropriate part of the profit accrued where the strategic decisions had been made i. e. in the 'principal' company in Switzerland and not abroad where tax rates were, as a rule, higher. In retrospect, the project had one major drawback for it made structures more complicated and clumsy so that in the end business was made more difficult and customer friendliness suffered as a result.

A second major aspect of the 'Prinzipal' project was centralization in Switzerland. At the same time, through *Prinzipal*, it was ensured—and that was the positive aspect—that in Switzerland strategic competence was in place so that the companies abroad basically could not run their business without Switzerland, which was the effect aimed at. Apart from process and cost optimizing, 'Prinzipal' also aimed at—in martial terms—unmanning the 'opposition' in Germany. Those are harsh words, but they were consistent with reality.

After the takeover of Hoechst's Specialty Chemicals, Frankfurt had secretly ranked as Clariant's second head office. In truth, there were two central offices: Muttenz and Sulzbach—a situation which the company could not afford in the long run. Four of the six divisions in the beginning were situated in the 'big canton', i. e. three quarters of the company was not even administered from Switzerland.

It was now planned to pool the entire business and incorporate it in a uniform structure in order to really create *one* company from two companies. The measure was to go towards creating a situation where in future the group would no longer be co-managed from Germany, but directed only from Switzerland. From now on, Clariant's principal strategic management and offices were to be focused in the Corporate Centre in Muttenz so that internal communications would improve. Thus the group was to become more efficient and flexible and be in the position to react more quickly to the needs of the market, which in turn would strengthen its competitive position in a sustainable way.

The move

The new organisation had an impact on where quite a number of employees worked. In the course of Project *Move*[268] more than 350 management person-

---

268 *Clartext* 2/2004, p. 18; Gerhard Lerch: "Wie man sich auf einer Völkerwanderung fühlt," in *Clartext* 3/2005, pp. 34–35.

nel relocated to Muttenz. Functional Chemicals, Pigments & Additives, and Textile, Leather & Paper Chemicals, in particular, divisions which so far had been located in Germany, were affected. In concrete terms that meant employees, especially from Sulzbach and Höchst, but also from Leinfelden, Gersthofen, Griesheim and from other European sites, going as 'guest workers' to the Alpine Republic.

It was important, therefore, not only to encourage the management personnel who resided in the Rhine-Main region to move from there to 'the back of beyond' but also to persuade their spouses and children to leave their work and their circle of friends behind. To make moving house a little easier for them, the Board of Management invited the staff and the families concerned to Basel on 5 and 6 June 2005. During these 'Basel days' the guests had the opportunity to become familiar with the new surroundings, and meet new colleagues, explore potential living areas in the tri-border region and to obtain information on the law, taxes, the cost of living, the job market, education and childcare.

The journey by special train from Frankfurt to Basel, the boat trip on the River Rhine on board the MS *Baslerdybli* and the MS *Lällekönig*, the tour of the plant, the excursions into the surrounding countryside and a tour of the city were organised by an event company. The response was very favourable and in the end more visitors than expected decided in favour of the move, which was to take place in the course of the following two years. A warehouse, Building no. 904 on the plant premises, was converted into an office building for the newcomers and during the construction work it was given the name of 'the Prussian bunker' by the permanent staff there. (The word 'Prussian' is frequently used in the south, particularly in Bavaria, to refer to anyone from the north and east of Germany).

Rifts

The measures impacted; there were many changes for the better. But it became obvious after a while, especially in the case of CPIP, that the first rifts had developed, Wellauer relates. At the operational level of the company management there were complaints about the personnel measures in particular. They moaned about not having enough people. The programme continued to be implemented but there were still times when new units were approved with the result that in some places there were reductions in staff in line with the target set while in other places there was an increase in the number of workers. This meant that the absolute figures did not decrease the way they should have. In Wellauer's opinion the CEO should have taken more drastic measures: "Mr Lösser was more of a moderator for the Management Board than a proper CEO. He was a person who banked rather heavily on consensus and frequently shied away from imposing strong measures on his own people." Lösser backed the programme to the hilt but if a colleague came to him begging desperately for more staff for a fantastic project, he often found it hard to refuse.

Over time a certain stagnation set in and in spring 2005 Wellauer reckoned the moment had come to set off the next stage of the programme, for which no money had been available at first. He outlined his ideas extensively in a letter to Raeber and Lösser. Above all, the measures were to include a reassessment of the sites. He estimated that of approx. 100 sites worldwide around 50 were superfluous; many of these had come into the company's possession when Clariant had acquired BTP. There were plants with a long tradition and local significance which had long since become uneconomical but continued to run for socio-political and local historical reasons. For example, Wellauer spoke out even then in favour of closing Hüningen.

Up to that point no one had dared part from entire sites and only partial closures had been undertaken. Thus it was not uncommon for individual buildings, which stood on factory premises consisting of several buildings, to be closed one by one over a long period of time, but the overly-large infrastructure and the vastly oversized supply plants continued to operate with full input, even when perhaps only a single building from the entire complex was still in use. In such cases drastic closures were called for. A further recommendation in Wellauer's proposals was for example that the company should try hard to find partners in China for certain divisions.

Lösser and Raeber did not precisely reject Wellauer's recommendations but were of the opinion that it was too early to implement the second stage. They preferred to wait a little in order to give the staff a little breathing space. "Mr Lösser was or is a very optimistic person who has many strong points but when it came to Clariant's future he was just too optimistic," is Wellauer's evaluation of the decision reached by the top management.[269]

---

269 Flavian Cajacob: "Mit Optimismus stimmt die Chemie," in *Handelszeitung*, 29 Oct. 2003.

Executive search

The search for a new CEO began about spring 2005 for it was planned that Roland Lösser should take over the office of Chairman of the Board of Directors from Robert Raeber who was retiring on grounds of age. Consequently, a headhunter was commissioned to find a suitable successor. At the same time, however, Lösser approached Wellauer and asked him if he would be interested in the post. Wellauer replied in the affirmative—but on condition that the measures he had proposed would be implemented. "I have been approached and have thought deeply about the matter," he said later in an interview for *Finanz und Wirtschaft*.[270]

Lösser confirmed that his proposals would be tackled, but first they would be put on hold for a while. In a talk with Lösser just before the personnel decision was due, Wellauer demanded a definite promise from the Board of Directors that his programme would be continued systematically and expanded otherwise he would not be available for the post of CEO.

Many within the company regarded Thomas Wellauer[271] as the ideal candidate and the favourite for the succession. He was highly experienced, straight, assertive and charismatic. As an economist and doctor of chemical engineering Wellauer looked back not only on many years of experience in banking and insurance but he was also very familiar with the pharmaceuticals and chemicals industry. After working in the financial consultancy group of McKinsey for ten years he was appointed Head of Winterthur, the insurance group, in 1997. After the group was taken over by Credit Suisse, Wellauer, as a member of the senior management, was in charge of the insurance business and then he took over the management of the Financial Services Division in 2000. Lukas Mühlemann, the then Head of Credit Suisse, promoted the amalgamation with the Allfinanz group which brought the bank to the brink of ruin with the result that both Mühlemann and Wellauer had to step down in 2002.

Eventually Lösser summoned him to Clariant, where he did a very difficult and necessary job between 2003 and 2005. However, there was a justifiable fear (which was not unfounded) that, in the event of a decision in favour of Wellauer as CEO, business leaders in Switzerland would be up in arms for his reputation was tainted by the stigma which the losses by Winterthur Versicherung had left in the financial sector. As many things at Clariant still needed

270 Andreas Meier/Franziska Pedroietta: "Die Spezialchemie operiert unter extremen Bedingungen," in Finanz und Wirtschaft, 29 Oct. 2005, no. 86, p. 27.
271 Albert Steck: "Machtnetz von Thomas Wellauer: Der Allrounder," in *Bilanz* 6/2006, 9 May 2006.

clarification and many problems required a speedy solution, the Board of Directors had grave reservations[272] about how the market- whether the public or the financial market—would react to a man like Thomas Wellauer with such a past. The decisive question was how to deal with such doubts and whether the industry and the media would react more favourably if they were presented with a new face as CEO.

The expertise which the chemicals engineer, analyst and financier could draw on and his profound knowledge of Clariant's problems, which he had acquired in three years of detailed work at the various sites worldwide, did not tip the balance. After taking into consideration his qualifications and the supposed risks connected to his person, the committee increasingly focussed on an external candidate.

At that time the concept of the ideal CEO in the chemicals industry in northern Switzerland was influenced by a German management expert, who had recently moved to a neighbouring company in Basel. It was this model which latently served as the standard for the search.

A few years into the millennium, a trend became evident that more and more northerners from Scandinavia were rising to top managerial positions in Swiss companies. One of the first was Ulf Berg from Denmark, who was elected Chairman of the Board of Directors at Sulzer in autumn 2004. Further candidates, to mention but a few, were Jouni Heinonen from Finland, who became Head of Gurit, the plastics group, in mid-2000 and Bo Risberg, from Sweden, who took charge of Hilti, the constructional engineering group, in 2007.

The popularity of individuals from the far north can be put down to the fact that they were noted for qualities such as perseverance, an urge to discover, a high standard of education, language skills, social competence and experience in dealing with trade unions and they could be relied on to achieve results. Scandinavian managerial staff was even more interested in consensus than their Swiss counterparts, Clemens Hoegl, Managing Partner at Egon Zehnder International, claimed in an interview.[273]

Chairman Robert Raeber, CEO Roland Lösser and Tony Reis, a member of the Board and a former CEO of Swiss IBM were on the Compensation & Nomination Committee at Clariant. These three agreed to consider people not only from the inner circle but also to start searching for an executive in the normal way. The profile of the ideal candidate was that first and foremost

272   Victor Weber: "Die stille Läuterung des Thomas W," in *Cash*, 17 Nov. 2005, p. 15.
273   Andreas Güntert/Sibylle Veigl: "Leuchten aus dem hohen Norden," in *Facts*, 1 Jun. 2006.

he had to be an experienced personality from the chemical industry; Clariant was not looking for a Swiss or a German but a personality. These were the parameters of the commission given to Zurich-based headhunter Egon Zehnder. There were a number of candidates put forward for consideration. For example, a Briton from ICI, who made a very good impression, was a hot favourite, but the procedure seems to have taken too long or he received a more lucrative offer in the meantime for he backed out. Talks were also held with a Frenchman and an American but finally the decision was made in favour of a northerner from Sweden, Jan Secher.[274]

An industrial engineer from Stockholm with considerable work experience abroad, Secher could already look back on a career lasting more than 20 years[275] which had begun at ASEA, now ABB, the Swedish electrical engineering group. After various managerial jobs in sales and distribution, marketing and product management, he became one of the Executive Committee at ABB, where he was in charge of the Robot and Retailing Division until 2002. In 2003 Secher moved as CEO to the SICPA group, a leading manufacturer of printing inks worldwide which had its head office in Lausanne and which had forged its way to a leading position on the global market for printing inks for packaging and printer's proof inks for bank notes. SICPA generated turnover of around CHF 1 billion and had approx. 3,500 employees.

Secher joined Clariant in December 2005. Wellauer[276] recalls that in the talks he held with Secher about CPIP, it became obvious that the future CEO had different ideas and wanted to concentrate increasingly on the market whereas, in his eyes, austerity measures tended to have a demotivating impact. As a result, Wellauer regarded his mission at Clariant as completed. At Lösser's request he remained for the next three months until the new CEO took up office in the company. He continued to take care of the programme but only in a part-time capacity and in this period became aware that the enthusiasm for a systematic and tough implementation was receding drastically. At the end of March 2006 Wellauer left Clariant once and for all. A few weeks later Daniel Vasella appointed him Head of Corporate Affairs on the Board of Management of Novartis, the foundation of which Wellauer had actively supervised as head of the McKinsey consultation team in 1995/1996. Since October 2010 Thomas Wellauer has been COO and member of the Management Board of Swiss Re, a reinsurer.

---

274 "Neuer Chef bei Clariant: Jan Secher sticht Thomas Wellauer aus," in *Tages-Anzeiger*, 16 Oct. 2005.
275 Stock, Oliver: "Schwedisches Comeback," in *Handelsblatt*, 4 Nov. 2005.
276 Thomas Wellauer, 17 Sept. 2010.

2006–2008

Self-assessment

Jan Secher joined the Board of Management in January 2006 and at the end of the Annual General Meeting he assumed the office of Chief Executive Officer as of 7th April. Simultaneously Robert Raeber stepped down as Chairman and member of the Board of Directors on grounds of age. He was succeeded by Roland Lösser, who had been CEO until then. Furthermore, Clariant announced a further change in the Board. Peter Chen, professor of chemistry at the ETH in Zurich, took over from Dieter Seebach, who was also retiring. There was also a major change in the Board of Management due to the appointment of Patrick Jany, who succeeded François Note as CFO.

Despite the extensive restructuring measures initiated by Lösser as CEO, which entailed the shedding of 6,000 jobs, Clariant did not succeed in extricating itself completely from the unfortunate situation it had landed in due to taking over BTP. Moreover, the situation was aggravated by the rising price of raw materials. This was a problem which the entire industry had to contend with because it could not pass on these costs in full to the customers.

Basel-based economic journalist Felix Erbacher interviewed every CEO and Chairman at Clariant, and that also included Jan Secher.[277] In retrospect, the journalist thinks that Secher's assumption of office was anticipated with considerable optimism—there were high expectations attached to the Swedish manager as a representative of a new generation. However it must be remembered that he arrived at a time when the specialty chemicals industry was facing a crisis. Erbacher reports that as the previous CEO, Roland Lösser had it somewhat easier because as a financier it must have been relatively clear to him what had to be done: In view of the messy situation with BTP, simply to

---

277 Felix Erbacher, 26 Feb. 2010.

Jan Secher, CEO at Clariant from 2006 to 2008

build up from nothing. Whereas in Lösser's case the starting points were apparent—namely cutting costs—Secher's activities fell into a phase where the company was faced with powerful players, comparable to Ciba, both on the customer and on the supplier side. Clariant found itself hedged in entirely and into the bargain Secher inherited a huge variety of products.

Jan Secher[278] reports that the most fundamental problem facing him when he assumed office was the unrealistic self-assessment of the group. Clariant assumed that it was a specialty chemicals company. This was also the conviction conveyed by Raeber and Lösser in their talks with him.

Thereupon the new CEO initiated a comprehensive review of Clariant's management systems: over a period of months, an internal task force under his management travelled all over the world to the sites belonging to the company, polled the management there and put the strategy to the test. In no way did the result indicate a specialty chemicals company but rather painted an entirely different picture.[279] The term 'specialty' only applied to around 60 percent of the goods manufactured by the company while the remainder consisted of mass-produced goods where the main distinctions were not the quality but the price. Under these circumstances the new CEO felt compelled to subject the strategy and the efficiency of the organization, its portfolio and its

---

278 Conversation with Jan Secher in Essen on 15 Mar. 2011.
279 Sergio Aiolfi: "Jan Sechers Sanierungsplan für Clariant," in *Neue Zürcher Zeitung*, 28 Dec. 2007.

operations to a thorough inspection, examining the company from three different perspectives—the industry, customers and employees.

One of Secher's first official acts was the sale[280] of Pharmaceutical Fine Chemicals to the investment company of Tower Brook Capital Partners. This was a business unit which was overvalued in the books and not part of Clariant's core competences. After approval by the competition watchdogs the disinvestment was completed at the end of June 2006.

Masterbatch

In contrast, one acquisition did serve to strengthen the main activities: in October Clariant announced plans to acquire the masterbatch business[281] from Ciba Specialty Chemicals, thus putting paid to speculations about an imminent merger of the two competitors. While the Masterbatch Unit tended to play a minor role at Ciba, Clariant was already one of the leaders in the sector with a market share of 13 percent worldwide and in the first half of 2006 had again managed to increase turnover in this segment by 9 percent. The stock markets reacted favourably to the announcement of the acquisition with the result that the share price of both companies went up. The takeover was effected on 1 December 2006.

The term masterbatch is used to describe the business with mixing additives or pigments which are highly concentrated in polymer substrates, i. e. in interlinked molecules. The colour concentration for plastic materials is the reason why a drinks container, for example, is red, green or yellow.

Insight into the world of masterbatches is afforded by the story of the stadium seats,[282] which goes back to the Sandoz era when the World Cup was held in Italy in 1990. To cope with the 2.5 million spectators who were expected at the matches, new stadiums were to be built or existing stadiums were to be enlarged and refurbished at the twelve venues chosen for the various matches. The seating was created by Designer Giancarlo Venelli, who envisaged the stadium as a huge living room with comfortable coloured seats, which were to provide the spectators with the greatest possible safety. The prototype united a

---

280 Sergi Aiolfi: "Clariant verkauft Teil des Life-Sciences-Geschäfts," in *Neue Zürcher Zeitung,* 29 Apr. 2006.

281 Sergi Aiolfi: "Ciba-Masterbatch-Bereich geht an Clariant," in *Neue Zürcher Zeitung,* 5 Oct. 2006; Pierre Weil: "Übernahme beendet Fusionsfantasien. Clariant kauft Masterbatch-Geschäft von Ciba Spezialitätenchemie," in *Basler Zeitung,* 5 Oct. 2006.

282 *Sandoz Bulletin 1990,* no. 91, pp. 34–35.

number of features which hitherto had never been met with in the antiquated Italian stadiums: the ergo metric seat was cast in a single piece with a smooth surface and had no 'edges' which largely ruled out the risk of injury.

Building the model in series, however, proved to be difficult and in the end Venelli contacted Wegaplast in Bologna. After the physical properties of various materials were checked for their performance with respect to heat, atmospheric effects and impact resistance to vandalism, polypropylene was chosen. Wegaplast then had to look for a further partner for the chemical properties of the seats and found Sarma: The seats were to be coloured, not oxidised, protected from ultra-violet rays and supple, not liable to crack and conform to the highest requirements of fire protection laws.

Established in Pogliano Milanese in 1953, Sarma had been developing and manufacturing masterbatches, additives for chemical products and pigments in the form of granules and pastes since the early 1960s and became part of Sandoz in 1979. Sarma's fortunes were largely determined by Venetian chemist and agronomist Antonio Saletti, who was the Division Manager in 1980 and became a Delegate of the Board of Directors at Sandoz's Sarma SpA as of 1987.

Due to Saletti's main area of interest, Sarma had always been familiar with research, but the problem of the stadium seats proved to be new and complex. It was a question of producing a masterbatch or, even better, of creating a package which contained both the pigments and the necessary additives. The development work lasted months until at long last, on 9 January 1989, a new product could be patented in Italy: *Combibatch*. Thanks to this material hundreds of thousands of red, green and yellow seats finally came off the production lines. The first seat was of course fitted in San Siro Stadium, which is today known as Giuseppe-Meazza Stadium, in Milan. Fans even sat on these seats in the Stadio Olimpico in Rome, when on 8 July 1990 the German team under their coach Franz Beckenbauer became world champions after defeating Argentina 1:0. It says much for the efficiency and quality that 20 years after the events just described the spectators at the last World Cup in South Africa likewise sat on stadium seats for which Clariant is responsible.

The strategy 'Clariant 2010'

In November 2006, after six months of evaluation, Secher presented his new strategy under the motto *Clariant 2010—Launching world-class perfor-*

Masterbatch, stadium seats

mance.[283] This contained elements of growth and innovation and a reduction in complexity and costs. The target was to achieve a much higher performance level, whilst at the same time, tightening the strings and reducing net working capital, and to position Clariant with their added value of less than 25 percent among the best competitors in the field of Specialty Chemicals. Secher intended to spend about CHF 500 million on the strategy in the coming four years.

The first stage was to generate an above peer return on invested capital by 2010. At the same time the operating margin was to rise to 9 percent. For this purpose numerous measures were introduced which included amongst other things a 25 percent cut in the number of products—at that time there were around 50,000 different products. Over and above that, 130 manufacturing sites were to be shut down. These were principally in Europe because Clariant was focussing on the fast-growing markets outside Europe such as China, India and North America. While sales and distribution were to be geared

283 Jürgen Dunsch: "Clariant streicht stellen in Europa und expandiert in Asien," in *Frankfurter Allgemeine Zeitung*, 15 Nov. 2006; Sergio Aiolfi: "Weiterer personeller Aderlass bei Clariant. Neue Wachstumsstrategie bringt den Abbau von 2.200 Stellen," in *Neue Zürcher Zeitung*, 15 Nov. 2006; Bruno Schletti: "Streichkonzert in Moll – Debüt des neuen Clariant-Dirigenten," in *Tages-Anzeiger*, 15 Nov. 2006, p. 25; Andreas Meier: "Clariant will Vielseitigkeit des Geschäfts nutzen," in *Finanz und Wirtschaft*, 18 Nov. 2006.

much more to customers and markets, functions which were necessary for all sections of the company were to be centralized. Apart from a reduction in sales costs and overheads, the strategy was to lead to further staff cuts of 10 percent by the end of 2009; however, it was hoped that redundancies could be avoided by simply not filling positions which had become vacant.

Building upon the strengths in the dye sector and in surface and performance chemicals, investments were to be made in the next four years in developing businesses that offer customers maximum added value by providing applications, advisory and solution services and for which the customer would pay accordingly. In addition Secher intended to inject the company with enhanced customer orientation.[284] More customer awareness was to be achieved by wage structures, which correspondingly put the managers under pressure.

Assistance in the implementation of this concept was offered by "best-in-class" methods for segmenting the markets and determining the value contribution. The price management system PRIMA which is geared to the needs of the company helped in optimizing pricing and added value. Besides, all sales staff was to undergo intensive training at the newly established *Clariant Academy*. To boost long-term innovative power it was planned not only to exploit the creative potential within the company but also to build on its alliances with start-up companies and universities and on an active exploration of new technologies.

Nina Baiker, a chemicals analyst at the Zurich Kantonalbank, gave Secher's reorganisation plan good marks and ascertained: "The new programme is a continuation of the previous restructuring programme CPIP."[285] This was also confirmed by Jan Secher[286] when he was asked what had happened to CPIP while he was in office. He told the *NZZ am Sonntag* on 19th November that his plans had not been rocket science, for the answers to the problems lay within the company.

While the stock exchange received the proposed new course of the company favourably with the result that the share price increased by 3 percent at times, the ambitious aim was regarded sceptically by some analysts. On account of its plans to streamline the company, Clariant was rated as a potential takeover target.[287]

At the presentation of its strategic aims in November 2006 Clariant adopted

284 Birgit Voigt: "Ein neuer Gärtner für den Clariant-Wildwuchs," in *Neue Zürcher Zeitung am Sonntag*, 19 Nov. 2006.
285 "Kahlschlag bei Clariant," in *Handelsblatt*, 14 Nov. 2006.
286 Jan Secher, 15 Mar. 2011.
287 Oliver Stock: "Clariant geht in die zweite Sparrunde," in *Handelsblatt*, 15 Nov. 2006, p. 22.

a new approach. Instead of inviting investors, analysts, journalists and employees to a conference hotel, as was the usual mode, a temporary pavilion was erected at the head office in Muttenz which was used concurrently to put the Clariant brand centre stage and boost its image. The purpose behind the new kind of presentation was to facilitate the launching of new products and services, the tapping of new markets and customer penetration. Every division and the Group Function Technology unit showed highlights from their innovation pipeline. The exhibits ranged from ceramic composites and recycling concepts for airports to the latest DVD generation for the high-definition TV format HDTV.

Secher's way of presenting his strategy *Clariant 2010* was infectious and he swept his team off its feet. Everyone was immensely impressed. The audience had the impression: Wow, for the very first time *everything* has been thought of and it is not just one part or other that has been optimized again. Yes indeed, that could work. Secher was a chap that could fill others with enthusiasm; he brought new life to the company. Many were in good spirits, convinced that the company would develop in the right direction.

After this successful event, the year ended with good news: Clariant appeared to have reached a point where, with a value adjustment of CHF 179 million, it could draw a line under the BTP adventure because it had finally got rid of the mortgage from that time. What had once promised to provide access to the life-science business, which in former times had been so sought-after, saddled the company with a goodwill the last instalment of which was not paid until the end of 2006.[288]

How Jürg Witmer came to be at Clariant

Jürg Witmer[289] had actually never had any contact to the company before he joined the Board of Directors at Clariant in 2007. It was only from the newspaper that, like others, he had learned in passing that Clariant had developed from a spin-off from Sandoz and that after the merger with Hoechst and the acquisition of BTP it could not exactly look back on a glorious history.

Specialty chemicals constituted a world with which he was entirely unfamiliar, even though his career had started in the chemicals industry in Basel.

---

288 Sergio Aiolfi: "Schlussstrich unter das BTP-Abenteuer von Clariant," in Neue *Zürcher Zeitung*, 8 Nov. 2006.
289 Interview with Jürg Witmer in Pratteln on 6 Sept. 2010.

After studying law and political science Witmer qualified as a lawyer and joined the legal department of Roche in Basel in 1978. There he soon became personal assistant to Fritz Gerber, the Chairman, who quickly recognized Witmer's potential and sent him on a career through the Roche Group lasting two decades. This took him from Hong Kong via Basel to Vienna and then to Geneva in 1999 where in his capacity as CEO he floated Givaudan in June 2000. As far as it goes, there had been practically no connection to the specialty chemicals sector in Basel.

Witmer's first personal contact to Clariant was through Peter R. Isler, who had been on the Board of Directors since 2004. When Witmer stepped down from his post as CEO at Givaudan, Isler approached him about the possibility of joining the Board of Directors at Clariant. At that point, however, the matter did not proceed any further.

In 2005 Witmer took over as President of the Givaudan Group and gained access to the vaccine industry as the designated President of the Swiss Serum- and Vaccine Institute Berna Biotech. After the company was sold off to a Dutch company, Witmer retained a temporary mandate on the Board of Directors. In 2006 he was elected onto the Board of Directors of the Syngenta Agro Group, where he became Deputy President in 2008. Thus the wheel had come full circle and Witmer was back in the chemicals industry in Basel after 22 years.

In 2007 Witmer was contacted by Roland Lösser and asked if he would be prepared to join Clariant's Board of Directors. It was known that the company was not doing well and, with his mandates at Givaudan and Syngenta, Witmer was not exactly looking for a new one. Nevertheless, he met Roland Lösser and the then CEO Jan Secher. The talk with Peter R. Isler that followed induced him to join the Board of Directors in 2007 after all, because in spite of the difficult situation in which the company found itself, he saw potential for a favourable development and the chance to make a difference in Muttenz. Furthermore, the specialty chemicals industry seemed to Witmer definitely to complement the fields of activity with which he was already familiar. Besides, he held no executive office at that time and consequently he was in a position to accept a further mandate on a Board of Directors.

What do you need?

Secher proved to be a real marketing guy so that it was possible to break away from old traditions—for example in advertising—and develop new ideas. A comparison of Clariant's self-assessment in four different phases within a period of 13 years shows a real quantum leap. In 1996, when the *Faces* posters were designed, Clariant was still searching for its 'face'; still looking for its own identity. Parallel to the collages which formed the faces, the company increasingly made use of little piles of pigments as advertisements i. e. made use of images or themes closely related to products but not solution-driven (see pages 86/87).

The acquisition of Hoechst was the stepping stone to the big, wide world so that in 1998 they could be confidently proud of the global footprint, although test tubes and safety helmets were still frequent objects in advertising. Teaming up the already existing slogan "Exactly your Chemistry" with the logo identifying Clariant was introduced around 2004. The visualisation of the expanding advisory activity as a basic part of the business and its presentation turned out to be rather generic and universal.

An adequate form of expression that succeeded in posing performance as a unique characteristic was only to become significant under Secher, when advertising devoted more and more attention to the market. In 2006 there was a so-called branding road show and on the employee platform *Connection*[290] an article appeared worldwide on the object and meaning of logos, identifiers, brand management etc.

Wirz, the Zurich advertising agency, was entrusted with the task of portraying the applications, the partnerships with customers, the products, the market advantages for sellers and the areas in which Clariant was actively engaged and where they offered solutions. In a global campaign in eight languages—including Chinese and Japanese—Clariant consequently disclosed what it actually achieved and what its advantages were. Such a campaign was practically unknown in this part of the world but the purpose was to employ image and product advertising and tacticals especially on the covers of the international finance and trade press. The already familiar crucial question 'What do you need?' which was founded on service and innovations formed a platform for advertising motifs which have by now grown to 70 in number and for a corporate 'image' film.

'Tell me what you need' was the slogan coined by Walter Vaterlaus in 1997/1998 and introduced "after various communications agencies had produced no really sparkling ideas." The claim, which is still valid today, underpins Clariant's strengths: customer orientation, customized service packages, dialogue, partnership and innovative energy.

---

290 Clariant *Connection* 3/2006, pp. 14–18.

Under Secher, regulations were enforced which meant that all advertising measures were designed, written, translated and prepared centrally, placed in a trade press title both locally and in the regions, and made available electronically. Thus it was not only the employees in charge of marketing communications at Clariant but also external booth builders, product designers and desktop publishers who had access to the web-based platform, the so-called Corporate Identity Net.

In addition to the international advertising campaign Clariant also got to the heart of its business with an 'image' film underpinning its strategic significance. A film was made about the company in which the main features of Clariant were portrayed evocatively in the style of a music video. The dynamic film, edited to be in time with the sound track of 'Heroes' by pop musician David Bowie, highlights Clariant's individual characteristics in various scenes.

Co-operation with advertising agency Wirz began in 2007 when Clariant again started to operate in the black due to a net profit of CHF 5 million. However, the profit could be mainly put down to lower taxes and a better financial result, whereas the actual profitability was still suffering from the increase in the price of raw materials and energy and in unfavourable effects from foreign-currency exchange rates. Compared to the 5 percent increase in the price of raw materials, retail prices only rose by 1 percent so that the gross margin dropped by 1.5 percent compared with the previous year. Even a reduction in sales costs and overheads could not prevent a drop in the operating profit before exceptionals.

Although the turnaround was a long time in coming, the restructuring process went according to plan. Half of the downsizing planned until 2010 was effected and the portfolio streamlined by more than 20 percent. After the Pharmaceutical Fine Chemicals Division had been sold off in the previous year, the Life Science Chemicals Division was finally dissolved and the remaining activities, i. e. Specialty Fine Chemicals, were transferred to the FUN Division. Clariant now consisted of only four divisions.

The Pigments & Additives Division was the first division where the plans to separate product-driven bulk commodities and service-driven specialties were put into operation. Similar separations were then undertaken in TLP and FUN but not in Masterbatches. The separation was not always easy to accomplish as the manufacture of specialty products was often closely related to the production of bulk commodities.

The group made two purchases in 2007: Toschem de Colombia, a supplier of chemicals and services to the oil, gas and industrial water treatment market in Columbia, and Masterandino, a manufacturer of masterbatches which was also located in Columbia. Furthermore Clariant sold off its Masterbatches, Textile, Leather and Paper businesses in Australia and its shares in Abieta Chemie GmbH in Germany. Moreover the company sold the activities of Site Services, Energy Supply, ESHA Services and Enterprise Functions of its subsidiary Industriepark Gersthofen Servicegesellschaft.

That year special emphasis was placed on personnel management. The Clariant Academy trained around 1,850 sales managers in value-based selling, an approach towards negotiating higher prices with customers based on greater added value for the customer. Very many regarded the measure with considerable scepticism and had no faith in the training course because they were afraid of losing valuable customers if prices were increased and of having to account for such losses. Secher,[291] however, encouraged his staff not to be afraid of losing customers or returning home from negotiations without an order.

Service-orientated businesses proved to be profitable and with a reduction in inventories it was possible to increase the cash flow from current operations. But for some analysts these measures did not seem to be sweeping enough to really solve the problems of the company. After the publication of the third quarterly report which lagged behind expectations, one financial expert imagined in a report in the *Neue Zürcher Zeitung*[292] that Clariant was an airship that was running out of fuel while the crew was still trying to repair the passenger seats.

At the end of the fiscal year, however, prospects for a further implementation of Secher's reorganisation programme eventually gave rise to optimism, albeit very restrained optimism, but it did help provide a slight impetus to the ailing share price.

The last of the "first men appointed"

In February 2008, only nine months after accepting a mandate on the Board of Directors at Clariant, Jürg Witmer found himself faced unexpectedly with the choice of succeeding Chairman Roland Lösser who was retiring for personal reasons.

---

291 Jan Secher, 15 Mar. 2011.
292 Sergio Aiolfi: "Jan Sechers Sanierungsplan für Clariant," in Neue *Zürcher Zeitung*, 28 Dec. 2007.

To start with, Lösser was the man who, as CEO, had made a decided contribution to Clariant's fortunes over many years. After his objections to the acquisition of BTP had fallen on deaf ears, he stuck to his decision to step down from office and to retain only his mandate on the Board of Directors. However—it is almost an irony of fate—when Clariant was plunged into a crisis by BTP, Lösser was the one chosen to step in. He accepted the challenge to take over the reins as CEO and get the company out of the mess. Due to his efforts he succeeded in refinancing and more or less put Clariant back on its feet.

Lösser was one of the "Founding Fathers." Under the guidance of Rolf W. Schweizer and in the company of Martin Syz, Hanspeter Knöpfel, Peter Brandenberg, Herbert Link and Albert Hug, he boarded that little uncomfortable boat that was released by Sandoz like a tiny nutshell onto the high seas of the chemical industry.

Apart from Peter Brandenberg, a member of the group management who seemed to weather every storm in the company, Lösser was one of the last founding fathers and to a certain extent the only remaining leading figure: 'The Last of the Mohicans.' He was imbued with traditional habits and he was one of the old school: a German with a Sandoz heart beating in his chest, as was still said of him even 12 years after Sandoz had ceased to exist. Nevertheless, his people followed him, obeyed him and he was mostly indulgent and forbearing towards them.

The turning point

At the time when Witmer[293] was confronted with the choice of succeeding Lösser as Chairman, three analysts at Vontobel[294] rated Clariant among potential Swiss takeover targets in 2008/2009. Although he was advised by many not to jeopardize his reputation by becoming chairman of a company in financial difficulty, Witmer decided to accept the challenge but on condition that he could have a say in replacements for the Board of Directors. With Lösser's retirement and the departure of Tony Reis and Kajo Neukirchen from office, there was a natural gap in the Board of Directors, which he hoped to turn to good use.

---

293 Corinne Amacher: "Machtnetz von Jürg Witmer: Chemische Verbindungen," in *Bilanz* 21/2009, 20 Nov. 2009.
294 Vontobel Equity Research (Ed.): *Aktienmarkt Schweiz*, 15 Feb. 2008.

Following the ordinary Annual General Meeting of 10th April 2008 Jürg Witmer took over from Roland Lösser as Chairman. As agreed with the designated Vice-Chairman Rudolf Wehrli, Witmer suggested three new members, Carlo G. Soave, Dominik Köchlin and Hariolf Kottmann for the three future vacancies. Moreover he asked for a certain freedom to act in his capacity as Chairman: "The worst thing you can do is acquire responsibilities without also having the opportunity to achieve something," Witmer comments.

And so a successful Swiss entrepreneur took the helm as the new Chairman and everyone hoped that after many turbulent years Clariant could get back on an even keel and move forward financially under its own steam.

The new chairman had already announced in advance that the restructuring and cost-cutting measures set out in Jan Secher's strategy *Clariant 2010* were to be continued. However, as these were unlikely to be adequate, there would, in addition, have to be some serious, fundamental thinking on the entire Clariant portfolio. "In the short term these decisions could be painful, but in the long term they ought to pay off," Witmer told the *Handelszeitung*.[295]

Unlike CEO Jan Secher, who a few months earlier had compared Clariant with an aeroplane which is about to take off but still gathering speed on the runway,[296] Witmer was more cautious in his comments and wanted to give the new Board of Directors enough time to examine the situation thoroughly. Basically, however, there were many things he called into question.

In the first six months of 2008 the company continued to systematically implement the strategy set out in *Clariant 2010*. Of the planned 2,200 job cuts 1,800 had been shed by mid-year. Following the target "price over volume," all four divisions continued to raise prices perceptibly, which in many areas enabled the company to compensate for an increase of 11 percent in the price of raw materials. Furthermore, great efforts were made to steer unprofitable businesses back into the black or else to give them up.

In the Pigments & Additives Division it was mainly the coatings business which recorded the strongest growth in turnover thus retaining the gross margin generated in the same period of the year before. The profitability of the TLP Division was impaired by a drop in volume and by the sharp rise in the price of raw materials in the paper business. Moreover, a drop in demand in all three divisions led to a decrease in turnover, especially in North America and Europe, which could not be offset by the favourable growth in some major Asian markets.

295 Valentin Handschin: "Neuer Präsident stellt vieles in Frage," in *Handelszeitung*, 4 Mar. 2008.
296 Valentin Handschin: "Clariant ist bereit zum Durchstarten," in *Handelszeitung*, 17 Oct. 2007, no. 42, p. 7.

The Masterbatches Division had to struggle with the slowdown in the economic trend and a drop in demand particularly in the USA but in Europe and Asia, too. This applied principally to the automotive market, whilst the business conditions in retail markets for packaging and consumer goods remained stable as these were less subject to cyclical influences. With selective price rises the division managed to offset the rise in the cost of raw materials and to increase the gross margin compared with the same period of the year before. What is more, with Rite Systems and Ricon Colors, Clariant acquired two leading suppliers of masterbatches in the USA. These acquisitions were to strengthen the position in the market segments packaging and consumer goods.

Due to the sharp focussing on markets connected with infrastructure and basic consumer requirements, FUN was perceptibly less impaired by the global economic slowdown. Clariant also moved the head office of its global business divisions Oil Services and Mining Services to Houston, Texas to bring them even nearer to the oil-services market which was booming due to the high demand for energy worldwide.

Mid-year there were signs that the Clariant share would be excluded from the Swiss Market Index (SMI).[297] Clariant reacted with deliberate composure to the imminent exclusion. "It would not have any great impact on us," Chief Communication Officer Arnd Wagner claimed and added that the market had already expected this scenario in the previous summer. Besides, Clariant primarily boasted major institutional investors for whom it was a matter of indifference in which index the share was included. However, this view was contradicted by observers, who stated that it was definitely important whether a share was included on the best-known share index in Switzerland or not: on the one hand many private investors are oriented towards the leading index which contains the 20 largest and most liquid shares in Switzerland and on the other hand, the guidelines of certain pension funds or investment funds prescribe that investments may only be made in companies which are represented on the SMI. Then on 7 July 2008 it finally happened: Clariant no longer had a place on the Swiss Market Index, because it had been ousted by the biotech company Actelion from Allschwil.[298]

Only a few days after Clariant was excluded from the SMI, the new Chairman—after being in office for only three months—suggested at an annual management meeting of the Board of Directors in Brunnen at the Vierwaldstättersee that they replace the CEO.

---

297 Valentin Handschin: "Actelion vor Grosserfolg," in *Basler Zeitung*, 4 Jul. 2008.
298 Carla Palm: "Bankaktien weiter zurückgeworfen – Actelion verdrängt Clariant aus SMI," in *Finanz und Wirtschaft*, 9 Jul. 2008.

Although it had been sensed since Witmer's taking up office as Chairman in April that he could not always agree with Secher on future strategy, the CEO's resignation came as a surprise to the general public. Witmer gave his reasons[299] for the change in leadership in a press release and was available to answer questions from the press: Secher had made a decisive contribution to the reorientation of the company but facts had to be faced. Witmer had undertaken an in-depth assessment of the situation with the Board of Directors and had come to the conclusion that in view of the changes in the economic environment a step forward had to be taken in order to strengthen performance management and to create sustainable added value through innovations, too. Securing this sustainability had top priority. For this reason Witmer thought the time had come for the reins to be handed over to a personality with management experience in Specialty Chemicals. The Chairman told the press[300] that it was entirely a question of who was best able to develop Clariant further in the changing economic environment. In his eyes, Hariolf Kottmann seemed to be the ideal solution for this position: to imbue the company with a new spirit.

The former candidate

Two years before Hariolf Kottmann[301] took office as CEO of Clariant on 1 October 2008, he had been approached by a headhunter because Capvis Private Equity Partners in Switzerland was looking for a German chemicals manager for the Board of Directors of their subsidiary SF-Chemie in Muttenz. SF-Chemie had been established under the name of Säurefabrik Schweizerhall in 1917 as the joint manufacturing plant of Sandoz, Ciba, Geigy and the chemical factories of Schweizerhall and Uetikam. After the spin-off of Clariant and Syngenta, the company had been owned by both but was sold to Capvis in 2004.

Kottmann was selected and as a member of the Board of Directors at SF-Chemie met Rudolf Wehrli in 2006, when the latter became Chairman there. The former CEO of Gurit was no stranger to Kottmann because as chairman of SGL Carbon he had once met Wehrli for a lengthy talk to test the waters regarding a possible takeover of Gurit.

299 Clariant *Press Release*, 4 Sept. 2008; Franziska Pfitser: "Jürg Witmer erläuterte seine Gründe für den Führungswechsel," in *Finanz und Wirtschaft*, 6 Sept. 2008, p. 21.
300 Valentin Handschin: "Die Chemie-Gerüchteküche brodelt," in *Basler Zeitung*, 6 Sept. 2008.
301 Hariolf Kottmann, 1 Sep. 2010.

After about a year SF-Chemie was sold and the Board of Directors was dissolved. For a while Kottmann lost sight of Wehrli but then in November 2007 he had a phone call from him. Wehrli was by then on Clariant's Board of Directors and made Kottmann an offer that he should join, too. Having received consent from SGL Carbon Hariolf Kottmann took up his mandate on the Board of Directors at Clariant in Muttenz in April 2008.

In July of the same year, a strategy meeting of SGL Carbon which was to take place in Asia clashed with a similar Clariant event which was to take place in Brunnen at Vierwaldstättersee. At the end of July Kottmann met Jürg Witmer who wished to inform him of the results of the meeting. Witmer took the opportunity to inquire whether he would be interested in succeeding Jan Secher. Kottmann accepted the offer and has been in office as Chief Executive Officer at Clariant since October 2008.

Corporate culture

The success of a company does not depend on mere economic factors but is fundamentally influenced by its culture, too. In view of wide geographical diversification it is useful to know how people in other cultures think. One would actually think that with increasing globalisation corporate cultures shaped by national identity would lose significance. But what happens when there is already a lack of communication between direct neighbours?

In the two years of extensive investigations for this book, the author has met no one who would have claimed that Rolf W. Schweizer had managed to invest the new group with its own identity and culture. But what does identity consist of; what is the meaning of corporate culture?

Corporate culture[302] underlies all the norms, values and attitudes which shape the behaviour of the employees and thus the image of a company. These are reflected in the visible structures and processes, which for example find expression in the manners, the language and the clothing of the employees, in the architecture, the furnishings and equipment of the buildings, in the technology, the design of business documents, and also in the anecdotes and stories which circulate. All these criteria also impact on dealing with external business partners and create the picture the general public has of a company.

The creation of a corporate culture must unite the three main currents in the modern company: corporate targets, employee satisfaction and customer orientation—the better these are coordinated, the better the company can assert itself on the market.

---

302 See Violeta Nareski: *Zum Einfluss der Unternehmenskultur auf die Motivation der Mitarbeiter in der New Economy*, Hamburg 2003, p. 56 ff.

It shouldn't cost anything

Schweizer's motto was: It should not cost anything. Consequently everything was limited to the bare essentials and so there was little room for cultural matters which could have promoted a community spirit. Schweizer was a technocrat: that is how Felix Erbacher described him on a number of occasions.

Thrift and thinking in terms of frugality were meant to find their way into all business divisions and that applied to office routine, too. After the IPO, for example, Clariant continued to make use of Sandoz's customary business paper and printed matter; the old blue logo was merely pasted over with the new four-coloured Clariant logo. Many a customer may well have drawn his own conclusions when he received such a document.

For this reason the advertising department, which was later dissolved, produced self-adhesive memo-pads for the textile dyes and chemicals business. These were attached to the brochures, which were originally intended for use by Sandoz, before they were sent to customers. Each sticker had the following notice printed on it in three languages: "Auch wenn wir einen neuen Namen tragen, haben wir etwas gegen Verschwendung. Deshalb benützen wir das vorhandene Material, bevor wir neues produzieren.—Un nouveau nom n'est pas synonyme de gaspillage: les stocks des documents existants seront donc

Self-adhesive note appealing for economy, 1995–1997

épuisés.—We've changed our name, but hate to be wasteful. That's why we're using the old before we bring in the new."

This was meant to tell the customers: our name might be Clariant now but you are receiving the old Sandoz brochure because the new catalogue with the Clariant logo will not be produced until the old ones have been used up. Vaterlaus was annoyed that even years later some Sandoz brochures were still being used and in the end, after minor rebranding i. e. after Hoechst was taken over by Clariant, issued an ultimatum to head of the division Hans Peter Piringer to scrap the left-overs once and for all.

But economy was of the utmost importance in other areas, too. In the works canteen there was a sign which said: 'Only one napkin per customer, please,' or in the washrooms the following could be read: 'One paper towel is enough to dry two hands.'

Self-promotion

Corporate culture also means the perception you have of yourself i. e. what you think of yourself, how you see yourself in the public eye and how you present yourself visually. An impression of Clariant's perception of itself is revealed in the *Faces*,[303] the posters with a face from 1996—not a particularly attractive sight.

How Clariant expressed its own performance tended to be rather modest initially. Felix Erbacher[304] recalls that the group's press conference on financial statements was a decidedly tame affair in the beginning. The first conferences took place in Muttenz, but then Rolf W. Schweizer moved them to Basel. Reinhard Handte also held them in Basel.

Why a global company held its press conference on financial statements in the back of the beyond, and not where the stock exchange on which it was listed was situated, can be explained by the fact that "Clariant was always a little anxious; it was not a big company as far as Swiss economic journalists were concerned. It was argued that if the conference were held in Muttenz or Basel, then the journalists from Zurich would not come to Basel," Erbacher reports. Roland Lösser was the first to present his figures in Zurich, at the World Trade Center in Oerlikon.

303   Cf. images on pp. 86/87.
304   Felix Erbacher, 26 Feb. 2010.

The law of mass action

When the Chemicals Division was managed by Martin Syz [305] and still belonged to Sandoz, there was an excellent working atmosphere even though the employees were always under pressure from Marc Moret to deliver outstanding performance. Even after Clariant was established, the employees were still part of a close-knit community, in which there was trust and no envy. The employees were proud of their comparatively small Swiss company. Therefore, many found it strange when, after the merger with Hoechst's Specialty Chemicals, numerous new colleagues joined the company and suddenly there were almost 21,000, i. e. twice as many, German employees to 8,500 Swiss. "That is the law of mass action, as the chemist would say, and integration is difficult," Martin Syz recalls. It was not easy to find a common spirit and sense of direction.

Nevertheless, the Chairman and the outgoing CEO gave the good news in April 1998 that integration had been completed. Paul Gemperli,[306] the experienced fiscal policy maker from St. Gallen who rightly described the merger as "too big", believes that people may have been too ready to accept the verbal declaration: "We are integrated; we have merged the two cultures." However, he personally never had the decided impression that the integration and merger of the two cultures had really taken place. His perception of the matter was rather that there were Germans on one side and Swiss on the other side of the Board of Directors and an in-depth discussion was hardly possible.

Gemperli was proud of being on the Board of Directors of a company whose turnover suddenly soared from CHF two billion to about ten billion. "Turnover and total assets rose perceptibly; that was impressive and was very gratifying, but occasionally I was worried that I did not have enough overview of what Hoechst, with all its associated companies, was contributing. Perhaps that is why merging was not tackled aggressively enough."

The Board of Directors was of the opinion that if you started to look properly, then you would find that the whole thing was too big to gain a real idea of. Gemperli retired from the Clariant Board of Directors at the end of the fiscal year 1998, i. e. in March 1999. It is worth noting that Steve Hannam describes the situation that he experienced in person as of March 2000 in just the same way as the fiscal policy maker from St. Gallen did.

305 Martin Syz, 10 Dec. 2009.
306 Paul Gemperli, 24 Jun. 2010.

Herculean task

Quite a number of mergers fail because employees' interests are ignored. Integrating Hoechst did not fail but rather it was an unprecedented Herculean task that was not tackled with the necessary courage and determination.

The clash of the two corporate cultures triggered enormous conflicts especially since the differences were not identified and their significance was ignored. Setting a target to unite the two businesses under one roof by a certain date and to change the name plates and logos on the buildings is still a long way from integration in the social sense and certainly not at a human level. Only a person who identifies with the culture of the other on account of the situation he or she finds him- or herself in and in the ideal case adopts it as his/her own or who finds common ground with his or her partner can be satisfied. This was not the case at Clariant in the 20th century.

The cultural divergences delayed a successful merger; a common third culture[307] was not built up systematically but only emerged under rather painful circumstances. The common aim to survive at all costs united the 'children' of 'old' Clariant and Specialty Chemicals Hoechst, both of whom had been cast off by their 'mothers,' but it took a long time for them to become partners and share a common vision. The two partners managed to survive due to the merger but they had not the least intention of letting go, closing old doors behind them and opening new ones together.

The Sandoz spirit lives on

An organisation functions through social networks. In the case of a merger, it is logical for those brought together to link their networks and to pull together in every way possible. An important element in integration and an indispensible tool in its implementation is clear communication.

In 1997/1998, after the merger, Schweizer travelled with Seifert through the various countries to signify: "Look, both of us have come to show you that we now belong together. So please follow suit." The controller in one of the countries where two-thirds of the turnover was generated by Hoechst and one third by Clariant recalls that the President and his CEO pointed out emphati-

---

307   See Arne König: *Die Bedeutung von Unternehmenskulturen für den Erfolg von internationalen Megafusionen*, e-book, Leuphana University Lüneburg 2003.

Production facilities in Muttenz

cally in their speech that one should make use of the best in both cultures and combine the technical and commercial strengths of both in the 'new' company. However, after the dinner which followed the event, Schweizer took him aside and said: "But you will see to it, won't you, that the Sandoz spirit lives on here, in this country?"

'Old' Clariant employees defined the Sandoz spirit self-confidently as the aggressive style of the entrepreneur. Hoechst did not possess this entrepreneurial acumen because it was very, very bureaucratic. The paths towards a decision were much longer. Once a decision was reached at Sandoz, it was implemented, end of discussion. When a decision was reached at Hoechst, then that was just the start of a discussion. In no way did Sandoz or 'old' Clariant have this policy-making style which was peculiar to Hoechst. That was the big difference, an old hand elucidated.

For Schweizer one thing was certain: The other side had a completely different culture and he deliberately intervened by drumming into his own people: "You are here to see to it that the old Sandoz spirit doesn't die out." Why stir up the spirit of persistence at the beginning of a huge integration challenge?

Discrepancies

A further discrepancy in the integration process, which was not concealed in any way but openly expressed in normal language, was the officially used but incorrect term for the business which had been effected. The deal between Clariant and Hoechst was in actual fact an acquisition which Clariant made by buying the specialty chemicals business from Hoechst. For *tactical* reasons the word 'acquisition' was rarely used. The Hoechst men were not to be given the feeling of having been acquired: instead there was only ever talk of a 'merger.' For political reasons, that was a deliberate euphemism. The situation was thus politely glossed over as if Clariant wanted to apologise for the takeover.

Merger, takeover, acquisition—in the end individual feeling eclipses every technical definition and the need for recognition makes itself felt. For example, Seifert said to Lösser on many occasions: "My dear Roland, you didn't buy Hoechst. We sold ourselves to Clariant because we wanted to get away from Hoechst; because we saw the chance to go public immediately and to get decent salaries in Swiss francs. It wasn't you who bought us. It was we who ensured that we were bought by Clariant!"[308]

In analysing the constellation of that time, the question arises whether at that period another company of a similar size might have been interested in Hoechst's Specialty Chemicals or might have bought this traditional chunk with Seifert at its head? Seifert ponders for a moment, leans back in his chair and replies: "There was absolutely no one. I had talks with companies like Ciba and Hüls in Marl. They all declined."

A further contrast between the two merged companies was how they dealt with money: While Clariant was always very cautious when it came to expenditure and also paid relatively low salaries, the Hoechst men had lived in

---

308 Karl-Gerhard Seifert, 3 Feb. 2010/20 May 2010.

greater style and smiled to some extent at the austerity measures of their Swiss colleagues. Indeed they did not want to give up such privileges as a company car and a generous expense account. Besides, some Hoechst managers had a clause in their contracts which ensured first-class travel by plane. Once, at a fiscal meeting on efficiency and cost effectiveness, Lösser is said to have declared in front of everyone: "Gentlemen, I, too, only fly business class; I don't have to fly first class." That just shows how different the two cultures were when it came to cost awareness.

Communication

In autumn 1995 Walter Vaterlaus joined Clariant as Chief Communications Officer and Secretary to the Board of Management and left the company in mid-2001 whereupon the management of Corporate Communications was taken over by Philipp Hammel, who had been Head of Investor Relations since 1996.

Afterwards Patrick Kaiser[309] joined Clariant and looked after the Communications Department but left the company when Lösser took over from Handte as CEO. As an interim measure the department was placed under Peter Brandenberg, the Head of Human Resources, until a suitable replacement could be found: Walter Vaterlaus re-entered Clariant as spokesman in 2003 and stayed until Jan Secher introduced a new communication style within the company in the person of Arnd Wagner.

Communications from Clariant quite often aroused expectations which were not fulfilled. It always sounded a little as if at any moment the big breakthrough would happen, the sudden new start, the huge cost savings—but the promises never had any impact on the profit and loss account. Especially after acquiring BTP, Clariant adhered to this line for a considerable time. Vaterlaus distanced himself from this practice by saying "No thank you" when Schweizer asked him to stay after all.

All in all communication was less proactive or strong; much of the work was outsourced and given to agencies. Of course, there were also positive examples. When Hoechst was permitted to place its shares on the market, many thought that the transaction would have a decidedly negative impact on the share price but the secondary offering passed off quite positively: Liquidity on

---

309   Cf.: "Patrick Kaiser – der neue Mann bei Corporate Communications," in *Palette* 3/2002, p. 9.

the market suddenly expanded significantly which was certainly due to good communications, which together with Investor Relations made a remarkable contribution.

Seed without soil

At Clariant, no position at the top was filled so frequently and as diversely as the Head of Human Resources. It is also true that today nearly all the former HR managers are rather embarrassed when they speak of the circumstances in which they discharged their duties. Scarcely one of them worked in the job full-time; personnel matters were an appendage to the other tasks in hand.

The reason for this procedure was to be found in the spin-off in 1995: not one of the leading staff in Human Resources at Sandoz had remained at Clariant but had changed to Novartis. It is no secret that the issue most shabbily treated at Clariant was personnel matters. The saying 'Seed without soil' is probably particularly apt for a company where Human Resources have been neglected to such an extent. There was an endless coming and going of personnel managers and in the so-called pioneering days i. e. in the phase between IPO and BTP, head office was not very responsive to the topic of systematic training programmes for talented new blood.

IT specialist Heiner Meier[310] for example, who had worked at Sandoz under Marc Moret as an in-house auditor in the overhead value analysis as of 1981, was the second person to hold the post of personnel manager after Ruedi Muehlemann—but not for long, because when Hoechst was taken over by Clariant, he felt extremely uncomfortable as the buffer between the extremely divergent opinions of Rolf W. Schweizer and Karl-Gerhard Seifert. He says himself that he would have worn himself out sooner or later and was delighted to be able to move to the USA as Head of Finance.

Meier was actually at home in the IT department, but even an experienced HR expert could not fail to notice that the field of human resources development at Clariant was of secondary importance. The same thing happened to the former Hoechst employee Claus Hefner,[311] when he joined Clariant in 1998. Prior to that he had spent two years working for Hoechst in Asia where

310   Interview with Heiner Meier in Muttenz on 1 Mar. 2010.
311   Interview with Claus Hefner in Muttenz on 16 Feb. 2010.

his job was to look for workers, train them and bind them to the company. Upon his return, Hefner assumed responsibility for recruiting and for HR development at Clariant Germany. He still vividly recalls the first presentation that he gave with Personnel Manager Alexander Klak in Muttenz almost six months later. The aim was to explain to the staff responsible for HR work in Switzerland and a few other countries what was understood by personnel work in Germany and to give them an overview of the seminars held in the past.

On this occasion a Swiss colleague took the opportunity to ask: "When do you actually start in a company to deal with human resources and skills development?" Hefner did not need to think long about how he would answer the questions because as far as he was concerned human resources and skills development began the moment an employee entered the company. He also regarded the probationary period as an important phase to ease the new staff member into the company and its culture so that he could feel at ease. Hefner quickly realized that there was a completely different philosophy in Switzerland when his colleague replied that it took six to eight years to see what an employee's potential was. Only when it was clear what the employee was capable of, did the company begin to invest in him or her.

In order to accelerate the integration process, the Germans would have welcomed much closer co-operation, especially at the beginning, which would have made it easier for everyone to get to know each other and would also have facilitated the exchange of staff. But it was only from 2000/2001 onwards that the issue of human resources was gradually perceived as a task to be shared.

The frequent change in the global management of human resources must have been a definite disadvantage for the entire group: HR was a function without clearly defined parameters. Developing a common culture and a common system for personnel work would have required at least three years or even longer. Hefner, however, remembers that there was a new global HR manager every eighteen months or so, which inevitably led to overthrowing existing systems and to introducing new approaches.

Heiner Meier, who supervised the period of acquisition, was relieved when he was able to get rid of his job as Personnel Manager in Muttenz after about two years. He was replaced by a successor from outside the company. Jürg Helg came from the insurance sector and brought with him some very advanced approaches, especially in the field of further training. However, there were differences of opinion with the Board of Management as to how this should be implemented and since he was not allowed to put his ideas into action, he left the enterprise after only eighteen months. In 2001 his post was assumed by a

Frenchman, François Note, who likewise only stayed one and a half years and then changed to CFO on the Board of Management. Thereupon the post was filled by Dominik von Bertrab, who worked with great commitment but gave it up two years later after being promoted to Head of the Masterbatches Division. After Peter Brandenberg had held the post of global HR manager also for a mere two years, Johann Steiner, a young compensation and benefits specialist, was eventually appointed in 2006. Steiner joined Clariant in the Lösser era. At the same time, he was the first personnel manager to become, under Secher, a member of the Board of Management. In this period, various HR concepts for staff in the top management were systematized globally, but it was also overshadowed by several huge waves of restructuring and downsizing.

In retrospect Hefner has the impression that for a long time human resource management at Clariant was regarded as nothing but an administration and service department which was responsible for hiring and firing and payroll accounting while the management, training and development of employees never progressed beyond the initial stages. This may have been suitable when 'old' Clariant with its 8,000 employees was still manageable, but it is no longer advisable when a company exceeds a certain size. In this case, it may have been that perceptions on both sides had become contorted: on the one side there were the Hoechst staff with their many tools, systems and structures which were geared towards a group with 160,000 employees, on the other side the comparatively small 'old' Clariant that knew its people and had to pay more attention to cost containment.

Demoralised

The constellation of Clariant-BTP was a disastrous alliance: The acquisition of the British company not only brought the Muttenz employees to the brink of financial ruin but also had a completely demoralising effect on the staff. Schweizer risked a great deal, particularly the trust of his staff. Personal ties and personnel management practices did not exist and those who held the post of HR Manager did not possess the expertise of a personnel manager. Thus was no one in periods of crisis to support the employees and give them adequate advice, which only aggravated the situation even more.

Things had gone too far and faith in the company had been destroyed. In the period after the BTP deal, numerous competent employees turned their backs on the firm. Many who would have made good managers felt they had been well and truly betrayed; they were deeply shocked that BTP had been purchased at all and that Steve Hannam had not only been made a Divisional Manager but a member of the Board of Directors into the bargain.

The BTP business, which became a millstone round the company's neck, is roundly condemned by the majority nowadays. The topic is still cloaked in secrecy. When anyone involved at the time speaks of BTP, the listener is aware of feelings of anger, reserve and inner conflict. There is mention of laboratories with clay floors; there is talk of pre-war generators and of a leaking, seeping dam in the conurbation of Manchester; there is reference to an unethical product with bleaching propensities. Rumours, legend, or simple fact?

A two-headed monster

As we already find ourselves in the realm of fables, we can report on the two-headed monster which was at home at Clariant for seven years. This imperceptible being was not the product of the imagination but inconceivable reality.

As a result of the retainment clause a single precarious situation developed after the Hoechst deal, because Clariant was ruled doubly for seven years and during this period, unparalleled things happened. The 'new' Clariant suffered enormously from merger syndrome,[312] which was characterised by demotivation, stress, frictional losses and counter-productivity. Added to this there was a large portion of cynicism which nipped many things in the bud.

There are frequent reports that the men from Hoechst did what they wanted and the Swiss in Muttenz just sat there with mouths wide open saying: "But it was we who bought you. You should be doing what we want and not the other way round." The Muttenz employees were completely bewildered and could not quite grasp what was happening even though it was they who were actually the bosses. This situation led to high degree of frustration among the Swiss and the Hoechst men did not make the slightest effort to avoid it. Quite often the Swiss were met with smiles of derision and arrogance. They could read the attitude in the others' faces: You are not capable of running this company.

The two-headed monster nourished the opposition from the colleagues in Sulzbach to the extent that they behaved really counter-productively when they came to briefings at head office. New arrangements were made in Mut-

---

312   See Kerstin Barnikel: *Post-Merger Integration*, e-book, Ludwig-Maximilian-University, Munich, 2006.

tenz but no sooner were the managers sitting in the plane on their way back to Frankfurt than they laughed at the parameters which had been decided on and brought out their own, old figures.

Monkey cage

With CPIP and 'Prinzipal' or rather the end of the seven-year retainment clause, the double-headed monster was finally disposed of and Clariant's secret head office in Sulzbach was disbanded. Clearly, the move was a late but essential step towards integration. It was only after innumerable calamities— such as the failed merger with Ciba, BTP, and disinvestment—that the two cultures finally started to merge.

During the 'Basel Day' those who were relocating had no contact to the future colleagues in Muttenz; they only met with those who had been appointed to look after them or were part of the organisation team. Even today female employees who were working in the management block that day complain that behind the closed windows of Building 907 they felt as if they were in a monkey cage when this crowd of guests arrived at the factory premises. Curiosity and very probably pleasure but also reservations, when faced with the new and unknown, triggered a desire to make contact, which was, however, considered undesirable at that point. The staff was not even allowed to go into the yard but had to continue to work in the offices while Armin Meile, the manager of the site, welcomed the 250 guests and took them on a sightseeing tour of the area and a guided tour of the plant.

It is amazing how a decision can arouse such different feelings: some were offended and perhaps even suspicious, others enjoyed the invitation and made hopeful plans for the future. Most of those who had come from Frankfurt regarded the two days in Basel in a very favourable light and mainly remember that at the different stages—whether professional, organisational or cultural— food and drink were plentiful.

Entertaining

Rolf W. Schweizer was one who at a personal level maintained a close relationship to his top people. Within the company there was a very special circle of people he occasionally entertained at his home in Oberwil and who report in appreciative remembrance that the host, with an apron on, stood in the kitchen cooking for his guests. His son, Juerg Schweizer,[313] only grins when he hears that and describes his mother's efforts beforehand to ensure that her husband could take up his pose—sometimes with an apron on and sometimes with the carving set in his hands—just before the guests arrived. He relied entirely on his wife to organise everything in the background and cater for the wellbeing of the guests. The evenings usually ended in the 'grotto'—the bar in the cellar. It was said that whoever belonged to the chosen few had made it. There were not very many who enjoyed this honour and as a rule it was the so-called 'territorial rulers,' the heads of group companies, who Schweizer favoured with his recognition.

One of those in the circle of favoured few, still in Sandoz times, was the Italian Toni Saletti from Sarma, who was the initiator of the stadium seats for the World Cup in Italy in 1990. It is possible that Schweizer's enthusiasm for the masterbatch sector and the special promotion of this division stem from there. After the IPO the circle of those who were entertained included Nico Gontha, responsible for Indonesia; Donat Autsch, likewise responsible for Indonesia and also for Hong Kong, Japan and Mexico; Hans Wyss was responsible for Spain; Raymond Bilger was in charge of Turkey; Farhat Mirza managed the National Company Pakistan and Ken Brewton represented the USA, to name but some of the favoured few.

Manoeuvrable mass

Rolf W. Schweizer was almost invisible to most of the staff that did not belong to the top management and to those who worked in production. They were more likely to set eyes on Handte, and Lösser was everywhere. Secher, for example, even joined the staff in the canteen. Schweizer, by contrast, maintained a low profile and avoided public appearances. There were employees who had never met him personally, not even at employee meetings but had at most caught a glimpse of him at a press conference or on the intranet. But this was not enough to be able to get an idea of what he was like. On the other hand, Schweizer had very specific ideas about his people and did not mince his words when he talked about them.

---

313   Telephone conversation with Juerg Schweizer on 2 Jun. 2011.

After the failed merger with Ciba, at Carnival time, he was asked by *Cash*[314] about the negotiations with DyStar, which had come to nothing. The economics magazine asked: "What about the motivation of the employees in Switzerland? Originally Clariant wanted to sell the textile dye unit. Just because you aren't getting the price you wanted, you are keeping the division. The people must feel like a sheer manoeuvrable mass."

Schweizer pointed out the resilience of the Clariant employees by referring to a historical factor: "The employees in the Dye Division are former Sandoz people. There have been plans, twelve times already, to sell Sandoz Dyes—and they are still alive. These employees have developed a thick skin in the meantime. Besides, the earnings position in the dye unit is good. That is additional motivation."

But do the employees of a division which has been up for sale twelve times still feel motivated or is it not more likely that they are resigned and have inwardly handed in their notice long since? Surely, that is the question here.

Colours

Dyes were a highly sensitive matter both at Sandoz and at Hoechst; in fact they were virtually a political issue. 'Dye' was a word with strong emotional connotations especially at the River Main: with the label "Höchst the Colour Town"[315] the local government wanted to deflect from the image of a putrid chemicals location and instead arouse the positive feelings which the word 'colour' evokes.

Even Goethe[316] highlighted in his *Theory of Colours* the sensual-ethical effect of colour, which in its great diversity has a great attraction independent of its composition or its material properties. That is why colour as an element of art can be used to realise the highest aesthetic objectives.

'Rotfabriker' (red dye factory worker) is a traditional term and also an epithet for everyone who worked at the dye works in Hoechst, later Hoechst AG. In the manufacture of fuchsine, but also of aldehyde green, very fine emissions of dye developed in the factory and these pigment crystals even penetrated the skin. They could not be removed properly even by thorough washing but

---

314 Judith Raupp/Victor Weber, 1999.
315 Blum 1991.
316 Johann Wolfgang von Goethe: *Philosophische und naturwissenschaftliche Schriften No. 758, 1808–1810*, Edition Elibron Classics, Adon Media Corporation 2006, pp. 76–117, p. 89.

were gradually exuded through the pores, which usually took three or four days.[317] "I can still remember the time when my grandfather was employed in the dye works and he would sometimes come home red, green, blue or yellow. We children thought it was great fun," former keeper of Hoechst's archives Wolfgang Metternich,[318] who experienced the company in the third generation, relates. When the men came home from work on a winter evening, they left a long red trail in the snow.

Today pigment crystals—and not just red tones but also lilac and yellow for trendy products or their packaging—are still manufactured in the Main metropolis. However, the label 'Rotfabriker' lost its actual meaning after the Second World War because this method of producing dyes stopped when self-contained, tightly sealed oxidation and reduction systems were introduced during the 1950s.

Factory museum *Unicum*

As with Hoechst there were also stories and objects at Sandoz and later at Clariant which were related to dyes; moreover, there is a place where their history has found a home: a museum.

In the mid-1980s, Cesare Sgueglia, an employee in the waste disposal department at Sandoz and its subsidiary MBT, came in contact, again and again, with old discarded objects which were to be got rid of. His first find was a pair of old wooden scales which he liked so well that he—contrary to regulations— put them aside and saved them from being scrapped.

Together with his colleague Rolf Buchschacher, who shared Sgueglia's passion for collecting and his fondness for relicts from the past, he amassed a considerable collection of old technical gadgets and instruments, documents and other objects in the plants in Muttenz and Basel over the years. In his leisure time Sgueglia restored the equipment, colleagues carefully helped repair parts and others procured missing operating instructions. A photograph and a brief description of each object and the story relating to it were

---

317 Wolfgang Metternich: *Die städtebauliche Entwicklung von Höchst am Main*, Frankfurt a. M. 1990, p. 85.
318 Interview with Wolfgang Metternich in Kriftel on 3 Mar. 2010. The sobriquet for the company and its employees developed soon after 1863. It is known that at that time housewives in Hoechst complained that the washing left on the "Schützenbleiche" right beside the factory to be bleached was soiled by dyes. However, that not only applied to the washing, it also applied to the workers, Metternich reports; Bäumler 1988.

stored in a data bank. To make their treasures available to a wider public, the two collectors, with the help of colleague Jean-Pierre Zürcher and with the consent of Clariant's Board of Management, set up an exhibition in the basement of Building 906 in Muttenz: thus a collection of historical exhibits was born which was appropriately named *Unicum*. The museum opened its doors to visitors for the first time in December 1999. This journey through the company's development, which in part recalled long forgotten episodes, events and persons, was received with great interest by both employees and guests.

However, in times of a shortage of staff and a lack of resources, it became more and more difficult to maintain such a project despite the commitment of volunteers. The situation was aggravated by the waning interest on the part of the public so that in the end the institution had to be closed.

However, a wind of change blew through the rooms when research began on this book in 2009 for the stocks from the museum provided numerous sources and valuable information on the history of the company. Therefore, Clariant is at present giving thought to a viable solution for the future destination of the historic material. A search has been started for institutions that could take charge of objects of interest as bequests or as permanent loans to be passed on to posterity. A sensible relocation of the *Unicum* or a possible integration of the exhibits in a future museum of local industries would be a feasible solution.

The first step in this direction has already been taken. From May until October 2011, there was a special exhibition entitled 'Here and there. Basel in the 20th century,' in the goods depot of the station at St. Johann. It was sponsored by the two cantonal governments of the city of Basel and Basel Region, by the 'Gesellschaft für das Gute and Gemeinnützige' (the 'Society for the Good and the Charitable', a private social and cultural institution) and the Göhner foundation and had about 20 exhibits from the works museum *Unicum* on public display.

Across generations

If it were possible to make some of the objects from the *Unicum* talk, then they would tell quite a story: the piston burettes from Sandoz's own glazier's workshop, the analysis regulations from the 1920s, the pattern cards, the old company magazine the *Sandoz Bulletin* and its successor the *Palette,* which was discontinued three years ago, and even the old in-house telephone directories and lists of authorized signatures, and the two-metre-long time-worn stir stick made of acid-proof tropical wood dating from the time when Rolf W. Schweizer's father was deputy director—if all the objects in the museum could be brought to life, we would learn how many generations of families had been and still are employed at Clariant and its preceding companies.

If part of a group develops in such a way that it can exist autonomously on the market, it gets a new name, a new appearance and in no time there is a new arrival in the trade register, a 'start-up' for which the clock has been re-set to zero. But what happens to its past? Where is its early history? Do such companies and their business history fall by the wayside in historiography? Simply because the company has been given a different name does not mean that its history has dissolved into thin air. History does not end, it is not discontinued.

And what about the hundreds or thousands of employees worldwide who are in the second or third generation in the company i. e. who were or are employed at Sandoz, Hoechst and Clariant? Take Michaela Patz,[319] for example, whose grandfather Karl Patz was born in 1912 and worked as a ships fitter and cook at Meister Lucius & Brüning for 30 years and spent half his life on a barge. Does she not have a long company history?

What happens to the many years of service of people like Michaela Patz, whose other grandfather Werner Ludwig thoughtfully reminded the 16-year-old again and again: "Pet, think of your pension, go and work in the 'red factory', there you'll have a job for life!"? This grandfather, who was born in 1924, also earned his living in Höchst and as a heavy worker soldered reaction boilers for over 40 years. There was milk in the plant in abundance to neutralize the lead which had been inhaled and he frequently came home very red when he had to step in at the dye works.

As an apprentice trainee 23 years ago Patz used to go swimming with her colleagues from Pratteln in the 'Farbwerkbad' (a swimming pool donated by Farbwerke Hoechst to celebrate the 600th anniversary of the town of Höchst) in Silostrasse in Frankfurt during her lunch breaks. How does she view the company's history? Where do the boundaries lie for her? Will she say:"My company is only 15 years old"?

Can there already be talk of a company history after fifteen years, since Clariant was founded? Whoever makes plans for the future takes experiences from the past—whether consciously or not—into consideration. What applies

---

319   Report by Michaela Patz in Pratteln on 11 Oct. 2010.

to the individual can be applied to a whole organisation or company. Clariant does indeed have bold plans for the future and draws its lessons from history. Or in the words of Basel historian Jacob Burckhardt: "What was once rejoicing and misery must now become knowledge and awareness."[320]

---

320 Jacob Burckhardt: *Weltgeschichtliche Betrachtungen*, edited and with an epilogue by Rudolf Marx, 7. ed., Stuttgart 1949, p. 10.

Epilogue

Just when I had finished a rather strenuous biography of an entrepreneur, I received the following email on 20th April 2009: "Hello, Ms Bálint, I would like to talk to you about the possibility of your writing a history of the Clariant Group. Would you be interested? Kind regards, Arnd Wagner, Head of Group Communications."

I did not know the person who had sent the email and as a consumer I was even less familiar with Clariant. I would have been more likely to react to Sandoz, for its calcium tablets were a household name in my childhood. I would probably have nodded like the dyer in the backwoods of India in Herbert Link's story and said: "Ah, Sandoz, yes we know."

Naturally I googled Clariant's provenance in a matter of seconds and just like Vaterlaus when he received Schweizer's offer in 1995 I recalled the TV photos of the fire in Schweizerhalle. I was studying in the southern German town of Freiburg in 1986 and I can still remember that first November weekend; there was a smell in the air which did not come from garden leaves on a bonfire, from a barbeque or from chimneys. It was only as the day progressed that I learned from the radio what was causing the smell and later there were the haunting pictures of the fire and the dead fish floating in the Rhine.

Mr Wagner and I conferred for over two hours in Sulzbach and after that I spent weeks researching before I presented him with a 20-page outline of the project setting out the main areas of focus and the technical parameters.

I discovered a company which in a difficult market environment was trying to infuse new life into itself. Why the situation was so serious could only be understood by looking at the past. It was my task to illuminate the stony path of Clariant's beginnings. However, I did not inevitably see the company's history as starting with going public in 1995 but rather as deriving from the history of how Sandoz and Hoechst developed. That was the historical aspect.

Reports by contemporary witnesses and interviews with persons who were actively and passively engaged in the three companies at first, second and third management level and who were to describe and explain their era were to provide authenticity. The original idea was to define the themes, to compile about two-thirds of the material myself and to engage guest authors from various disciplines to write short sections on some topics.

I contacted three historians as potential guest authors—two Swiss colleagues and a German one, who were not known to me personally. My literary research and the reading of their works had attracted my attention to them. What makes them eminently suitable are the focus areas of their research, their sphere of activity and the scope of their publications; they address such topics as chemicals, dyes, industry in Basel and corporate history as a matter of course. First of all, I phoned the three gentlemen, then wrote and asked to talk to them and looked forward to meeting them in person.

In May 2009 I got in touch with Alexander Engel, 'Akademischer Rat' (Academic Councillor, comparable to an assistant professor) at the Institute for Economic and Social History at the University of Göttingen. I chose him because of his dissertation in 2009 on the emergence of modern markets for dyes.[321] Engel found my request very daring, he agreed to cooperate but without imposing any conditions. The result is the first chapter of this book.

Tobias Straumann, private lecturer at the Institute for Empirical Economic Research at the University of Zurich, wrote his dissertation on *The History of Basel Chemicals (1850–1920)*[322] which appeared in 1995. I hoped very much that he would also agree and the conversation we had in his office in December 2009 took place in a very candid atmosphere. However, Straumann drew my attention to his tight teaching schedule and a book on which he himself was working; he consequently declined with thanks.

In January 2010 I met Christian Simon of the history department at the University of Basel. He is Professor of Modern General and Swiss History and was co-editor of the anthology *Chemie in der Schweiz. Geschichte der Forschung und der Industrie* (Chemicals in Switzerland. The History of Research and Industry). For that reason he appeared to me to have the necessary knowledge of the area and its history.[323] Mr Simon listened attentively to my

321 Engel 2009.

322 Tobias Straumann: *Die Schöpfung im Reagenzglas: Eine Geschichte der Basler Chemie (1850–1920)*, (Thesis, Zurich University, 1995), Basel/Frankfurt a. Main 1995.

323 Thomas Busset/Andrea Rosenbusch/Christian Simon (Ed.): *Chemie in der Schweiz. Geschichte der Forschung und der Industrie*, Basel 1997; Christian Simon: "Chemiestadt Basel," in: *Basel, Geschichte einer städtischen Gesellschaft*, ed. Georg Kreis/Bert von Wartburg, Basel 2000, pp. 364–383.

request and his feedback on my theme was refreshingly critical. He was very forthright and I was grateful to him for being so frank with me.

I was well able to understand Simon's criticism. At the time Clariant was in bad shape: strikes outside the head office, figures in the red, redundancies and plant closures and on account of press conferences and the Annual General Meeting security forces brought in to make the strikers see reason. At head office in Muttenz, where I was allocated a forlorn corner office, I found nothing but a desk and chair, the room was cleaned once a month and I brought with me my own writing materials and paper. I was soon given an idea of what austerity measures mean.

The CEO knew my style of writing and was convinced that it packed a punch; on the other hand, the Chairman was very sceptical about the book and wanted none of it. The project was only known to a few, there was no talk of it in-house for more than nine months and as a result I was aware of many resentful glances. Consequently, I was not at all keen to meet Jürg Witmer and so I gave him a wide berth, which worked well until one day, almost a year after the project started, he happened to look into the conference room where Arnd Wagner and I were discussing the constitution of the Board of Directors at zero hour.

My chance had come: With my illustrated Big-Linkers file in my hand I introduced myself to Witmer and took the opportunity to ask him to tell me something about the great names in the economy. With a broad smile he started to leaf through the file and made one or two pithy remarks about each of the nine heads. The ice was broken and a few months later he visited me in my writing workshop where books and files containing numerous press reports were stacked on shelves and the tables were covered with text modules and the walls plastered with photographs. It was at this late stage that he came to know the project and its author more closely. Only when he read the manuscript at Christmas 2010 did he learn in detail where his company comes from, what constituted it and what it consists of. His scepticism had evaporated in the face of the interesting history of the company.

Dear Mr Witmer and Mr Kottmann, I would like to wish you and your employees all the best for the future. May your company grow and your business flourish. Clariant clareant!

Biographies

Rolf W. Schweizer

Chairman and President of the Board of Directors
July 1995 to March 2002

CEO
May 1998 to May 2001

Rolf Walter Schweizer[324] was born in Basel in 1930. After studying economics and acting as an assistant at the University of St. Gallen he obtained his doctorate[325] (Dr. of Econ., HSG) in 1958.

In the same year the fledgling economist began his professional career at Sandoz AG in Basel, where over the years he climbed the career ladder rung by rung.

His first station was the dye department. There his responsibilities included the sale and distribution of dyes in Germany and Eastern Europe. After the amalgamation of the Dye and Chemicals Divisions in 1968, Schweizer was put in charge of Global Marketing.

In 1976 Schweizer turned his back on Basel for a few years. In 1967 Sandoz had begun to break into the dietetics market and had acquired Wander AG in Bern, a food manufacturer that had made a name for itself as the producer of Ovomaltine, the malt drink also known as Ovaltine. There Rolf W. Schweizer was appointed as a Delegate of the Board of Directors and at the same time Head of the Food Division at Sandoz. It was in this capacity that he was largely instrumental in the acquisition of Wasa, the famous producers of crisp bread, in 1982.

After returning to Basel in 1983, Schweizer took over management of the Chemicals Division which apart from the pharmaceuticals business was one of the mainstays of the company and became a member of the Board of Management. The takeover of Master Builders Inc. in the USA, which laid the foundations for the expansion of Sandoz's Construction Chemicals, was effected under his aegis.

---

324   Released by Juerg Schweizer on 2 Jun. 2011.
325   Rolf W. Schweizer: *Die Einkommensdisparität zwischen der Landwirtschaft und der Industrie* (Thesis, St. Gallen, Handels-Hochschule, 1958), Winterthur 1958.

In 1988 he was promoted to the office of Deputy Chairman of the Board of Management and in 1989 finally received a mandate on the Board of Directors of Sandoz AG. Four years later he was also elected onto the Board of Directors of the Schweizerischer Bankverein. In 1993 he was appointed Head of the core business of Chemicals & Environment.

When Rolf W. Schweizer was elected as a Delegate of the Board of Directors in May 1994 and assumed the post of CEO, many regarded him as the potential successor to Chairman Marc Moret. However, history ran a different course. In the course of focussing on the life-science business, a move which Moret had planned, Sandoz spun off its Chemicals Division in 1995 and created Clariant. Marc Moret placed Rolf W. Schweizer at the head of the newly established company. Rolf W. Schweizer, by then 65 years old, was a very experienced manager of whom it was said that he was more conversant with global chemicals than anyone else in the industry. Despite the meagre facilities and equipment Clariant had received from Sandoz, the young company made good progress. Due to the acquisition of Hoechst AG's specialty chemicals branch, which was more than three times the size of Clariant, in 1997 Schweizer clinched a deal which can justifiably be described as his greatest coup and which brought him to the zenith of his career. As a result, Clariant had become a leading global player in the field of specialty chemicals.

In the following years the President made a number of attempts to secure a further deal of similar size and he almost succeeded in merging with the Specialty Chemicals Unit of competitor Ciba in 1998.

In order to gain a foothold in the field of pharmaceutical intermediate products, which were considered to be especially lucrative, Schweizer made a final major acquisition in 2000: the takeover of the British chemicals group BTP debited Clariant's balance sheet to the tune of CHF 4 billion.

In the meantime, Schweizer at 70 years of age would normally have been obliged to step down from his office as Chairman of the Board of Directors. He handed over his post as CEO, which he had held in personal union since 1995, to the former Hoechst manager Reinhard Handte in May 2001 but a suitable successor to the Chairmanship had not been found and so Schweizer—contrary to the statutes—remained in office for another year until spring 2002 when he surrendered the chair to Robert Raeber and took his well-earned retirement. Nevertheless, Rolf W. Schweizer remained associated with the company for a while: as Honorary Chairman without a vote he could continue to participate in meetings of the Board of Directors when required.

Martin Syz

CEO
July 1995 to December 1996

Martin Syz[326] was the first man to head the Board of Management of the newly established Clariant. At that point he was able to look back on a career of almost 30 years at Sandoz where in 1990 he had become a member of the Board of Management.

Born in Zurich in 1936 and raised in Wallin, Martin Syz, as the descendant of an industrialist's family, had the advantage of a solid economic background. His ancestors on his mother's side were founders of the engineering factory of Oerlikam and of Alusuisse, his father's family descended from the co-founders of the Zurich Versicherungs Gesellschaft. Through his father, a graduate of the University of Zurich, who was a chemicals engineer and manager of a large aluminium plant, Syz came into contact with chemicals at a very early age. As he was particularly interested in this 'mystical' science subject at school, it was really a logical step after his 'A' levels for him to start studying chemistry at the University of Zurich.

After his PhD[327] under Professor Heinrich Zollinger in 1964 Syz was drawn first to California where he was engaged in contract research at Stanford Research Institute for two years before he had to return to Switzerland to do military service. Syz describes himself as an out and out military type who absolutely wanted to earn the title of captain, which was the rank he held. Upon his return to Wallis in 1967 he accepted employment with Ciba in Monthey and six months later he moved to Basel where he became factory manager of the Dye and Chemicals Department at Sandoz where Maurice Jacottet was CEO. This makes Syz one of those who experienced three generations of management—Jacottet, Dunant and Moret—at Sandoz, although it was Marc Moret with whom he became best acquainted.

---

326 Biography released on 7 Dec. 2010.
327 Martin Georg Syz: *Beitrag zur Kenntnis der Assoziationsbildung von organischen Farbstoffen* (Thesis, Zurich University, 1964) Zurich 1964.

The excellent training opportunities which the company offered its up-and-coming talents were of particular interest to Syz, which is why he took part in a two-year programme at the Centre d'Education Permanente (CEDEP), where he acquired additional qualifications in business administration and finance. This educational establishment had been established in 1970 by Yves Dunant from Sandoz and five other European business companies in co-operation with the prestigious French Business School INSEAD in Fontainebleau. Thanks to this further education opportunity Syz saw himself in the position of being able to undertake assignments which went beyond mere technology.

When he assumed responsibility for coordinating global production in his department, he gained experience on the international stage. During his innumerable trips abroad he got to know all the Sandoz factories. In the mid-1980s he was appointed Head of Marketing of his department and in 1993 the entire management of the Chemicals Division was assigned to him. Thus his appointment as CEO in the demerged company of Clariant in 1995 was a logical step.

As far as Syz is concerned, team spirit has always played an important role in business life. For that reason he felt it was vital to create a spirit of frankness and trust at the 'new' company of Clariant right from the very beginning. After the acquisition of Hoechst in 1997 Martin Syz handed over his post to his successor Karl-Gerhard Seifert at the end of 1996, in order to create a balance of the top positions of President of the Board of Directors and CEO. During the first year of transition he held the position of COO to aid integration and left the company at the end of 1997.

Karl-Gerhard Seifert

CEO
January/July 1997 to April 1999

Karl-Gerhard Seifert[328] was born in the north Hesse town of Reichensachsen in 1946. As the son of a chemist he came into early contact with this science and after taking his 'A' levels in 1966, he too began to study chemistry and left Göttingen University with a PhD in 1971. In 1972 he was drawn to California because IBM was searching for someone who was well-versed in the line of work that Seifert had described in his thesis.[329]

But as the 'American Way of Life' did not appeal to him in the long term, Seifert decided to return to Germany. In 1973 he gave up his original plans for a post-doctoral qualification in favour of employment at Hoechst AG where he was engaged in physical measurements. The job was not to his liking and at his own request he moved to the production sector where he first became assistant production manager and later plant manager. There he was able to put into practice the knowledge he had gained at IBM in the field of computerized control systems and automated the pigment plant AZO IV and further plants in Fechenheim and Offenbach. In 1979 Hoechst needed a manager in Suzano, Brasil, and there Seifert took charge of the production of pigments. However, Jürgen Dormann, the then Head of the ZDA, called him back to Hoechst two years later. There Seifert entered the department as 'Referent' (section head) and finally took over from Dormann as head of the entire department in 1984 when the latter moved up onto the Board of Management.

In 1988 Seifert was also appointed a member of the Board of Management of Hoechst AG, responsible for Agrochemicals and the Africa Region. One year later

---

328   Biography released on 7 Dec. 2010.
329   Karl-Gerhard Seifert: *Chemisch induzierte Kernspin-Polarisation, Temperaturabhängigkeit und Symmetrieeigenschaften* (Thesis, Göttingen Univ., 1971), Göttingen 1971.

he played a significant role in the foundation of the agro joint venture *AgrEvo* with Schering. A rival in this project was Rolf W. Schweizer of all people from Sandoz, which was on the brink of completing a contract with Schering but in the end was left empty-handed. In addition, Seifert as a member of the Board assumed responsibility for the Pharmaceuticals Division from 1991 on. During this time, the American company of Marion Merrell Dow was acquired and Hoechst AG was then able to expand its activities significantly in this area.

After disagreements between Dormann and Seifert on the subject of pharmaceuticals, Seifert took over Chemicals in 1996. At this time it was becoming evident that the Hoechst Group was to be converted into a strategic management holding. This did not meet with Seifert's approval, which is why he was one of the driving forces in the negotiations for the sale of the Specialty Chemicals Division to Clariant and on 1st July 1997 he took up his new office as CEO in Muttenz. The integration of approx. 21,500 former Hoechst employees into the 'new' Clariant also rested on him.

When in autumn 1998 Rolf W. Schweizer announced the planned merger with Ciba Specialty Chemicals and no post was envisaged for Seifert in the new management, he decided to leave Clariant. The fact that the merger did not go through in the end and that he could have continued in office did not alter Seifert's decision.

In 1999 Seifert entered Deutsche-Bank subsidiary Morgan Grenfell Private Equity Ltd. as Head of German Operations, but a year later he decided to start his own business as a consultant. In 2000 he acquired from Multikarsa in Indonesia the former fibres business of Hoechst AG, Trevira GmbH, which was later sold to Reliance. In 2001 he purchased Cassella with its sites in Offenbach and Fechenheim and parts of the plant in Griesheim from Rolf W. Schweizer. The company trades under the name of AllessaChemie and is engaged mainly in make-to-order production. Karl-Gerhard Seifert is Chairman of the Supervisory Board.

Reinhard Handte

COO, CEO
May 2001 to March 2003

Reinhard Handte[330] was born in Hirsau in Baden-Württemberg in 1946. After his 'A' levels and military service, the son of a master fitter began studying chemistry at the University of Stuttgart in 1967. After graduating with a PhD[331] in 1974, Handte entered the R&D unit of the Hoechst Group where, in the first few years, he applied himself to the synthesis of pesticides. From the plant in Höchst he moved to Westhofen in Bavaria and continued to work very successfully in the field of integrated pest management. The group owes several patents in this field to him. On his return to the parent plant he entered the ZDA at managerial level. Within this framework he was responsible for various research tasks in the business unit Dyes and Late-Stage Intermediates. He soon became Head of R&D and finally in 1995 he was promoted to Head of the entire business unit of Specialty Chemicals.

With the acquisition of the Specialty Chemicals Division by Clariant in 1997, Handte became Managing Director of Clariant GmbH in Frankfurt where there were around 8,500 employees. After the German subsidiary had been more or less established, Handte's activities gradually shifted to Muttenz. In addition to his position of Managing Director in Germany, Handte as a member of the Corporate Executive Board was responsible for R&D and Safety, Environment and Health. As research and development was in the hands of the individual departments, it was Handte's task to co-ordinate the various departments at group level, to develop common strategies with his team and to spot future trends on the market. The field of 'Environment, Safety and Health' also played a major role in the group. The primary aim here was to set global standards and to check these at regular intervals. For example, all the facilities at every production location had to be main-

330 Biography released on 11 Jan. 2011.
331 Reinhard Handte: *Synthese und Reaktionen von 2-Oxo-^3-pyrrolinen und 2H-2-oxo-pyrrolen* (Thesis, Stuttgart Univ., 1974), Stuttgart 1974.

tained in a technically correct manner, products examined according to the regulations and processes implemented properly. It was Handte who also developed a uniform auditing system to be used worldwide so that deficits could be recognised quickly and rectified. In all his activities it was of paramount importance to him to maintain contact to the plants and to speak directly to the employees in charge in the factories. He regarded himself as a boss who was there for everyone, who enjoyed working with people and convincing them of an idea.

In the middle of 1999 Handte changed to group head office where he took over as COO. At the same time he moved house to Muttenz. Together with Rolf W. Schweizer, Reinhard Handte was instrumental in the purchase of the British company BTP in 2000. This purchase was to facilitate the strategy approved by the Board of Directors to create a focus in Fine Chemicals but unfortunately this acquisition did not have the desired effect as was later to become all too apparent. In 2000 Reinhard Handte was also elected onto the Board of Directors of Clariant.

In May 2001 Handte took over from Schweizer as CEO. In this office this chemist of outstanding merit came increasingly under fire in the period that followed, due to an inconsistent information policy and imprudent statements in connection with the ramifications of the BTP purchase. Thus in the end the 56-year-old stepped down from office in March 2003 and left Clariant.

Roland Lösser

CFO
July 1995 to May 2001

CEO
April 2003 to April 2006

Chairman
May 2006 to April 2008

Roland Lösser[332] was born in Goslar, Lower Saxony in 1942. After studying economics he began his career in the business administration department of Vereinigte Leichtmetallwerke in Bonn.

In 1969 the management expert joined Sandoz Pharmaceuticals in Nuremberg where he first worked as a Team Leader and then a few years later as Head of the Organisation Department. Over time his department expanded so that data processing also fell within the scope of Lösser's responsibilities. In 1980 he was transferred to the parent company in Basel where he took office as Head of the Systems Management and Operation Research Department, which today corresponds to the function of Chief Information Officer.

In 1986 Roland Lösser returned to the Sandoz subsidiary in Nuremberg to assume a new area of responsibility as Head of Finances/Administration. In 1990 Lösser risked the 'jump across the pond'. As CFO of Sandoz Corporation in New York he gained valuable experience on the US financial markets in the following five years and deepened his knowledge of the various business divisions of the company.

During this period, at the end of 1994, a small circle of people who were in on the secret began to prepare the spin-off of the Chemicals Division to form Clariant. With his future colleagues, Roland Lösser, as designated CFO in the new company, also started preparations for the forthcoming IPO. In summer 1995 he

---

332   Biography released on 19 Apr. 2011.

returned from the USA and took up office as CFO at Clariant's head office in Muttenz.

Lösser remembers the IPO in 1994 as an exciting time and a great challenge. Accompanied by some colleagues he went on road shows throughout Europe and the USA to introduce the young company to potential investors. There was also a lot to be done in-house because departments such as Treasury, Investor Relations, Accounting, Controlling etc., which had been administered centrally at Sandoz, now had to be organised from scratch. Only two years later Lösser had another demanding task to master: the merger with Hoechst Specialty Chemicals meant finding a way to achieve the optimum integration of an organization almost three times the size of Clariant. With the sudden quadruplicating of its turnover Clariant became attractive to major investment houses.

In 2000 Roland Lösser also became a member of the Board of Directors of Clariant. A year later he handed over his post as Head of Finance to François Note but retained his mandate on the Board of Directors and his post on the Supervisory Board of Clariant GmbH in Germany, where he was Chairman from 2001 to 2006.

If the 58-year-old thought that he could devote himself first and foremost to his hobbies in the future then he was mistaken. When Clariant plunged into a severe crisis because of the BTP acquisition, it needed the help of an experienced financial expert, which was why Chairman of the Board Robert Raeber asked him in spring 2003 to take over the office of CEO from Reinhard Handte who was retiring. Thus it happened that Lösser returned to operative business at a very difficult time when it was his topmost priority to set the financial situation to rights and to improve operational performance.

In 2006 Lösser handed over the task of CEO to Jan Secher and succeeded Robert Raeber as Chairman of the Board of Directors. In April 2008 Roland Lösser stepped down from his office as President of the Board and finally retired at the age of 66.

Robert Raeber

Chairman
May 2002 to May 2006

Robert Raeber[333] was born in Baden near Zurich in 1936. After taking his 'A' levels in 1956 he did not intend to study but to earn money as quickly as possible, which was why he turned to journalism at first. However, after working for a small Swiss film gazette for two years, he looked for a job which would offer long-term perspectives. Consequently, he applied as a management trainee to Unilever, the foods and beverages group, and there he gained his first experience in marketing. After this training Raeber acquired the post of Creative Director in a European Advertising Agency Group. Some four years later he moved as a consultant to the customer services department of Advico Advertising Agency in Zurich, where he later became General Manager. While he was giving two presentations on behalf of the agency at Nestlé in Switzerland, Raeber attracted the attention of the management there. Nestlé appointed him Marketing Coordinator for Europe in 1967.

In 1974 he took charge of the Culinary Division in France and later became Commercial Director of Vittel. From 1979 on Raeber filled various management positions at Nestlé in Germany. In 1992 he became Chairman of the Managing Board of Nestlé Germany AG and finally in 1997 was appointed General Director of Nestlé AG in Vevey/Switzerland, responsible for the whole of Europe. He retained this post until his retirement in July 2001. However, he remained Chairman of the Supervisory Board in Germany until 2007. At the same time Raeber held a mandate on the Advisory Board of Dresdner Bank and on the Board of Directors of Maus Frères in Geneva and was the Chairman of CIAA, the Confederation of the Food and Drink Industries of the European Union.

In 2001 President Rolf W. Schweizer invited Raeber, known as a man of action, onto the Board of Directors of Clariant. Raeber, who lived in Lausanne, did not see

---

333 Biography released on 14 Dec. 2010.

himself as an 'executive' Chairman but as an 'active' Chairman. Unlike his predecessor, he did not want to encroach on the daily business of the Board of Management, but he did see it as the task of his committee to determine corporate strategies, to purposefully implement decisions and to fill the major offices in the company with the best possible people.

Raeber took up office at a difficult time, for the group was badly in debt due to the acquisition of BTP. Reducing this debt was of the utmost importance. Moreover he thought it imperative to reconsider the existing strategy thoroughly and to implement the current cost-cutting programme constantly. In addition Raeber wanted to put his long years of experience in industry to good use in order to set new impulses for improving customer orientation and strengthening customer relations in the long term and thus create added value.

Although he thought that the sale of certain business divisions was unavoidable, he did not see a solution to the problem in an excessive focussing of business. As Chairman he considered it to be important that the Board of Directors covered all the responsibilities pertaining to a company. For that reason he engaged new members from very varying areas whereby the theme of *Corporate Governance* which was gradually assuming greater significance was taken into consideration. At the same time, Raeber was anxious to lay down clear rules for the responsibilities of the Board of Directors and the Board of Management and develop an atmosphere of constructive debate.

Upon reaching retirement age Robert Raeber handed over the chairmanship to Roland Lösser in April 2006.

Jan Secher

CEO
April 2006 to August 2008

Jan Secher[334] was born in Sweden in October 1957. He completed his studies at the University of Linköping with a master's degree in industrial engineering.

He began his career in Sales and Distribution, Marketing and Product Management at the Swedish electrical engineering company ASEA in 1982. Part of his work involved a five-year stay in North America. In 1988 the company merged with the Swiss Energy Engineering Group Brown, Boveri & Cie to form ABB with its head office in Zurich. From 1989 Secher held various management positions at subsidiaries in Europe and Japan. In 2000 he was assigned to head office in Zurich where a year later as a member of the Executive Committee he assumed responsibility for the Manufacturing & Consumer Industries Unit, which had a turnover of CHF 5 to 6 billion and 30,000 employees.

In 2003, after a radical reorganization of the entire management, Jan Secher, after 20 years with ABB, moved to the Swiss SICPA Group, a manufacturer of special security printing inks which are used among other things in the printing of bank notes. Secher held office as CEO at SICPA in Lausanne for two years. The Swede had learned English, German and Japanese in the course of his numerous stays abroad and now French was added during his stay in western Switzerland.

After a headhunter drew Clariant's attention to him, Jan Secher joined the Board of Management in Muttenz at the end of 2005 and at the Annual General Meeting in April succeeded Roland Lösser as CEO. At that time Clariant was undergoing a phase of restructuring. After the crisis induced by the purchase of BTP, the situation of the company was slowly on the road to recovery but there was still a long way to go. Getting the ship back on course so that it could surge

334 Anon: "Jan Secher an der Spitze von Clariant," in *Clartext* 1/2006, p. 22; Felix Erbacher: "Im rauen Klima zu Hause," in *Basler Zeitung*, 14 Jan. 2006 p. 2.

ahead was therefore the paramount aim of Secher, who was an ardent yachtsman and former Canadian champion in the J24 class. Secher could quite definitely see parallels between the economy and yachting: as in sailing the strategy of managing a company had to be geared to the weather and environmental conditions. At first, Secher did in fact manage to bring a breath of fresh air into the company and motivate the employees. However, despite further restructuring measures and reductions in staff investors in particular were dissatisfied with the trend of the results. Consequently, Secher stepped down in autumn 2008 and handed over his post to Hariolf Kottmann.

In 2009 Jan Secher was engaged as Operating Partner with the US American private equity company Apollo Management L. P. in London. In 2010 he took up an offer from Ferrostaal, the Essen-based plant construction firm, whose longstanding chairman had been dismissed in view of serious corruption charges. On 1st June Jan Secher, who as an outsider was unencumbered by these events, assumed the chairmanship. His long years of service in international groups are to help re-focus the activities of the company on the customer and on operative business in future.

Appendix

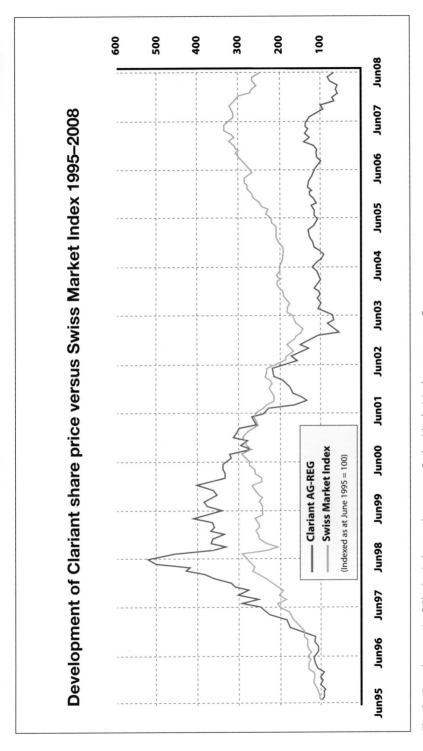

Fig. 65. Development of Clariant share price versus Swiss Market Index 1995–2008

Production sites
(including laboratories), symbols
represent each site's leading division

Textile, Leather & Paper Chemicals (TLP)

Pigments & Additives (PA)

Masterbatches (MB)

Functional Chemicals (FUN)

Life Science Chemicals (LSC)

Head office
of national branches,
100 or more employees

Laboratory Ten or
more employees

Administration or distribution
Five or more employees

Aberdeen

Northallerton
Oswaldtwistle   Selby
Beverley
Naas   Horsforth
Sandycroft   Wigan
Pentre
Denekamp
Pontypridd   Diemen
Louvain-la-Neuve
Lamotte
Mantes-la-Jolie   Knapsack
Höchst
Wiesbaden

Graulhet   Reinach
Me

Brignais   Origio
Porto   Bon Encontre
Tonneins   Pog
Igualada   Prat
Sant Andreu
Tarragona
Barcelona
Castellbisbal

Clariant sites in Europe 2005

Vantaa

Göteborg

Moscow

ise

Malmö

burg

Warsaw

Döbeln

Lodz

Prague

ndorf

Vienna

Budapest

ignano

co

Topkapi

Kemoks

Sefakoy

Vathi

Likovrissi

Interviews

Interviews and Techniques

At the beginning of the book project, the CEO sent a circular to around 30 people requesting them to participate in interviews to help define the content of the publication. The selection fell to Head of Communications Arnd Wagner.

One of the first to reply to the circular was Rolf W. Schweizer, with a memo: "May I ask you to let me have the questions in writing—I will reply to them by letter." He asked for a questionnaire to be compiled for him.

In the case of the live interviews, on the other hand, it was decided to avoid the widely practised question and answer model of conversation techniques or even of a questionnaire and to use narrative interviews instead to collect data. This method aimed at getting the interviewees to start talking and at keeping the account of their first-hand experiences flowing. The conversations which were tape-recorded began with a general request to relate, whereupon the partners in the dialogue reflected on their view of Clariant's past in the form of a biographical self-portrayal. The narrative soon started to flow and the interviewees were left to relive their past experiences. Due to the tricky relationships involved, it happened occasionally that the tape recorder had to be switched off. This, however, speaks for the need to communicate and the openness and honesty of the dialogues. An inquiry to prompt the telling of experiences and leafing together through the chronologically arranged set of photos for the future book were an additional instrument to elicit further information.

The circle of interviewees was enlarged by 20 persons with the result that there were 50 reports on tape to be evaluated. Half of the interviews lasted 2 to 2½ hours each. The remaining 50 percent were each 3 to 4 hours long. Four interviews lasted more than 6 hours each and one, minus the lunch break, stretched over 8 hours. The interviews took place at head office in Muttenz, later in Pratteln, in Sulzbach and in the offices of those participating in the interviews or in their homes.

The preparations for making contact, the contact itself, arranging times for meetings, the interviews, transcription, evaluation, the establishing of the text modules on the basis of the interviews, the sending of the text modules to those concerned and their release, and queries etc. extended over the entire length of the project, which lasted almost two years. Some of the statements and portrayals are, to a certain extent, congruent and for this reason not every opinion could be quoted. Sometimes only the gist of what was said has been reported and at other times direct quotations have been used but in both cases those interviewed were at liberty to edit the content of their text module, or in certain circumstances to revise or augment it. Release was granted by everyone; merely in two instances was permission granted on condition that the source of the text remained anonymous.

It would have been entirely illusory to compile a questionnaire for Rolf W. Schweizer, the 'father' of Clariant, right at the very beginning of the project because the knowledge and the amount of information were not nearly enough at that time to permit extensive and open questions.

Rolf W. Schweizer's advanced age and Clariant's economic development since the IPO were in the end a sound reason for a personal talk with the family and so a visit to Oberwil took place at the invitation of Mrs. Inge Schweizer in March 2010. During the four-hour conversation in which the elder son Juerg took part—not Rolf W. Schweizer, however—the family pointed out that despite his old age he was physically well but that his memory was not what it used to be.

Subsequently a last attempt was made and a questionnaire was eventually compiled in such a way that an elderly person could deal with it fairly easily. A richly illustrated age-appropriate catalogue, which reproduced the structure of the book along general lines, was prepared in painstaking detail. A few days after sending it to Rolf W. Schweizer the author received a letter from Inge Schweizer in reply: "My husband is now 80 years old, there has been no improvement in his powers of recall and therefore he is not in a position to answer your questions as, in view of their importance, they should be. We offer our most sincere regrets. If the situation had been different, my husband would have been able to make his views known in great detail and shed light on that period and the environment at that time … In all his actions my husband never thought of himself but of one thing only: and that was first and foremost Sandoz and then 'his' Clariant."[335]

---

335 Letter from Inge Schweizer on 8 Nov. 2010.

Interview partners

Talks recorded on tape

No.	Name	Date	Place
1.	Bertrab, Dominik von	17.2.2010	Muttenz
2.	Borgeaud, Pierre	28.7.2010	Winterthur
3.	Brandenberg, Peter	11.1.2010	Muttenz
4.	Breu, Raymund	27.1.2010	Basel
5.	Cuntze Ulrich	2.2.2010	Sulzbach
6.	Dietz, Erwin	1.2.2010	Sulzbach
7.	Dormann, Jürgen	17.2.2010, 3.5.2010	Winterthur
8.	Edlund, Björn	7.9.2010	Pratteln
9.	Erbacher, Felix	26.2.2010	Basel
10.	Gemperli, Paul	24.6.2010	St. Gallen
11.	Grom, Ewald	23.2.2010	Kelkheim
12.	Grosskopf, Michael	8.2.2010	Muttenz
13.	Hammel, Philipp	8.9.2010	Pratteln
14.	Handte, Reinhard	21.1.2010	Muttenz
15.	Hefner, Claus	16.2.2010	Muttenz
16.	Hug, Albert	13.1.2010	Muttenz
17.	Jany, Patrick	3.4.2010	Muttenz
18.	Kindler, Walter	14.6.2010	Muttenz
19.	Kottmann, Hariolf	1.9.2010	Wiesbaden
20.	Kowalewski, Ralf	18.2.2010	Reinach
21.	Link, Herbert	13.4.2010	Muttenz
22.	Lösser, Roland	2.1.2010	Muttenz
23.	Mäder, Christoph	1.3.2010	Basel
24.	Martin, Günter	8.11.2010	Pratteln
25.	Meier, Heiner	1.3.2010	Muttenz
26.	Meile, Armin	18.1.2010	Muttenz
27.	Merklein, Norbert	1.2.2010	Muttenz
28.	Metternich, Wolfgang	3.3.2010	Kriftel
29.	Metz, Günter	26.5.2010	Sulzbach
30.	Münch, Alfred	12.8.2010	Pratteln
31.	Ott, Ulrich	26.1.2010	Muttenz
32.	Raeber, Robert	12.5.2010	Frankfurt a. M.
33.	Reis, Tony	3.3.2010	Muttenz
34.	Reusch, Ingrid	22.2.2010	Sulzbach
35.	Schlömer, Henri	2.3.2010	Muttenz
36.	Schmieder, Klaus-Jürgen	18.3.2010	Sulzbach

37.	Seifert, Karl-Gerhard	3.2.2010, 2.5.2010	Frankfurt a. M.
38.	Sieber, Alexander	22.12.2009	Muttenz
39.	Syz, Martin	10.12.2009	Muttenz
40.	Tischhauser, Barbara	2.1.2010	Muttenz
41.	Vaterlaus, Walter	25.5.2010	Zürich
42.	Warning, Klaus	27.5.2010	Kelkheim
43.	Wellauer, Thomas	17.9.2010	Zürich
44.	Wiezer, Hartmut	24.2.2010	Sulzbach
45.	Winter, Thorsten	2.2.2010	Sulzbach
46.	Witmer, Jürg	6.9.2010	Pratteln
47.	Wohlmann, Herbert	9.2.2010	Muttenz

Talks not on tape

No.	Name	Date	Place
48.	Beyeler, Marianne	11.8.2010	Pratteln
49.	Flükiger, Werner	4.5.2010	Muttenz
50.	Hufschmid, Doris	14.4.2010	Oberwil
51.	Itin, Roland	9.2.2010	Muttenz
52.	Patz, Michaela	11.10.2010	Pratteln
53.	Rutte, Ralph	4.6.2010	Muttenz
54.	Schweizer, Inge und Juerg	24.3.2010	Oberwil
55.	Schweizer, Inge	1.4.2010	Muttenz
56.	Secher, Jan	15.3.2011	Essen
57.	Sgueglia, Cesare	11.3.2010	Muttenz
58.	Wagner, Thomas	17.2.2010	Muttenz

Telephone conversations

No.	Name	Date
59.	Kündig, Markus	19.3.2011
60.	Küster, Ulf	12.4.2010, 25.3.2011
61.	Privat, Beat	3.4.2010

Written interviews

No.	Name	Date
62.	Capron, Laurence	e-mail dated 10.12.2010
63.	Fava, Walter	e-mail dated 30.11.2010
64.	Hannam, Steve	e-mails dated 31.1.2011, 8.3.2011, 23.3.2011
65.	Heier, Hans-Bernd	e-mail dated 21.11.2010.
66.	Heier, Karl Heinz	e-mail dated 19.11.2010.
67.	Kochendörfer, Frank	e-mail dated 22.10.2010
68.	Meyer, Rolf A.	e-mail dated 3.8.2010

Passages from interviews and conversations in the form of text modules

Interview with Pierre Borgeaud in Winterthur on 28 Jul. 2010; text modules: *Amtszeit*, BTP, *Harzig, Über Moret und Rolf W. Schweizer* and *Wie Borgeaud zu Clariant kam*, released on 8. Oct. 2010.

Interview with Raymund Breu in Basel on 27 Jan. 2010; text module: *Going-public*, released on 18 Apr. 2011.

Interview with Jürgen Dormann in Winterthur on 17 Feb. 2010; text modules: *Bewerbung, Die Geschichte von Hoechst, DyStar, Gleichzeitig, NINO* and *Rhodia*, released on 15 Dec. 2010, 17 Dec. 2010, 19 Dec. 2010 and 27 Apr. 2011.

Interview with Björn Edlund in Pratteln on 7 Sept. 2010; text modules: *Rekrutieren, Im Bilde sein, Nase, Es war toll* and *Sich schätzen*, released on 1 Nov. 2010.

Interview with Felix Erbacher in Basel on 26 Feb. 2010; text modules: *Ein Hag dazwischen, Moret-Rolf W. Schweizer-China, Pressekonferenz* and *Secher*, released on 1 Sept. 2010.

Telephone conversation with Siegfried Fischer on 9 Mar. 2011; text module: *Betriebserlaubnis*, released on 23 Mar. 2011.

Interview with Paul Gemperli in St. Gallen on 24 Jun. 2010; text module: *Too big*, released on 21 Oct. 2010.

Interview with Michael Grosskopf in Muttenz on 8 Feb. 2010; text module: *Zweimal Heier*, released on 28 Oct. 2010, with permission from Karl Heinz Heier on 19 Nov. 2010 and by Hans-Bernd Heier on 21 Nov. 2010.

Interview with Philipp Hammel in Pratteln on 8 Sept. 2010; text module: *Hauptanlass*, released on 18 Mar. 2011.

Interview with Reinhard Handte in Muttenz on 21 Jan. 2010; text modules: *Andere Interessen, Von Müttern verstossen* and *Vita*, released on 5 Jan. 2011.

Interview with Claus Hefner in Muttenz on 16 Feb. 2010; text module: *Saat ohne Boden*, released on 5 May 2011.

Interview with Albert Hug in Muttenz on 13 Jan. 2010; text modules: *Euch verkaufen*, *Pferdefuss* und *Warum Hoechst?* released on 14 Nov. 2010, 15 Nov. 2010, 16 Nov. 2010.

Interview with Hariolf Kottmann in Wiesbaden on 1 Sept. 2010; text modules: *Einladung nach Muttenz* and *Wie Kottmann zu Clariant kam*, released on 2 Jan. 2011.

Telephone conversation with Markus Kündig on 19 Mar. 2011; text module: *Nachfolge regeln*, released on 22 Mar. 2011.

Interview with Herbert Link in Muttenz on 13 Apr. 2010; text modules: *Ah, Sandoz, Due Diligence* and *Schalmei*, released on 5 Jan. 2011, 31 Jan. 2011 and 14 Mar. 2011.

Interview with Roland Lösser in Muttenz on 2 Jan. 2010; text modules: *Du kriegst meinen Job*, *Schiff*, *Mit 60 gehen* and *Vita*, released on 17 Nov. 2010.

Interview with Christoph Mäder in Basel on 1 Mar. 2010; text module: *Handschrift*, released on 25 Mar. 2011.

Interview with Heiner Meier in Muttenz on 1 Mar. 2010; text module: *Saat ohne Boden*, released on 22 Apr. 2011.

Interview with Norbert Merklein in Muttenz on 1 Feb. 2010; text module: *ICI-Anekdote*, released on 2 Sept. 2010, and text module: *Giraffe*, released by Frank Kochendörfer on 22 Oct. 2010.

Interview with Wolfgang Metternich in Kriftel on 3 Mar. 2010; text module: *Rotfabriker*, released on 17 Jul. 2011.

Interview with Günter Metz in Sulzbach on 26 May 2010; text module: *Deutsch-Schweizer Chemiegespräche*, released on 17 Dec. 2010.

Interview with Alfred Münch in Pratteln on 12 Aug. 2010; text module: *Wie Münch zu Clariant kam*, released on 24 Sept. 2010.

Telephone conversation with Beat Privat on 3 Apr. 2010; text module: *Sponsoring*, released on 15 Jul. 2011.

Interview with Robert Raeber in Frankfurt a. M. on 12 May 2010; text modules: *Bewegung im Verwaltungsrat*, *Fuchs*, *Gestoppt*, *Streitkultur*, *Vita* and *Wie Raeber zu Clariant kam*, released on 14 Dec. 2010.

Interview with Ingrid Reusch in Sulzbach on 22 Feb. 2010; text module: *Kunststoffmesse*, released on 15 Nov. 2010.

Conversation with Juerg Schweizer in Oberwil on 24 Mar. 2010; text modules: *Bewirten*, *Treffpunkt Flughafen* and *Vita* (Rolf W. Schweizer), released on 4 Mar. 2011.

Interviews with Karl-Gerhard Seifert in Frankfurt a. M. on 3 Feb. 2010 and on 2 May 2010; text modules: *Brief von Rügen*, *Honigfabrik*, *Die besten Leute*, *DyStar 1998*, *Machte fifty-fifty*, *Rolf W. Schweizer kontra USA*, *Sich finden* and *Vita*, released on 14 Sept. 2010, 26 Oct. 2010 and 26 Jul. 2011.

Interview with Alexander Sieber in Muttenz on 22 Dec. 2010; text module: *Filetstücke*, released on 23 Nov. 2010.

Interview with Martin Syz in Muttenz on 1 Dec. 2009; text modules: *Brunnen, Massen-*

wirkungsgesetz, Neidlos, Roadshows, Sondern steigerte, Toms River, Viel Rauch, Vita und Von Nr. 1 zu Nr. 2, released on 23 Nov. 2010, 30 Nov. 2010 and 2 Dec. 2010.

Interview with Walter Vaterlaus in Zurich on 25 May 2010; text modules: *Visibility, Bekanntheit, Ciba Fusion, Erste Generalversammlung, Jungfrau Maria, Konzernleitungsausschuss, Rolf W. Schweizer geht nicht* and *4× Swoosh*, released on 1 Sept. 2010.

Interview with Klaus Warning in Kelkheim on 27 May 2010; text modules: *Blickwinkel* aund *Vorangetrieben*, released on 5 Dec. 2010.

Interview with Thomas Wellauer in Zurich on 17 Sept. 2010; text module: *2003–2006*, released on 1 Feb. 2011.

Interview with Hartmut Wiezer in Sulzbach on 24 Feb. 2010; text module: *Positiv eingestimmt* released on 22 Jul. 2011.

Interview with Jürg Witmer in Pratteln on 6 Sept. 2010; text module: *Wie Witmer zu Clariant kam*, released on 12 Dec. 2010.

Interview with Herbert Wohlmann in Muttenz on 9 Feb. 2010; text modules: *Drivers, Due Diligence, Fake, Hineingetrieben, Juristentreffen, Kommunikation, Rauhes Fahrwasser*, released on 16 Nov. 2010, and the text module: *Kommunikation*, released by Hans-Bernd Heier on 21 Nov. 2010.

List of literature and references

The contents of this publication are based on sources which are shown as footnotes in the text or in the bibliography. As for the rest, the contents are based on the author's research and on statements by numerous people involved in Clariant's history and interviewed in detail by the author.

The survey covered a wide field but was restricted to a certain framework. An inspection of the minutes of meetings of the Board of Directors and the Board of Management might have afforded greater insight but retention periods made this impossible.

Literature

Aeberli, Urs: "Da waren's plötzlich vier," in *Handelszeitung*, 1 Jun. 1995, p. 3.

Aiolfi, Sergio: "Clariant verkauft Teil des Life-Science-Geschäfts," in *Neue Zürcher Zeitung*, 29 Apr. 2006.

Aiolfi, Sergio: "Ciba-Masterbatch-Bereich geht an Clariant," in *Neue Zürcher Zeitung*, 5 Oct. 2006.

Aiolfi, Sergio: "Schlussstrich unter das BTP-Abenteuer von Clariant," in *Neue Zürcher Zeitung*, 8 Nov. 2006.

Aiolfi, Sergio: "Weiterer personeller Aderlass bei Clariant; Neue Wachstumsstrategie bringt den Abbau von 2,200 Stellen," in *Neue Zürcher Zeitung*, 15 Nov. 2006.

Aiolfi, Sergio: "Jan Sechers Sanierungsplan für Clariant," in *Neue Zürcher Zeitung*, 28 Dec. 2007.

Aiolfi, Sergio: "Ciba zum Letzten: Das Verschwinden einer 125 Jahre alten Industrie-Ikone," in *Neue Zürcher Zeitung*, 6 Apr. 2009.

Alperowicz, Natasha: "Dormann leads a revolution at Hoechst," in *Chemical Week*, 15 Jun. 1994.

Alperowicz, Natasha: "Transforming Hoechst," in *Chemical Week*, 22 May 1996.

Amacher, Corinne: "Machtnetz von Jürg Witmer: Chemische Verbindungen," in *Bilanz* 21/2009, 20 Nov. 2009.

Ammann, Manuel/Matti, Daniel/de Wyss, Rico: "Performance Schweizerischer Verwaltungsräte anhand der Aktienkursentwicklung," in *Financial Markets and Portfolio Management*, Issue 17, No. 1, March 2003.

Bäumler, Ernst: *Die Rotfabriker: Familiengeschichte eines Weltunternehmens*, Munich, 1988.

Barnikel, Kerstin: *Post-Merger Integration*, E-Book, Ludwig-Maximilian-University Munich, 2006.

Basler Zeitung (Ed.): *Die Katastrophe von Schweizerhalle; Zwei Wochen im November 1986: Eine Dokumentation aus Originalartikeln der Basler Zeitung*, compiled by Roger Berger, Basel 2006.

"Beteiligung schnell loswerden," in *Manager Magazin*, 1 Jun. 1999.

Behrens, Bolke: "Absturz vom Himmel," in *Wirtschaftswoche*, 24 May 2001.

Blum, Eva Maria: *Kultur, Konzern, Konsens: Die Hoechst AG und der Frankfurter Stadtteil Höchst* (Thesis, Tübingen Univ., 1991), Frankfurt 1991.

Burckhardt, Jacob: *Weltgeschichtliche Betrachtungen*, edited and with an epilogue by Rudolf Marx. 7. ed., Stuttgart 1949.

Busset, Thomas/Rosenbusch, Andrea/Simon, Christian (Ed.): *Chemie in der Schweiz: Geschichte der Forschung und der Industrie*, Basel 1997.

Cajacob, Flavian: "Mit Optimismus stimmt die Chemie," in *Handelszeitung*, 29 Oct. 2003.

Claassen, Dieter: "Clariant von Grossaktionär zurückgepfiffen," in *Tages-Anzeiger*, 14 Apr. 1999.

"Clariant holds on to textile dyes," in *Chemical Week*, 9 Sept. 1998.

"Clariant wird Götti," in *Palette* 1/2000, p. 11;

"Clariant Opfer des Eifers," in *Handelsblatt*, 16 Aug. 2001, no. 157, p. 18.

"Clariant hinterlässt ein ungutes Gefühl; Kapitalerhöhung angekündigt," in *Finanz und Wirtschaft*, 26 Feb. 2003, no. 16, p. 21.

"Clariant: Die Chemie stimmt nicht," in *Manager Magazin,* 13 Mar. 2003.

"Clariant mit hoher Sonderabschreibung," in *Handelsblatt*, 17 Jun. 2003, no. 114, p.15.

Commemorative Paper, Universiy of St. Gallen: Spoun, Sascha/Müller-Möhl, Ernst/Jann, Roger (Ed.): *Universität und Praxis. Tendenzen und Perspektiven wissenschaftlicher Verantwortung für Wirtschaft und Gesellschaft*, Zurich 1998.

"Das Pigment Violett 23 wird 50 Jahre. Ein farbechter Dauerbrenner," in *chemie.de*, 21 Jul. 2003.

Deutsch, Claudia H.: "Ciba Is Set for a Merger with Clariant" in *New York Times*, 10 Nov. 1998.

Dormann, Jürgen: "Akquisition und Desinvestition als Mittel der Strukturanpassung bei Hoechst," in *Zeitschrift für Betriebswirtschaft*, Supplement (Sonderdruck: Globalisierung und Wettbewerb) 2/1992, pp. 51–68.

Dormann, Jürgen: "Geschäftssegmentierung bei Hoechst," in the *Zeitschrift für betriebswirtschaftliche Forschung*, No. 45, 12/1993 (Rev. version of the lecture at the Schmalenbach conference in Neuss , 6 May 1992), pp. 1068–1077.

Dunsch, Jürgen: "Clariant streicht stellen in Europa und expandiert in Asien" in *Frank-furter Allgemeine Zeitung*, 15 Nov. 2006.

"Einbringung von Anteilen an Kapitalgesellschaften. Verhältnis der §§ 20 und 23 Um-wStG zu dem sog. Tauschgutachten des BFH, 16 Dec. 1958," in *Der Betrieb*, 24 Feb. 1995, Issue 8.

"Ein Querdenker blickt zurück," in *Palette*, no. 4/1998, p. 6.

Eisenring, Christoph: "Clariant im strategischen Vakuum: Neuer Konzernchef—keine Kapitalerhöhung," in *Neue Zürcher Zeitung*, 13 Mar. 2003.

Elkins, Ken: "Clariant adding two plants in $ 50M Gaston expansion," in *Charlotte Busi-ness Journal*, 7 Dec. 2001.

Engel, Alexander: *Farben der Globalisierung. Die Entstehung moderner Märkte für Farb-stoffe 1500–1900* (Thesis Göttingen Univ., 2009), Frankfurt a. M./New York 2009.

Enriquez, Juan/Goldberg Ray A.: "Transforming Life, Transforming Business: The Life-Science Revolution," in *Harvard Business Review*, vol. 78, no. 2, March-April 2000, pp. 94–104.

Erbacher, Felix: "Clariant hat in Asien Grosses vor," in *Basler Zeitung*, 27 Nov. 1996, p. 17.

Erbacher, Felix: "Clariant zieht bald die nächste Schublade," in *Basler Zeitung*, 17 Apr. 1999.

Erbacher, Felix: "Auf Schweizer folgt Schweizer," in *Basler Zeitung*, 17 May 2001, p. 19.

Erbacher, Felix: "Nagelneue Clariant-Fabrik wird nicht gebraucht" in the *Basler Zeitung*, 29 Jun. 2001.

Erbacher, Felix: "Einige Kritik auf der Clariant-GV," in the *Basler Zeitung*, 8 May 2002, p. 18.

Erbacher, Felix: "Im rauen Klima zu Hause,"in *Basler Zeitung*, 14 Jan. 2006, p. 2.

Erni, Paul: *Die Basler Heirat. Geschichte der Fusion Ciba-Geigy*, Zurich, 1979.

Festschrift Hoechst AG: Mitten im Leben, 125 Jahre Hoechst, Frankfurt a. M. 1988.

"Festschrift Sandoz: 100 Jahre für ein Leben mit Zukunft," in *Sandoz Bulletin*, vol. 22, 1986.

Finn, David: "A Conversation with Marc Moret," in *A Tribute to Marc Moret. A Collec-tion of Essays*, Preface by Daniel Vasella, New York 1996, pp. 71–80.

Fischer, Thorsten: "Einkaufslast erdrückt Clariant," in *St. Galler Tagblatt*, 16 Aug. 2001.

Fröndhoff, Jörg: "Krise in der Pharmabranche erfasst Zulieferer," in *Handelsblatt*, 4 Dec. 2002, no. 234, p. 14.

Goethe, Johann Wolfgang von: *Philosophische und naturwissenschaftliche Schriften No. 758, 1808–1810* [Edition Elibron Classics, Adam Media Corporation 2006].

Gross, Ekkehard/Haun, Jürgen: "Die wichtigsten Steuererleichterungen und Steu-erverschärfungen durch das Steuerentlastungsgesetz 1999/2000/2002," in *CH—D Wirtschaft*, no. 5/99, pp. 16–20.

Güntert, Andreas/Veigl, Sibylle: "Leuchten aus dem Norden," in *Facts*, 1 Jun. 2006.

Guerrera, Francesco: "Laporte's pounds 1.5bn deal founders on Hoechst veto," in *The Independent*, 14 Apr. 1999.

Handschin, Valentin: "Clariant ist bereit zum Durchstarten," in *Handelszeitung*, 17 Oct. 2007, No. 42, p. 7.

Handschin, Valentin: "Neuer Präsident stellt vieles in Frage," in *Handelszeitung*, 4 Mar. 2008.

Handschin, Valentin: "Actelion vor Grosserfolg," in *Basler Zeitung*, 4 Jul. 2008.

Handschin, Valentin: "Die Chemie-Gerüchteküche brodelt," in *Basler Zeitung*, 6. Sept. 2008.

Handte, Reinhard: *Synthese und Reaktionen von 2-Oxo-delta³-pyrrolinen und 2H-2-oxo-pyrrolen* (Doctoral Thesis Stuttgart Univ., 1974), Stuttgart 1974.

Hayes, Peter: "Vorwort," in Lindner 2005, pp. IX–XV.

Hengartner, Thomas: "Clariant braucht härtere Korrekturen. Auslastung zu tief, Kosten zu hoch. Potenzial von BTP falsch eingeschätzt," in *Finanz und Wirtschaft*, 18 Aug. 2001, no. 64, p. 23.

Hiltermann, Heiner: "Aus der Traum: Scheitern gehört zum Geschäft. Do it again Sam," in *Basler Zeitung*, 28 Dec. 2001.

"Historie: Zehn Meilensteine. Vom Start des Frankens bis zur Pharma-Fusion: die wichtigsten Weichenstellungen aus 150 Jahren Schweizer Wirtschaft," in *Bilanz* 4/2006, 28 Jan. 2006.

"Hoechst will Clariant-Anteile verkaufen," in *Spiegel Online*, 1 Jun. 1999.

Hofmann, Daniel M.: "Glänzende Clariant will Chancen nutzen," in *Neue Zürcher Zeitung*, 16 May 1998, p. 25.

Hofmann, Daniel M.: "Die neue Clariant will (noch) nicht glänzen; Weitverbreitete Skepsis in der Analytiker-Gemeinde," in *Neue Zürcher Zeitung*, 5–6 Dec. 1998, p. 27.

Hofmann, Daniel M.: "Clariant positioniert für Margenverbesserung," in *Neue Zürcher Zeitung*, 22 Mar. 2000, No. 60.

Honsel, Georg: "Die Hype-Zyklen neuer Technologien," in *SpiegelOnline*, 21 Oct. 2006.

Hug, Daniel: "Nachwehen einer überbezahlten Übernahme," in *Tages-Anzeiger*, 16 Aug. 2001.

Hume, Claudia: "Clariant's Laporte Acquisition is off," in *Chemical Week*, 21 Apr. 1999.

Hume, Claudia: "Clariant Sells Intermediates Unit to Former CEO," in *Chemical Week*, 28 Mar. 2001.

Hunter, David: "Clariant: Out on its own. Moving where the market is," in *Chemical Week*, 30 Aug. to 5 Sept. 1995, pp. 30–34.

Hunter, David: "BTP hard at work behind the scenes. BTP plc Company Profile," in *Chemical Week*, 10 Apr. 1996.

"110 Jahre Sandoz: Ein historischer Rückblick," in *Sandoz Bulletin*, no. 112 (last number), 1996, pp. 6–31.

INSEAD (Ed.): *Acquisition Wave in the Fine Chemical Industry: Clariant-BTP Acquisition (A)*, Case Study for Tuition by Laurence Capron and Andrew Horncastle, 2006

"Jan Secher an der Spitze von Clariant," in *Clartext* 1/2006, p. 22.

Jones, Chuck/Zamoyski, Andy: "The Giraffe Turns Forty!" in *Clariant Compact*, October 2010, S. 22.

"Kahlschlag bei Clariant," in *Handelsblatt,* 14 Nov. 2006.

Kepplinger, Hans Mathias: *Störfall-Fieber. Wie ein Unfall zum Schlüsselereignis einer Unfallserie wird,* Freiburg i. Br./Munich 1994.

Kirchhofer, Jan: Clariant: "Keine Doppelfunktion mehr," in *Basler Zeitung,* 20 Dec. 2000, p. 18.

Klose, Hans-Georg: "Alles CPIP oder was?" in *Clartext* 4/2004, p. 7.

Knechtli, Peter: "Schweizer unter Erfolgsdruck: Letzter Streich darf kein Flop werden," in *Online Reports,* 20 Apr. 1999.

Knechtli, Peter: "Mit der Clariant-Aktie sinkt auch Schweizers Stern. Experten werfen dem Präsidenten Managementfehler vor—schwierige Suche nach Nachfolger," in *Sonntagszeitung,* 19 Aug. 2001.

Knoepfli, Adrian: *Im Zeichen der Sonne: Licht und Schatten über der Alusuisse 1930–2010,* Baden 2010.

König, Arne: *Die Bedeutung von Unternehmenskulturen für den Erfolg von internationalen Megafusionen,* E-Book, Leuphana University Lüneburg 2003.

Kratz, Wilfried: "Wundersame Spaltung," in *Die Zeit,* 5. Mar. 1993.

Kreis, Georg/von Wartburg, Beat (Ed.): *Basel, Geschichte einer städtischen Gesellschaft,* Basel 2000.

Lanz, Kurt: *Weltreisender in Chemie,* 2nd rev. ed., Düsseldorf/Vienna 1980.

"Laporte breaks silence over merger failure," in *Chemistry and Industry,* 16 Aug. 1999.

Lerch, Gerhard: "Wie man sich auf einer Völkerwanderung fühlt," in *Clartext* 3/2005, pp. 34–35.

Lindner, Stephan H.: *Hoechst. Ein I. G. Farben Werk im Dritten Reich,* Munich 2005.

Mäder, Ruedi: "Es war wieder mal Zeit, anzurufen," in *Aargauer Zeitung,* 10 Nov. 1998, p. 37.

Mäder, Ruedi: "Clariant-Chef wirft das Handtuch," in *Aargauer Zeitung,* 13 Mar. 2003.

Meier, Andreas: "Britische BTP wäre ein guter Fang für Clariant," in *Finanz und Wirtschaft,* 22 Jan. 2000, No. 6.

Meier, Andreas: "Schwierige Nachfolgeregelung," in *Finanz und Wirtschaft,* 22 Mar. 2000.

Meier, Andreas: "Clariant speckt ab. Werk Cassella ausgegliedert. Polyvinyl-Bereich weg," in *Finanz und Wirtschaft,* 11 Jul. 2001, no. 54, p. 20.

Meier, Andreas/Pedroietta, Franziska: "Die Spezialchemie operiert unter extremen Bedingungen," in *Finanz und Wirtschaft,* 29 Oct. 2005, no. 86, p. 27.

Meier, Andreas: "Clariant will Vielseitigkeit des Geschäfts nutzen," in *Finanz und Wirtschaft,* 18 Nov. 2006.

Metternich, Wolfgang: *Die städtebauliche Entwicklung von Höchst am Main,* Frankfurt a. M. 1990.

Metternich, Wolfgang: *Der Maler Jakob Becker—Der Lehrer der Kronberger Maler,* Frankfurt a.M./Kronberg 1991.

Metternich, Wolfgang: *Jubiläumsschrift 2002: Vom Chemiewerk zum Industriepark. 100 Jahre Chemieproduktion in Gersthofen 1902–2002,* Gersthofen, 2002.

Metternich, Wolfgang: *Ideenfabrik: Von den Farbwerken zum Industriepark Höchst,* Frankfurt a. M. 2007.

Metternich, Wolfgang: "Höchster Farben—Lyoner Seide. Was den Damen der Pariser Gesellschaft die Tränen in die Augen trieb," in *Festschrift Höchster Schlossfest.* Frankfurt a. M.-Höchst 2011, pp. 38–42.

Meyer, Rolf A.: "Strukturwandel in der chemischen und pharmazeutischen Industrie. Neue Chancen für die Spezialitätenchemie" in Spoun, Sascha/Müller-Möhl, Ernst/ Jann, Roger (Ed.): *Universität und Praxis. Tendenzen und Perspektiven wissenschaftlicher Verantwortung für Wirtschaft und Gesellschaft der Universität St. Gallen zum 100-Jahr-Jubiläum,* Zurich, 1998, pp. 273–288.

Meyer, Werner/Erbacher, Felix: "Bei Sandoz pfeift ein anderer Wind: Interview mit Marc Moret," in *Basler Zeitung,* 9 Apr. 1983.

Milmo, Sean: "Hoechst Forces Clariant to End Possible Takeover of Laporte," in *Chemical Market Report,* 19 Apr. 1999.

Nareski, Violeta: *Zum Einfluss der Unternehmenskultur auf die Motivation der Mitarbeiter in der New Economy,* Hamburg 2003.

Neue Zürcher Zeitung, 16 May 1998, p. 25.

"No Chemistry between Clariant and Rhodia?" in *Swissinfo.ch,* 22 Nov. 2001.

"Neuer Chef bei Clariant; Jan Secher sticht Thomas Wellauer aus," in *Tages-Anzeiger,* 16 Oct. 2005.

Nollert, Michael: *Unternehmensverflechtungen in Westeuropa. Nationale, und transnationale Netzwerke von Unternehmen, Aufsichtsräten und Managern (Soziopulse, Studien zur Wirtschaftssoziologie und Sozialpolitik,* vol. 3) (Professorial Thesis, Zurich, Univ., 2002), Berlin/Münster 2005.

Owen, Geoffry/Harrison, Trevor: "Why ICI Chose to Demerge," in *Harvard Business Review,* Year. 73, No. 2, March-April 1995, pp. 132–142.

Owen, Geoffrey: "Parting of the Corporate Ways," in *Financial Times,* 13 Mar. 1995.

"P&G withdraws order for Clariant with the loss of SFR 100m," in *Chemical Business Newsbase,* 1 Aug. 2001.

Palm, Carla: "Bankaktien weiter zurückgeworfen—Actelion verdrängt Clariant aus SMI," in *Finanz und Wirtschaft,* 9 Jul. 2008.

"Patrick Kaiser—der neue Mann bei Corporate Communications," in *Palette* 3/2002, p. 9.

Petignat, Raymond: "Marc Moret—bewundert, verehrt, gehasst," in *Basler Stadtbuch 2006,* Christoph Merian Foundation (Ed.), pp. 74–77.

Pfister, Franziska: "Jürg Witmer erläuterte seine Gründe für den Führungswechsel," in *Finanz und Wirtschaft,* 6 Sept. 2008, p. 21.

Ploss, Emil Ernst: *Ein Buch von alten Farben,* 3. unchanged ed., Munich 1973.

Raupp, Judith: "Nach mir die Fusion. Was alternde Firmenchefs mit unternehmerischer Logik begründen, dient oft nur der eigenen Denkmalpflege," in *Cash,* 13 Nov. 1998, no. 46, p. 11.

Raupp, Judith/Weber, Victor: "Die Mitarbeiter haben mittlerweile eine dicke Haut," in *Cash*, 5 Mar. 1999.

Ridder, Knight: "Mount Holly, N. C., Clariant Plant Loses Detergent Additive Deal," in the *Tribune Business News*, 17 Jul. 2003.

"Rhodia ends talks with Clariant," in *Chemical Week*, 5 Dec. 2001.

Riedl-Ehrenberg, Renate: "Alfred Kern (1850–1893). Edouard Sandoz (1853–1928). Gründer der Sandoz AG, Basel," in *Schweizer Pioniere der Wirtschaft und Technik*, issue 44, ed. by the 'Verein für wirtschaftshistorische Studien Zurich' (Association for Economic Historical Studies), Zurich 1986.

Roberts, Michael: "Laporte travels the long, hard road from commodities to specialties," in *Chemical Week*, 18 Aug. 1993.

Roland, Heinz: "Ein Tauschhandel," in Clariant *Clartext*, 10 Jul. 2007.

Ruetz, Bernhard/Roos, Armin: *Carl Christian Friedrich Glenck 1779–1845: Salzpionier und Gründer der Saline Schweizerhalle*, Zurich 2009.

Salz, Jürgen: "Glut bewahren," in *Wirtschaftswoche*, 5 Jul. 2001.

Schäfer, Ulrich/Meier, Andreas: "Wir setzen alles dran, die Gewinnzahlen zu erreichen," in *Finanz und Wirtschaft*, 16 Jan. 1999, p. 15; Schlatter, Reto: "Auf Shoppingtour," in *Handelszeitung*, 26 Jan. 2000.

Schletti, Bruno: "Streichkonzert in Moll—Debüt des neuen Clariant-Dirigenten," in *Tages-Anzeiger*, 15 Nov. 2006, p. 25.

Schreier, Anna Elisabeth/Wex, Manuela: "Chronik der Hoechst Aktiengesellschaft 1863–1988," Special edition from: *Dokumente aus Hoechst-Archiven*, ed. by Klaus Trouet, Frankfurt a. M. 1990.

Schweizer, Rolf: *Die Einkommensdisparität zwischen der Landwirtschaft und der Industrie* (Thesis, St. Gallen, Handels-Hochschule, 1958), Winterthur 1958.

Scott, Alex: "BTP Buys Italy's Archimica," in the *Chemical Week* , 15 Jul. 1998.

Seifert, Karl-Gerhard: *Chemisch induzierte Kernspin-Polarisation, Temperaturabhängigkeit und Symmetrieeigenschaften* (Thesis, Göttingen Univ., 1971), Göttingen 1971.

Simon, Christian: "Chemiestadt Basel," in: *Basel, Geschichte einer städtischen Gesellschaft*, ed. by Kreis, Georg/von Wartburg, Bert: Basel 2000, pp. 364–383.

Smolka, Klaus Max: "Nach zwei Verlustjahren tauscht Clariant Vorstandschef aus," in *Financial Times Deutschland* vom 13.03.2003, Nr. S. 10.

Steck, Albert: "Der standhafte Patriarch. Rolf W. Schweizer," in *Facts*, 9/2003, p. 70.

Steck, Albert: "Novartis Teil 1, Die Fusion," in *Bilanz* no. 4/2006, 28 Feb. 2006.

Steck, Albert: "Machtnetz von Thomas Wellauer: Der Allrounder," in *Bilanz* 6/2006, 9 May 2006.

Stock, Oliver: "Schwedisches Comeback," in *Handelsblatt*, 4 Nov. 2005.

Stock, Oliver: "Clariant geht in die zweite Sparrunde," in *Handelsblatt*, 15 Nov. 2006, no. 221, p. 22.

Strasser, Wolfgang: *Erfolgsfaktoren für die Unternehmensführung*, Wiesbaden 2004.

Straumann, Tobias: *Die Schöpfung im Reagenzglas: Eine Geschichte der Baseler Chemie (1850–1920)* (Thesis, Zurich Univ., 1995), Basel/Frankfurt a. M., 1995.

Straumann, Tobias: "Die Novartis-Fusion aus historischer Sicht," in *Basler Stadtbuch* 1996, Christoph Merian Foundation (Ed.), pp. 37–42.

Streeck, Nina: "Falsche Formel," in *Bilanz*, 1 May 2003.

Sulzbacher, Lilly: "Unterstützung für drei Bergbauernfamilien," in *Presseinformation Winterhilfe*, 31 Jul. 2000.

Sutter, Markus: "Zwei starke Firmen werden zu zweit noch starker," in *Basler Zeitung*, 10 Nov. 1998.

Syz, Martin Georg: *Beitrag zur Kenntnis der Assoziationsbildung von organischen Farbstoffen* (Thesis, Zurich Univ., 1964), Zurich 1964.

Teuteberg, René: *Basler Geschichte*, 2nd ed., Basel 1988.

"The Investment Column: BTP," in *The Independent*, 9 Jun. 1999.

Tschudin, Peter: *Basler Papiermühle*, Schweizerisches Museum für Papier, Schrift und Druck, Basel 2002.

Vasella, Daniel: "Novartis—Spitzenleistung in 'Life Science'," in *Basler Stadtbuch 1996*, Christoph Merian Foundation (Ed.), pp. 11–17

Vasella, Daniel: "Nachruf. Dr. Marc Moret zum Gedenken," in *Novartis live*, 4/2006.

Vereb, Katalin: "Welttiertag: Ein Tier als Göttikind," in the *Coopzeitung*, 3 Oct. 2006, no. 40, pp. 8–9, 11, 13.

Vogt, Markus: "Dr Christo paggt y—und d Bänggler sinn derby," in *Basellandschaftliche Zeitung*, 22 Feb. 1999.

Voigt, Birgit: "Basler Chemie überflügelt alle," in *Tages-Anzeiger*, 10 Nov. 1998, front cover.

Voigt, Birgit: "Ein neuer Gärtner für den Clariant-Wildwuchs," in *Neue Zürcher Zeitung am Sonntag*, 19 Nov. 2006.

Vonhof, Holger: "Ein Beitrag zum Verstehen: Das Werk Höchst im Dritten Reich," in *Höchster-Kreisblatt*, 18 Mar. 2005, p. 14.

Vontobel Equity Research (Ed.): *Aktienmarkt Schweiz*, 15 Feb. 2008.

Weber, Victor: "Pluto macht Clariant ärmer und ärmer," in *Cash*, 23 May 2003, no. 21, p. 5.

Weber, Victor: "Die stille Läuterung des Thomas W," in *Cash*, 17 Nov. 2005, p. 15.

Wehrli, Bernhard: *Aus der Geschichte des Schweizerischen Handels- und Industrie-Vereins 1870–1970: Zum hundertjährigen Bestehen des Vororts*, Zurich 1970.

Weil, Pierre: "Übernahme beendet Fusionsfantasien: Clariant kauft Masterbatch-Geschäft von Ciba Spezialitätenchemie," in *Basler Zeitung*, 5 Oct. 2006.

"Wie warme 'Weggli'," in *Finanz und Wirtschaft*, 10 Jul. 1999.

Williams, Dede: "Digestive problems," in *ICIS Chemical Business*, 17 Feb. 2003.

Wilson, David M.: *Der Teppich von Bayeux*, Preface by Jean le Carpentier, 2nd. ed., Cologne 2005.

Winter, Thorsten: "Clariant baut in Höchst eine Produktionsanlage für Spezialwachse," in *Frankfurter Allgemeine Zeitung*, 9 Sept. 2004.

Winter, Thorsten: "Mitarbeiter helfen Clariant in Höchst beim Sparen," in *Frankfurter Allgemeine Zeitung*, 22 Nov. 2005.

Winter, Thorsten: "Wir standen vor zwei Jahren vor dem Abgrund," in *Frankfurter Allgemeine Zeitung/Rhein-Main-Zeitung*, 28 Jun. 2011.

Young, Ian: "Rhodias Tirouflet Sticks to his Guns," in *Chemical Week*, 19 Feb. 2003.

Zeller, Christian: *Globalisierungsstrategien: Der Weg von Novartis*, (Thesis, Hamburg Univ., 2001) Berlin/Heidelberg 2001.

Zeller, Christian: "Beyond Globalization: Scales and Speed of Production in the Pharmaceutical Industry," in: ESPACE. Economies in Space, Working Papers in Economic Geography no. 2007–2, Bern 2002.

"2–15–20–20" in *Clariant Direkt* 3/99d, 15 Feb. 1999.

"10 Jahre Clariant—eine dynamische Dekade," in *Palette* 2/2005, pp. 16–18.

Company reports, company magazines, commemorative publications

Clariant Aktionärsinfo (Information for Shareholders)

Clariant *Clariant Direkt*

Clariant Connect

Clariant Firmenzeitschrift *Clartext* (company magazine)

Clariant Firmenzeitschrift *Palette* (company magazine)

Clariant Annual Reports

Clariant Internal Communications

Clariant Media Releases

Hoechst Commemorative Publication 125th Anniversary, 1988

Hoechst Commemorative Publication Gersthofen 100th Anniversary, 2002

Hoechst Company Magazine *Hoechst heute*

Hoechst Company Magazine *Hoechst persönlich*

Hoechst Annual Reports

Hoechst Minutes of Board Meetings

Novartis *Novartis live*

Sandoz Commemorative Publication 100th Anniversary, 1986

Sandoz Company Magazine *Sandoz Bulletin*

Sandoz Annual Reports

Sandoz *Sandoz Internal Information*

University of St. Gallen Commemorative Publication 100th Anniversary, 1998

Newspapers and magazines

Aargauer Zeitung
Basellandschaftliche Zeitung
Basler Zeitung
Der Betrieb
Bilanz
Börsenzeitung
Cash
Charlotte Business Journal
CH—D Wirtschaft
Chemical Business Newsbase
(ICIS) Chemical Business
Chemical Market Report
Chemical Week
Chemistry and Industry
Coopzeitung
Facts
Financial Times
Financial Times Deutschland
Finanz und Wirtschaft
Frankfurter Allgemeine Zeitung
Frankfurter Allgemeine Zeitung/Rhein-Main-Zeitung
Handelsblatt
Handelszeitung
Harvard Business Review
Höchster Kreisblatt
The Independent
Internationale Politik
Tribune Business News
Manager Magazin
Neue Zürcher Zeitung
Neue Zürcher Zeitung am Sonntag
New York Times
Sonntagsblick
Der Spiegel
St. Galler Tagblatt
Tages-Anzeiger
Die Welt
Wirtschaftswoche
Zeitschrift für Betriebswirtschaft

Zeitschrift für betriebswirtschaftliche Forschung
Zeitschrift für Unternehmensgeschichte
Die Zeit

Serials

Basler Stadtbuch (Municipal Chronicle of the City of Basel)
Documents from Hoechst's Archives
European University Publications
Financial Markers and Portfolio Management
Jahrbuch Basel (Almanac of the City of Basel)
Schriften aus dem Max-Planck-Institut für Gesellschaftsforschung (Publications by the Max-Planck-Institute for the Study of Societies)
Pioneers in Economics and Technology
Series by the 'Arbeitskreis für Management und Wirtschaftsforschung' (Workgroup for Management and Economic Research
Soziopulse—Studien zur Wirtschaftssoziologie und Sozialpolitik (Studies on Economic Sociology and Social Policy)

Reference works

Brockhaus: Wirtschaft. Betriebs- und Volkswirtschaft, Börse, Finanzen, Versicherungen und Steuern, (Economics: Business Administration and Economics, Stock Markets, Finance, Insurance and Taxes) 2nd rev. ed., Mannheim/Leipzig 2008

Duden: Wirtschaft von A bis Z: Grundlagenwissen für Schule und Studium, Beruf und Alltag, 4th ed., Mannheim 2009 (Duden: Economics from A to Z: Basics for School, University, Profession and Everyday)

Hessische Biografie (Hessian Biographies)

Historisches Lexikon der Schweiz (Historical Lexicon of Switzerland)

Neue Deutsche Biographie (New German Biographies)

www.wikipedia.de

www.wirtschaftslexikon24.net

Archives consulted

Basel-Stadt Staatsarchiv, Basel (Town Archives)

Basler Zeitung Archiv, Basel (Newspaper Archives)

Clariant Firmenarchiv (Company Archives) Pratteln and Werksmuseum (Plant Museum Unicum) Muttenz

Novartis Firmenarchiv, Basel (Company Archives)

Hoechst GmbH Unternehmensarchiv, Frankfurt a. M. (Company Archives)

Schweizerisches Wirtschaftsarchiv der Universität Basel (Swiss Economic Archives of the University of Basel)

Universitätsarchiv St. Gallen (University Archives)

Further reading

Adelshauser, Werner (Ed.): *Die BASF. Eine Unternehmensgeschichte*, Munich 2002.

Bäumler, Ernst: *Ein Jahrhundert Chemie*, Düsseldorf/Vienna 1963.

Bäumler, Ernst: *Farben, Formeln, Forscher; Hoechst und die Geschichte der industriellen Chemie in Deutschland*, Munich 1989.

Barran, Jördis: *Zwischen Ethik und Interesse. Soziale und pädagogische Motive der Gründer der Farbwerke Hoechst AG* (Europäische Hochschulschriften, Reihe: Studien zur Erwachsenenbildung, Bd. 14), Frankfurt a. M./Berlin 1997.

Bartmann, Wilhelm: *Zwischen Tradition und Fortschritt: Aus der Geschichte der Pharmabereiche von Bayer, Hoechst und Schering von 1935–1975*, Stuttgart 2003.

Berghoff, Hartmut: *Moderne Unternehmensgeschichte*, Paderborn 2004.

Berner, Christiana: *Der Topmanager zwischen Anspruch und Realität: Aufgaben, Image, Selbstverständnis,* (Doctoral Thesis, Kassel Univ., 2001), Marburg 2003.

Bertrich, Fred: *Kulturgeschichte des Waschens*, Düsseldorf/Vienna 1966

Billerbeck, Ewald: "Forscher, Förderer und Fabrikarbeiter. 100 Jahre F. Hoffmann-La Roche", in *Baseler Stadtbuch* 1996, Christoph Merian Stiftung (Ed.), pp. 43–47.

Borschberg, Edwin: *Die Diversifikation als Wachstumsform der industriellen Unternehmung* (Professorial Thesis, Fribourg Univ., 1965), Bern/Stuttgart 1969.

Buntz, Andreas: *Das Führungsverständnis der deutschen Spitzenmanager: Eine empirische Studie zur Soziologie der Führung,* (Doctoral Thesis Hohenheim Univ., 2005), Frankfurt/Berlin/Bern 2005.

Cascorbi, Annett: *Demerger-Management. Wertorientierte Desintegration von Unternehmen,* (Doctoral Thesis Hamburg Univ. der Bundeswehr, 2003), Wiesbaden 2003.

Döring, Claus: "Kettenreaktionen in der internationalen Chemie: Fokussierung und Life-Science-Orientierung prägen die neunziger Jahre," in *Börsen-Zeitung,* 31 Dec. 1997, p. 14.

Dormann, Jürgen (in conversation with Jürgen Dunsch): "Beim Life-Science-Konzept haben wir uns in der Zeitperspektive vertan," in *Frankfurter Allgemeine Zeitung*, 13 Dec. 2000, p. 49.

Drost, Ralf: "Die Farbe Lila," in *Welt Online*, 28 Apr. 2001.

Enzweiler, Tasso: "Jürgen Dormann, 'Magic Dorman', öffnete die Festung Hoechst" in *WeltOnline*, 16 Mar. 1999.

Erni, Paul/Huber, Georg: *Die unternehmerische Wertschöpfung. Gedanken zum industriellen Management in der globalen Technokultur*, Preface by Marc Moret, Lucerne 1989.

Eugster, Karin/Martínez, Larissa Marolda: "Informationsasymmetrie im Vorfeld von Umstrukturierungen," in *Gesellschaft- und Kapitalmarktrecht* 1/2007, pp. 39–53.

Forter, Martin: *Farbenspiel. Ein Jahrhundert Umweltnutzung durch die Basler chemische Industrie* (Doctoral Thesis Basel Univ., 1998), Zurich 2000.

Forter, Martin: *Falsches Spiel. Die Umweltsünden der Basler Chemie vor und nach „Schweizerhalle*, Zurich 2010.

Freye, Saskia: *Führungswechsel. Die Wirtschaftselite und das Ende der Deutschland AG* (Schriften aus dem Max-Planck-Institut für Gesellschaftsforschung, Bd. 67- Papers of the Max-Planck-Institute for the Study of Societies Vol. 67), Frankfurt a. M. 2009.

Galambos, Louis/Hikino, Takashi/Zamagni, Vera: *The Global Chemical Industry in the Age of the Petrochemical Revolution*, New York 2007.

Goldberg, Ray A./Knoop, Carin-Isabell/Sunder, Srinivas Ramdas: "Novartis: Betting on Life Science," in *Harvard Business Review*, Year 76, Dec. 1998.

Grand, Simon/Bartl, Daniel, *Executive Mangement in der Praxis. Entwicklung—Durchsetzung—Anwendung*. Foreword by Jürgen Dormann. Frankfurt a. M. 2011.

Hemmerich, Kai-Uwe: "Einblicke in den Europäischen Betriebsrat der Clariant-Gruppe," in Niederst, Noelle/Schack, Axel (Ed.): *Europäische Sozialpolitik. Die richtige Antwort auf die Globalisierung? Wiesbadener Gespräche zur Sozialpolitik, Tagungsband*, Heidelberg 2009, pp. 263–267.

Höpner, Martin/Krempel, Lothar: "Ein Netzwerk in Auflösung: Wie die Deutschland AG zerfällt," in *Max-Planck-Institut für Gesellschaftsforschung-Jahrbuch* 2003/04, Cologne 2005, pp. 9–14.

Holtbrügge, Dirk: "Akkulturation in länderübergreifenden Unternehmungskooperationen. Das Beispiel Aventis," 2002 (Lecture).

Jeffreys, Diarmuid: *Hell's Cartel: IG Farben and the Making of Hitler's War Machine*, New York 2008.

Jenewein, Wolfgang/Morhart, Felicitas: "Wie Jürgen Dormann ABB rettete," in *Harvard Business Manager*, Year. 28, No. 9, Sep. 2007, pp. 22–32, also printed in: ibid. Edition 4/2009, pp. 68–76.

Klotzsche, Mario: "Indigo und die schweizerische Farbenindustrie. Grossprojekte von Ciba und Geigy" in *Zeitschrift für Unternehmensgeschichte. Journal of Business History*, no.1/2009, Vol. 54, pp. 3–25.

Knittel, Melanie: *Cultural Due Diligence. Analyse, Methoden und Anwendung*, E-Book, Zeppelin University Friedrichshafen 2002.

Kreis, Georg/von Wartburg, Beat (Hrsg.): *Basel, Geschichte einer städtischen Gesellschaft*, Basel 2000.

Leuthold, Dieter: "Unternehmensgeschichte als Kernelement der Unternehmenskultur" in *Schriftenreihe des Arbeitskreises für Management und Wirtschaftsforschung*, Vol. 5, Bremen 2006.

Lüönd, Karl: *Erfolg als Auftrag. Ems-Chemie: Die Geschichte eines unmöglichen Unternehmens*, Bern 2011.

Menz, Wolfgang/Becker, Steffen/Sablowski, Thomas: *Shareholder-Value gegen Belegschaftsinteressen. Der Weg der Hoechst-AG zum "Life-Sciences"-Konzern*, Hamburg 1999.

Novartis International AG (Ed.): *Die Geschichte des Firmensports bei Novartis*, Basel 2009.

Oetter, Joachim: *Strukturveränderung im Konzern durch Spaltung. Eine Studie zur Spaltung der Hoechst AG* (Europäische Hochschulschriften, Series 2: Rechtswissenschaft, Vol. 3821), Frankfurt a. M./Berlin/Bern 2003.

Prinz, Eberhard: *Färberpflanzen. Anleitung zum Färben, Verwendung in Kultur und Medizin*, Stuttgart 2009.

Sarasin, Philipp: "Basel auf dem Weg zur modernen Industriestadt (1833–1914)", in: Basel 1501–2001, 179th Neujahrsblatt der Gesellschaft für das Gute und Gemeinnützige Basel," (New Year's Gazette of the GGG Society for the Good and Charitable), Basel 2000, p. 141–152.

Schmieder, Klaus-Jürgen: "Spin-off als Instrument der Unternehmenspolitik" in *Börsen-Zeitung*, 19 Apr. 1997 (Speech at the press conference on financial statements on 12 Mar. 1997 in Jahrhunderthalle Hoechst, Frankfurt).

Schwedt, Georg: *Chemie zwischen Magie und Wissenschaft. Ex Bibliotheka Chymica 1500–1800* (= Exhibition Catalogue, Herzog-August-Bibliothek Wolfenbüttel 1991), Weinheim 1991.

Siegwart, Hans/Neugebauer, Gregory (Ed.): *Mega-Fusionen: Analysen, Kontroversen, Perspektiven*, Bern/Stuttgart/Vienna 1998.

Streeck, Wolfgang/Höpner Martin (Ed.): *Alle Macht dem Markt? Fallstudien zur Abwicklung der Deutschland AG* (Schriften des Max-Planck-Instituts für Gesellschaftsforschung Cologne, Vol. 47), Frankfurt a. M. 2003.

Tenfelde, Klaus u. a.: *Stimmt die Chemie?* Essen 2007.

Tuor, Urs: *Spezialitäten- und Feinchemie, Sektorstudie der Bank Sarasin & Cie AG*, April 2003.

Vasella, Daniel: Novartis-Spitzenleistung in *"Life Science"* in *Basler Stadtbuch* 1996, Christoph Merian Foundation (Ed.), pp. 11–15.

Verg, Erik/Plumpe Gottfried/Schultheiss, Heinz: *Meilensteine. 125 Jahre Bayer 1863–1988*, Bayer AG (Ed.), Cologne 1988.

Vita, Giuseppe: "Wachstumsindustrien Gen- und Biotechnologie. Life Sciences als internationale Zukunftschance," in *Internationale Politik*, 8/1998, Online-Edition.

Vitols, Sigurt: "Viele Wege nach Rom? BASF, Bayer und Hoechst," in Streeck/Höpner (Ed.), 2003.

Volonté, Christophe: *Wie hat sich die Struktur des Board of Verwaltungsrates Schweizer Firmen in den beiden letzten Jahrzehnten verändert*, Master's Thesis, Universität Basel 2007.

Watter, Rolf/Roth Pellanda, Katja: "Die 'richtige' Zusammensetzung des Verwaltungsrates" in Rolf H. Weber (Ed.), *Verantwortlichkeit im Unternehmensrecht III* (Europa Institute Zurich, Vol. 67), Zurich 2006, pp. 47–95.

Watter, Rolf/Rhode, Thomas: "Die Spendenkompetenz des Verwaltungsrates," in Roger Zäch (Hrsg.), *Individuum und Verband—Festgabe zum Schweizerischen Juristentag 2006*, Zurich 2006, pp. 329–345.

Wehnelt, Christoph: *Hoechst. Untergang des deutschen Weltkonzerns*, 3rd ed., Oberstdorf 2009.

Yergin, Daniel: *The Prize. The Epic Quest For Oil, Money & Power*, New York/London 1999/2008.

Index of photos and illustrations

Copyrights

© Tino Briner, Basel: p. 132

© The British Library Board: p. 12

© Clariant AG, Muttenz: pp. 38, 43, 52, 57, 61, 86/87, 97, 108, 111–116, 127, 147, 151, 156, 157, 163, 184, 198, 201, 214, 218, 239–255

© Deutsches Textilmuseum (German Textile Museum) Krefeld Inv. Nr. 16044: p. 18 (l)

© Estate of Pablo Picasso/Artists Rights Society (ARS), New York: p. 19

© Financial Times: p. 24

© Galleria d'Arte Moderna Milano, Collezione Grassi: p. 16

© Gemeindeverwaltung (Municipal Administration), Mund/Wallis: p. 10

© Hoechst GmbH Company Archive, Frankfurt a. M.: pp. 18 (r), 76, 78, 84, 243 (picture: Dirk Reinartz)

© IHS: p. 68

© KEYSTONE/MARTIN RUETSCHI: p. 173

© KEYSTONE/SCIENCE PHOTO LIBRARY/PASCAL GOETGHELUCK: p. 1

© Museum Georg Schäfer, Schweinfurt: p. 20

© Bequest Nico Cadsky, Solothurn: p. 138

© Bequest Hans Geisen, Minusio/Ticino: p. 23

© Novartis AG Basel: pp. 29–36 with the kind permission of the company archives of Novartis AG.

© Staatsgalerie Stuttgart, Inv. Nr. 3301: p. 21

© The town of Bayeux: p. 11, with special permission from the town of Bayeux.

© Stadtbibliothek (Municipal Library) Nuremberg, Amb. 317b.2Â°, f. 272v: p. 15

© Rheinisches Bildarchiv Cologne rba_c010867: p. 13

© The Trustees of the British Museum: p. 22

© Kurt Wyss, Basel: p. 89

Public domain/no license required: pp. 2, 25, 29, 30, 33

Board of Directors and Board of Management
1995–2008

Board of Directors	11 : 6	Board of Management
Rolf W. Schweizer Chairman and President	1995	Martin Syz CEO
Eric André		Roland Lösser CFO
Truls Berg		Peter Brandenberg
Pierre Borgeaud		Albert Hug
Urs Bühler		Hanspeter Knöpfel
Hans-Ulrich Doerig		Herbert Link
Paul Gemperli		
Jean-Claude Gisling		
Markus Kündig		
Marcel Ospel		
Pierre de Weck		
Alfred C. Münch Secretary		Walter Vaterlaus Secretary

Board of Directors	9 : 7	Board of Management
Rolf W. Schweizer Chairman and President	1996	Martin Syz CEO
Eric André		Roland Lösser CFO
Truls Berg		Peter Brandenberg
Pierre Borgeaud		Hanspeter Knöpfel
Urs Bühler		Albert Hug
Paul Gemperli		Herbert Link
Jean-Claude Gisling		Victor Sanahuja
Markus Kündig		
Georges Streichenberg		
Alfred C. Münch Secretary		Walter Vaterlaus Secretary

Board of Directors	11 : 11	Board of Management
Rolf W. Schweizer Chairman and President	1997	Karl-Gerhard Seifert CEO
Eric André		Roland Lösser CFO
Truls Berg		Peter Brandenberg
Pierre Borgeaud		Reinhard Handte
Utz-Hellmuth Felcht		Hanspeter Knöpfel
Paul Gemperli		Joachim Mahler
Jean-Claude Gisling		Ulrich Cuntze
Markus Kündig		Günther Hencken
Klaus-Jürgen Schmieder		Reinhart S. Meyer
Claudio Sonder		Victor Sanahuja
Georges Streichenberg		Hartmut Wiezer
Herbert Wohlmann Secretary		Walter Vaterlaus Secretary

Board of Directors	8 : 11	Board of Management
Rolf W. Schweizer Chairman and President	1998	Karl-Gerhard Seifert CEO
Eric André		Roland Lösser CFO
Truls Berg		Peter Brandenberg
Pierre Borgeaud		Reinhard Handte
Paul Gemperli		Ulrich Cuntze
Markus Kündig		François Dennefeld
Klaus-Jürgen Schmieder		Günther Hencken
Claudio Sonder		Joachim Mahler
		Reinhart S. Meyer
		Victor Sanahuja
		Hartmut Wiezer
Herbert Wohlmann Secretary		Walter Vaterlaus Secretary

Board of Directors	8 : 11	Board of Management
Rolf W. Schweizer Chairman, President, CEO	1999	Reinhard Handte COO
Eric André		Roland Lösser CFO
Truls Berg		Peter Brandenberg
Pierre Borgeaud		Ulrich Cuntze
Markus Kündig		François Darrort
Tony Reis		François Dennefeld
Klaus-Jürgen Schmieder		Günther Hencken

Claudio Sonder   Joachim Mahler
                                                  Reinhart S. Meyer
                                                  Victor Sanahuja
                                                  Hartmut Wiezer

Herbert Wohlmann Secretary   Walter Vaterlaus Secretary

Board of Directors	8 : 12	Board of Management

Rolf W. Schweizer Chairman, President, CEO 2000   Reinhard Handte COO
Eric André   Roland Lösser CFO
Truls Berg   Peter Brandenberg
Pierre Borgeaud   Ulrich Cuntze
Reinhard Handte   François Darrort
Markus Kündig   François Dennefeld
Roland Lösser   Steve J. Hannam
Tony Reis   Günther Hencken
                                                  Joachim Mahler
                                                  Reinhart S. Meyer
                                                  Victor Sanahuja
                                                  Hartmut Wiezer

Herbert Wohlmann Secretary   Walter Vaterlaus Secretary

Board of Directors	9 : 10	Board of Management

Rolf W. Schweizer Chairman and President   2001   Reinhard Handte CEO
Pierre Borgeaud   François Note CFO
Steve J. Hannam   Peter Brandenberg
Reinhard Handte   François Darrort
Markus Kündig   François Dennefeld
Roland Lösser   Nico Gontha
Robert Raeber   Joachim Mahler
Tony Reis   Reinhart S. Meyer
Dieter Seebach   Günther Hencken
                                                  Hartmut Wiezer

Herbert Wohlmann Secretary   Walter Vaterlaus Secretary

Board of Directors	8 : 9	Board of Management
Robert Raeber Chairman	2002	Reinhard Handte CEO
Pierre Borgeaud		François Note CFO
Heinrich Bossard		Peter Brandenberg
Reinhard Handte		François Dennefeld
Steven J. Hannam		Nico Gontha
Roland Lösser		Günther Hencken
Tony Reis		Joachim Mahler
Dieter Seebach		Reinhart S. Meyer
		Hartmut Wiezer

Herbert Wohlmann Secretary

Board of Directors	6 : 8	Board of Management
Robert Raeber Chairman	2003	Roland Lösser CEO
Pierre Borgeaud		François Note CFO
Heinrich Bossard		Dominik von Bertrab
Roland Lösser		Peter Brandenberg
Tony Reis		Siegfried Fischer
Dieter Seebach		Nico Gontha
		Joachim Mahler
		Uwe Nickel

Herbert Wohlmann Secretary

Board of Directors	7 : 10	Board of Management
Robert Raeber Chairman	2004	Roland Lösser CEO
Heinrich Bossard †		François Note CFO
Peter R. Isler		Dominik von Bertrab
Roland Lösser		Peter Brandenberg
Kajo Neukirchen		Siegfried Fischer
Tony Reis		Nico Gontha
Dieter Seebach		Joachim Mahler
		Uwe Nickel
		Hartmut Wiezer
		Peter Piringer

Herbert Wohlmann Secretary

Board of Directors	7 : 9	Board of Management
Robert Raeber Chairman	2005	Roland Lösser CEO
Peter R. Isler		François Note CFO/Patrick Jany CFO
Klaus Jenny		Dominik von Bertrab
Roland Lösser		Peter Brandenberg
Kajo Neukirchen		Siegfried Fischer
Tony Reis		Nico Gontha
Dieter Seebach		Joachim Mahler
		Uwe Nickel
		Hartmut Wiezer
Herbert Wohlmann Secretary		

Board of Directors	7 : 8	Board of Management
Roland Lösser Chairman	2006	Jan Secher CEO
Peter R. Isler		Patrick Jany CFO
Klaus Jenny		Dominik von Bertrab
Kajo Neukirchen		Peter Brandenberg
Tony Reis		Siegfried Fischer
Dieter Seebach		Uwe Nickel
Peter Chen		Peter Piringer
		Hartmut Wiezer
Herbert Wohlmann Secretary		

Board of Directors	8 : 7	Board of Management
Roland Lösser Chairman	2007	Jan Secher CEO
Peter Chen		Patrick Jany CFO
Peter R. Isler		Peter Brandenberg
Klaus Jenny		Dominik von Bertrab
Kajo Neukirchen		Siegfried Fischer
Tony Reis		Okke Koo
Rudolf Wehrli		Johann Steiner
Jürg Witmer		
Herbert Wohlmann Secretary		

Board of Directors	**8 : 6**	**Board of Management**
Jürg Witmer Chairman	2008	Hariolf Kottmann CEO
Peter Chen		Patrick Jany CFO
Peter R. Isler		Peter Brandenberg
Klaus Jenny		Dominik von Bertrab
Dominik Koechlin		Siegfried Fischer
Hariolf Kottmann		Okke Koo
Carlo G. Soave		
Rudolf Wehrli		

Index of names

Index